Harrington William Holden

John Wesley in Company with High Churchmen

Harrington William Holden

John Wesley in Company with High Churchmen

ISBN/EAN: 9783743329751

Manufactured in Europe, USA, Canada, Australia, Japa

Cover: Foto ©ninafisch / pixelio.de

Manufactured and distributed by brebook publishing software (www.brebook.com)

Harrington William Holden

John Wesley in Company with High Churchmen

JOHN WESLEY

IN COMPANY WITH

HIGH CHURCHMEN.

BY

AN OLD METHODIST.

"If it be possible, for one hour lay prejudice aside; give what is advanced a fair hearing."—WESLEY'S *Appeal to Men of Reason and Religion.*

LONDON:
CHURCH PRESS COMPANY,
13, BURLEIGH STREET, STRAND.

1869.

Dedication.

TO ALL

MY BROTHER PRIESTS

AND

BROTHER METHODISTS:

To the former,

AS A HAND-BOOK OF CHURCH PRINCIPLES,

BACKED BY FAMOUS AUTHORITY

FOR PAROCHIAL USE;

To the latter,

AS A DEFENCE OF CHURCH PRINCIPLES,

BY THE FOUNDER OF THEIR

SOCIETY,

JOHN WESLEY.

INTRODUCTION.

THE circumstances of the day encourage an old Methodist to contribute his mite towards determining the opinions, and allaying the scruples, of many men of sober minds, who wish, apart from prejudice and misrepresentation, to know what to think about the many matters of Doctrine, and Ritual, which now engage so large a share of the public attention.

Mr. Wesley's principles and religious convictions are so little known by professed Churchmen, and even by his own people "called Methodists," as to make any careful statement of them of considerable interest, especially as he lived in a day when these points came before him unattended by "the din of controversy and the strife of tongues," and were calmly considered in the light of Holy Scripture, and, as he professes, "the purest ages of the Church."

This fact alone, that the conclusions he arrived at were after most careful study of the Holy Scriptures and their best Comment, the Practice and Records of the Apostolic Churches, and without prejudice (except, considering the age and nation, so far as it was adverse), together with his known integrity, and pure zeal for Apostolic Christianity, must, for a large portion of the religious public, give to them and the pages in which they are embodied a peculiar claim to candid consideration.

This is the Author's hope; and also that others who entertain the same principles and religious convictions, and are therefor, like Wesley, denounced, may receive for this, if for no better reason, a little more of that Christian charity which, as all now unite in deploring, was meted out in such scant measure to the Founder of Methodism.

To exhibit their just claim to equal charity on the ground of this identity, it may be best to set forth in order a declaration of those things which by High Churchmen are most surely believed; and in a parallel column to give a corresponding declaration on the part of John Wesley. This will prove, even to the most·incredulous, that John Wesley was, and ever remained—his own *Works* being witness—a High Churchman.

In the execution of this plan the Author may perhaps be taxed with quoting from writings which, though included in Mr. Wesley's *Works*, are not his own—*i.e.*, *Thomas à Kempis's Christian Pattern*, *Dr. Brevint's Treatise on The Christian Sacrifice*, and *The Manners of the Ancient Christians*: but the answer is conclusive in each instance.

The *Christian Pattern* is not Thomas à Kempis's Christian Pattern, but Mr. Wesley's expurgated edition of it; and the character of the omissions shows that he acted on the principle of admitting only what was suited to his purpose and agreeable to his mind. Moreover, he required all his Societies to be supplied with this book, "which ought," said he, "to be in every house;" had it sold by his preachers in every place; and earnestly advised every member of the Connexion to make it a regular part of his devotional reading. *Min.* i. 16, 40.

For the *Treatise on the Christian Sacrifice* the case is even stronger. This Treatise was deliberately adopted by Mr. Wesley as a formal statement of Eucharistic Doctrine, and carried the sanction of his name into all his Societies from the year 1745 until after his death. For its "Sacramental Principles" Mr. Wesley is even more responsible than Dr. Brevint himself, as ten times over during these fifty years the Treatise was given to his Societies afresh, accompanied by the "Sacramental Hymns of John and Charles Wesley," which are little more, as Methodists themselves confess, "than paraphrases of the prose text:" indeed, in them these principles are further developed, as a close comparison will show, besides having given to them the pointed advantage, among such a people as the early Methodists, of a poetic form.

As to *The Manners of the Ancient Christians*, by a French author, the extracts which Mr. Wesley was pleased to make therefrom, and publish in English for his Societies, were necessarily acceptable to himself: for in the case of these works published under his name, for the instruction of his people, he avowedly excluded all matter of which he did not approve, for the reason he assigned—to preserve in his teaching "a consistency throughout." Whilst for such others towards which he did not assume this paternal relation, and exercise this expurgatory power, *e.g.*, *The Christian Library*, he formally disavowed anything beyond a *general* agreement.

It may also be observed that quotations from none of these stand alone, but have ample confirmation from Mr. Wesley's other writings.

Perhaps it is not unnecessary to remark respecting the *Arminian Methodist Magazine* that it was commenced by Mr. Wesley in 1778, carried on during his life under his strict supervision, and continued by his coadjutors—the Wesleyan Conference—after his death, on the same plan of rigidly excluding therefrom whatever was not in accordance with the spirit and principles of Methodism. So jealous was Wesley to preserve this "consistency throughout," in all Methodist publications, that none of his preachers might print anything even on his own account, which had not previously received correction at head-quarters and the stamp of entire approbation.*

The same reasons which make it necessary to fortify with

---

* "Let none print anything of his own till it has been approved by the Conference" (*Conference Minute*, 1763): "Print nothing without my approbation" (*Conf.*, 1765): "Without my consent and correction." (*Conf.*, 1781.) Contributions intended for the *Magazine* had first to receive the approval of three of the Preachers who were appointed by the Conference "to read and to sanction or reject" them. They were then forwarded to

authority, quotations from the above sources, make it desirable that one general remark should be made respecting the manner in which this work has been performed:—Wishing nothing so much as to cut off that last resort of disabled critics, which is to run off upon a word, a point of detail, a solitary instance of misapprehension, the Author has, in endeavour, been most scrupulously exact, and preferred always to tolerate an awkwardness of style rather than by a mere change of person, or an inversion of order, in a quotation to avoid it. Nevertheless, where necessity required he has of course supplied connective particles, and also, for the sake of brevity omitted extraneous matter or mere alliterative sentences. If for these, any one is in haste to raise the charge of interpolation or mutilation, he will do well first to read a page anywhere in Mr. Wesley's *Works*, where quotations from Scripture occur, and consider how far such a charge can be allowed to be sound, and of general application.

That some diversity of expression might be pointed out even in Wesley himself, is evidently probable, and for the most natural of reasons: "Considering," says Wesley, that "during these last thirty years ... I was answering so many different objectors, frequently attacking me at once, and one pushing one way, another that, with all the violence they were able:" but notwithstanding such occasional diversity of expression, and an acknowledged diversity of sentiment also, between the years before 1738 and the years after, there is nothing in all Mr. Wesley's *Works* which would substantially affect the following tabulated statement of his principles and religious convictions—this being wholly derived from, or defended by Wesley during those fifty-three years of his life as to which he acknowledged no change in his teaching whatsoever. Whilst any attempt at showing the contrary, were it even apparently successful, would exhibit the Founder of Methodism to the world as the most self-contrarious of

"the London Committee," who had the further power "to make alterations, excisions, &c.," at their discretion, or else to signify the limited approbation attached to them by publishing such contributions with the names of those who sanction them. (*Conf.*, 1801.) This shows the nature of the censorship over the Methodist Press even as it continued after Mr. Wesley's death.

religious teachers, a charge which the Wesleyans have always warmly repelled, and be in irreconcileable hostility to his own honest words—"I have uniformly gone on for fifty years, never varying from the doctrine of the Church at all."

All Saints' Day, 1869.

The Works and Editions used are

Wesley's Works. Pine, Bristol. 1773. XXXII. Vols.	quoted thus	x. 25.
Wesley's Works. 3rd Edition. London. 1829. XIV. Vols.	,,	*Vol.* x. 25.
Wesley's Journal. Original Edition, in XXI. Parts	,,	*Jl.* x. 25.
Wesley's Notes on the New Testament. 1805. III. Vols.	,,	*Notes* ii. 25.
Wesley's Sermons. 10th Edition. II. Vols.	,,	*Ss.* ii. 25.
The Arminian Methodist Magazine. From 1778-1869	,,	*Mag.* ii. 25.
Hymns on the Lord's Supper, by J. & C. Wesley. 7th Edition. 1776 . . .	,,	*H.* No. xxv.
Minutes of the Methodist Conferences. XIV. Vols.	,,	*Min.* ii. 25.

All others quoted in full.

CONTENTS.

	PAGE
INTRODUCTION	v

CHAP.

		PAGE
I.—Of the Catholic Faith		1
II.—Of the Sacraments		3
III.—Of Holy Baptism		4
IV.—Of Confirmation		7
V.—Of Holy Communion		9
1. The Real Presence		9
2. The Eucharistic Sacrifice		11
3. Eucharistic Adoration		14
4. Benefit and Grace of the Holy Eucharist ...		15
5. Fitness and Preparation for Reception ...		18
6. Daily Celebration		18
7. Duty of Constant Communion		21
8. Administration to Young Children		23
9. The Mixed Chalice and Unleavened Bread ...		25
10. Choral Celebration		26
11. Repelling Evil-Doers		27
VI.—Of Confession		29
1. Practice of Confession		29
2. Benefit of Confession		34
3. Shame: a Hindrance to Confession		39
4. Secrecy in Confession		40
5. Objections against Confession		41
6. Of Penance		43
7. Of Sacerdotal Absolution		44
VII.—Of Anointing the Sick with Consecrated Oil		46
VIII.—Of Holy Orders		47
1. The Virtue of Ordination		47
2. The Apostolic Succession		50

CHAP.	PAGE
IX.—Of the Celibate State	57
X.—Of Fasting	61
1. Obligation of Fasting	61
2. Need of Fasting	62
3. Times of Fasting	64
XI.—Of Justification by Faith	66
XII.—Of the Communion of Saints	72
XIII.—Of Prayers for the Dead	74
XVI.—Of the Order of Public Services and of Church Arrangements	78
1. Daily Service	78
2. Weekly or Daily Communion	81
3. Separation of the Morning Services	85
4. Baptisms and Catechizing openly in Church ...	86
5. A Weekly Offertory	88
6. No Pews, but Benches free alike for Rich and Poor	89
7. Separation of the Sexes	91
XV.—Of Ritual	93
XVI.—Of Honour where Honour is Due	105
XVII.—Of Obedience to Church Authority ...	109
1. Obedience to Rubrics	109
2. Obedience to Bishops	112
XVIII.—Institution and Design of Methodism ...	115
XIX.—Alleged Violations of Church Order ...	118
XX.—Opposition to Methodism	120
1. False Accusations	120
2. "Putting down" Methodism	125
XXI.—A Call to Candid Consideration	133
XXII.—Stedfast unto the End	136
1. In the Church's Doctrine	136
2. In the Church's Fellowship	137
XXIII.—Methodism in Separation	144
XXIV.—Methodism again in Unity	155

JOHN WESLEY

IN COMPANY WITH

HIGH CHURCHMEN.

CHAPTER I.

OF THE CATHOLIC FAITH.

HIGH CHURCHMEN.*

IN loyalty thereto, High Churchmen unhesitatingly affirm—That which every Christian is bound to believe in is, "The Faith once (for all) delivered to the Saints," as taught and interpreted by those whom God hath commissioned to teach it, to all nations, even to the end of the world.

This, Holy Scripture sufficiently contains for salvation, but needs, as a guard against false interpretations, as well as an independent witness to Apostolical "traditions, whether by word or by epistle," what God has provided—the authoritative teaching of the Church. In these two we have a complete rule of Christian faith and practice. These, jointly,

WESLEY, 1735-1774.†

IN like manner, Wesley, the "defender of the Catholic Faith," as he avows himself, affirms the necessity of its acceptance as by the Church received and taught. "'The Faith that thou hast heard of me, among many witnesses, the same commit thou to faithful men, who shall be able to teach others also.' Thus was 'the Faith once delivered to the Saints,' thus was the Church, the whole body of Christians from the beginning, 'the ground and pillar of truth,' of all the truths contained in the oracles of God. In the writings, therefore, of these, not of modern reasoners and disputers, are we to search for that sense of Scripture, hard to be

---

* The *plural* is used without apology, as the unanimity of High Churchmen (of the newer school) in these and the following sentiments is sufficiently known to justify an individual writer in the use of it.

† The significance and the great importance of these dates, which accompany the chapters throughout, are determined by two facts:—

1. Mr. Wesley never allowed that there was any change in his doctrinal sentiments after 1738, and constantly maintained that he had been uniform in his teaching during the fifty years before his death—*e.g., Journal* xxi. 145.

2. Dr. Rigg, who, as Editor of the *London Quarterly Review*, holds the highest literary position in Methodism, has lately affirmed that " Wesley, up to 1738, had been a High Church sacramentalist; all his life afterwards he taught the Evangelical doctrine of salvation by faith:" in other words, "that Wesley ceased to be a High Churchman fifty years before his death." (*The Relations of John Wesley, &c.*, pp. 40, 60).

Mr. Wesley died in 1791.

B

High Churchmen.	Wesley.
"are the authority we appeal to, thither we refer our case, and can heartily conclude with that dictum of Vincentius Lirinensis, 'That is to be held which hath been believed everywhere, always, and by all.'" In accordance with this, High Churchmen believe and teach.	understood, which was received from the Apostles, and the Apostles from Christ." ix. 10. "The Rule of Faith (is) delivered to us in the oracles of God, *and* in the writings of the ancient Fathers of the Christian Church." (*Mag.* xxi. 401.) Thus did the Wesleyans reiterate Mr. Wesley's language—one parallel only need be quoted:—" Let us

therefore hold fast the sound doctrine 'once delivered to the Saints,' and delivered down by them *with* the written Word to all succeeding generations." *Ss.* i. 127.

"Faithful (were) the witnesses in those primitive times; and with purity of intention, simplicity, benevolence, and charity did they 'earnestly contend for the Faith once delivered to the Saints.'" (*Mag.* xx. 199.) Fitting exactly Mr. Wesley's words:—" The most authentic commentators on Scripture, as being both nearest the fountain, and eminently endued with that Spirit by Whom all Scripture was given." (x. 130.) "May we be followers of them in all things, as they were of Christ." *Jl.* xvii. 47.

To Dr. Middleton, who said (apparently in reference to Mr. Wesley's own words, xv. 361), "If the Scriptures are a *sufficient* rule, we do not want the Fathers as guides; nor, if clear, as interpreters." Wesley replies, "I reject the word *sufficient*, because it is ambiguous. The Scriptures are a complete rule of faith and practice; and they are clear in all necessary points. And yet their clearness does not prove that they need not be explained, nor their completeness that they need not be enforced." (xviii. 162.) In truth, Holy Scripture is a sufficient rule, or it is not, according as it is interpreted *with* or *without* the aid of the Fathers and the living voice of the Church. To this consistent principle Mr. Wesley held. Speaking of the early Methodists, he said, "From five to seven (each morning) we read the Bible together; carefully comparing it —that we might not lean to our own understandings—with the writings of the earliest ages." (xxvi. 106.) Thirty years later he said of the same people, It is "their one desire and design to be downright Bible-Christians—taking the Bible *as interpreted* by the Primitive Church and our own for *their whole and sole rule.*" (xv. 376). To sum up all, "Scripture and indubitable antiquity are the authority we appeal to; thither we refer our case, and can heartily conclude with that (saying) of Vincentius Lirin., 'That is to be held which hath been believed everywhere, always, and by all.'" xix. 102.

In accordance with this, Wesley believed and taught.

CHAPTER II.

OF THE SACRAMENTS.

High Churchmen.

Sacraments are the means of grace appointed by God for the *conveyance* of His grace to man.

Our use of them is necessary to salvation, since though God be not tied to them, *we are.*

Repentance and faith on our part do not supersede, but entitle us to, the use of them, and are requisite to their beneficial effect.

Wesley, 1756.

"By *means of grace*, I understand outward signs, words, or actions ordained of God, and appointed for this end to be the ordinary channels whereby He might convey to men preventing, justifying, or sanctifying grace."

"A Sacrament is 'an outward sign of inward *grace*, and a *means* whereby we receive the same.'" *Ss.* i. 154.

Wesley reminds people that not by "believing *only*," but by their faith leading them to use the means of grace, can they expect salvation. "If you say, 'Believe, and thou shalt be saved.' True; but how shall I believe? You reply, 'Wait upon God.' Well? But how am I to wait? In the means of grace, or out of them?" *Ss.* i. 156.

And to that hackneyed objection about "Trusting in them," he replies, "What do you mean by 'trusting in them'? Looking for the blessing of God therein? Believing that if I wait in this way I shall attain what otherwise I should not? So I do. And so I will, God being my helper, even to my life's end." *Ss.* i. 161.

CHAPTER III.

OF HOLY BAPTISM.

High Churchmen.

(*a*) Baptism is the means whereby God grants remission of sins and a new and spiritual birth.

The child of wrath is therein made a member of Christ, the child of God, and an inheritor of the Kingdom of Heaven.

(*b*) Before Baptism, infants are not in a state of salvation; and as Baptism is the only appointed means of washing away the stain of original sin, and consequently the only ordinary way by which they can enter Heaven, Baptism is for them, as it is for *all men*—*i.e.*, "*generally*—necessary to salvation."

(*c*) *Regeneration* is so properly the grace of *Baptism*, that either word is used indifferently in Holy Scripture to express the same thing. "Baptized into Christ," "by the washing of Regeneration," is equally expressed by "Regenerated into Christ, by the washing of Baptism." And so has the Church always taught. Correctly speaking, Regeneration never takes place without Baptism; and *vice versâ*, Baptism is never duly received without Regeneration.

Wesley, 1756-1790.

(*a*) "What are the *benefits* we receive by Baptism? The first of these is the *washing away the guilt of original sin* by the application of the merits of Christ's death. 'As by the offence of one, judgment came upon all men to condemnation, so by the righteousness of One, the free gift came upon all men to justification of life.' And the virtue of this free gift, the merits of Christ's life and death, are applied to us in Baptism. 'He gave Himself for the Church, that He might sanctify and cleanse it with the washing of water (Eph. v. 25, 26), by the Word'—namely, in Baptism, the *ordinary instrument of our justification*." xix. 279, 280.

"By Baptism we are admitted into the Church, and consequently made *members of Christ*, its Head. For 'as many as are baptized into Christ,' in His Name, 'have thereby put on Christ' (Gal. iii. 27)—that is, are mystically *united* to Christ, and made *one* with Him. For 'by one Spirit we are all baptized into one body' (1 Cor. xii. 13)—namely, 'the Church the Body of Christ.' From which spiritual, vital union with Him proceeds the the influence of His grace on those that are baptized."

"By Baptism we, who were by nature children of wrath, are made the *children of God*. And this *Regeneration*, which our Church in so many places ascribes to Baptism, is more than barely being admitted into the Church, though commonly connected therewith; being ' grafted into the body of Christ's Church, we are made the

Wesley.

children of God by adoption and grace.' By *water*, then, as a means—the water of Baptism—we are regenerated, or born again: whence it is also called by the Apostle, 'the Washing of Regeneration.' Our Church, therefore, ascribes no greater virtue to Baptism than Christ Himself has done. Nor does she ascribe it to the outward washing, but to the inward grace, which added thereto makes it a Sacrament."

"In consequence of our being made children of God, we are *heirs of the Kingdom of Heaven*. 'If children (as the Apostle observes), then heirs; heirs with God, and joint heirs with Christ.'" xix. 281-2.

(*b*) "It has been already proved that this original stain cleaves to every child of man; and that hereby they (infants) are children of wrath, and liable to eternal damnation. It is true the second Adam has found a remedy for the disease which came upon all by the offence of the first. But the benefit of this is to be received through the means which He hath appointed—through Baptism in particular, which is the ordinary means He hath appointed for that purpose; and to which God hath tied us, though he may not have tied Himself." xix. 284.

(*c*) "Familiar as a household word," amongst the early Christians, was the connection between Baptism and Regeneration, insomuch that they used either of the two words indifferently to express the double truth. Wesley reminds us of this, "The word Regeneration is the name of Baptism"—so Clemens Alexandrinus; and "Irenæus, who asserts that infants were regenerated into God," does, "in the usual phrase of those times," so speak of their Baptism. And himself, in correcting the Rev. Mr. Potter's inaccurate language on the subject, says, "The terms, of being regenerated, of being born again, of being born of God—in Scripture—*always express* an inward work of the Spirit, *whereof Baptism* is the outward sign:" also, "that the outward sign duly received is *always* accompanied with the inward grace." xix. 319, 320; xvii. 11; xxx. 352.

Those who fly off, vaunting the objection, "Why, then, don't the new-born bring forth the fruits of the New Birth in their after life?" Wesley silences, by pointing out that the objection is of equal force when turned against the excellency of preaching and their own favourite doctrine—Conversion: "The preaching like an Apostle, without joining together those that are awakened and *training them up in the ways of God*, is only *begetting children for the murderer*."

Indeed, no work of the Spirit can reasonably be expected to be permanent and abiding, unless it be duly nurtured by careful Christian training: and if not in riper years, how much less in infancy, when the subjects of it are wholly dependent upon others. The charge, then, which we foolishly make against God, of withholding

Wesley.

His grace from the means, is one which returns to our own door. xxxi. 247.

To an attempt to refine away the express teaching of S. John iii. 5, "Except a man be born of water and the Spirit he cannot enter into the Kingdom of God," Wesley replies, "Vain philosophy! The plain meaning of the expression, 'except a man be born of water,' is neither more nor less than this, 'except he be baptized.' And the plain reason why he ought to be thus *born of water* is because God hath appointed it." "In the ordinary way there is no other means of entering into the Church, or into Heaven." xix. 231, 282.

Passages from Mr. Wesley's *Sermons* are sometimes quoted against himself; as might be expected, in utter contempt of the context: Sermons XVIII., "The Marks of the New Birth;" and XXI., "The New Birth." In the former he says: "The question is, not what you were made in Baptism (do not evade), but what are ye now? ...... I allow you were 'circumcised with the circumcision of Christ,' as S. Paul emphatically terms Baptism. But does the Spirit of Christ and of glory *now* rest upon you? Else 'your circumcision is become uncircumcision.'" "Baptized gluttons and drunkards," &c. "Lean no more on the staff of that broken reed, that ye *were* born again in Baptism. Who denies that ye were then made 'children of God and heirs of the Kingdom of Heaven'? But notwithstanding this, ye are now children of the Devil. Therefore, ye must be born again. And let not Satan put it into your heart to cavil at a word, when the thing is clear." (pp. 183, 184.) Language which no High Churchman shrinks from addressing to those who put Baptism in the place of holiness of life. In the other Sermon, Wesley properly guards the Church's doctrine of Baptismal Regeneration from an equally ignorant conception of it: "Baptism is not the New Birth; they are not one and the same thing. ...... A man may possibly be born of water, and yet not be born of the Spirit. There may sometimes be the outward sign where there is not the inward grace. I do not now speak with regard to infants. It is certain, our Church supposes that all who are baptized in their infancy are at the same time born again; and it is allowed, that the whole Office for the Baptism of infants proceeds upon this supposition." (pp. 209, 210.) Moreover, Wesley begins these Sermons on the New Birth by setting down the doctrine of Baptismal Regeneration as an elementary truth, too certain to be questioned: "That these privileges—the being born again, born of God, born of the Spirit; the being a son or a child of God, or having the Spirit of Adoption—are ordinarily annexed to Baptism, we *know*." (p. 175.) Together with his *Sermons*, Wesley's *Notes on the New Testament* are the doctrinal standard to which his Societies are bound. In every edition of these, he says on Acts v. 16 (one example will suffice), "Be baptized and wash away thy sins: Baptism administered to real penitents is both a means and seal of pardon. Nor did God ordinarily in the Primitive Church bestow this on any, unless through this means." That Wesley never varied from this, he repeatedly declares—*e.g.*, in 1789 and 1790, "I have been uniform in doctrine for above these fifty years," "never varying from the doctrine of the Church at all."

CHAPTER IV.
OF CONFIRMATION.

High Churchmen.

"Confirmation, or Laying on of Hands," is the means through which God offers to the baptized the gift of the Holy Ghost—not barely the gift of grace, but the gift of the Spirit of Grace; and being given for a permanent purpose—that we may be filled with all the fruits of the Spirit, and be holy, "knowing that we are the temple of God"—it is a permanent ordinance, and is accordingly classed by S. Paul (Heb. vi. 1, 2) among the principles and foundations of the Christian Religion.

Infants, the Primitive Christians being witness, are proper subjects of Confirmation; and as they, as well as others, were anciently confirmed immediately after Baptism, renewal of solemn vows was impossible in the one case, unnecessary in the other, and therefore is no part of the Ordinance, however proper to it where Confirmation has been delayed.

The Church of England, herein following the Church of Rome, delays Confirmation until the child shall have been taught the first elements of Christian faith and duty: but requires the priest, on baptizing any infant, straitly to charge "the Godfathers and Godmothers"—"*Ye are to take care* that this child be brought to the Bishop to be confirmed by

Wesley, 1744-1754.

In a description of the manners of the Ancient Christians, taken from a French author, Wesley says, "And having been thus prepared they were baptized on ... the Eve of Pentecost, that they might be ready *to receive the Holy Ghost*. When the persons baptized were infants, their sureties or sponsors (as Tertullian calls them) answered for them. Immediately after baptism they were presented to the Bishop to be *Confirmed*, by prayer and Imposition of Hands." ix. 17.

Against "a current opinion that 'Christians are not now to receive the Holy Ghost,'" he quotes from the Office of Confirmation, and adds, "From these passages it may sufficiently appear, for what purposes every Christian, according to the doctrine of the Church of England, does *now receive the Holy Ghost*"—viz., not to work miracles, but to be filled with the fruits of that Blessed Spirit. (xiv. 230, 276, 283.) With this exception, the Gift and its main purpose remain the same now as at first: "Such a receiving the Holy Ghost as that was at the Day of Pentecost, I do, in part," mean; "but," even with regard to this necessary exception of extraordinary powers, "it is needful to observe this, that even in the

High Churchmen.	Wesley.
him, *so soon as he can say* the Creed, the Lord's Prayer, and the Ten Commandments in the vulgar tongue, and (then to) be further instructed in the Church Catechism set forth for that purpose." That pernicious abuse on the part of English Bishops of requiring all to be "further instructed" before they be confirmed, and even then denying them the grace of Confirmation unless they be of the full age of fifteen, has for its direct consequences that, 1st, One-half of the number of children so baptized are never "brought to be confirmed" at all; and, 2nd, Two out of three of those so baptized are never "admitted to the Holy Communion."	infancy of the Church, God divided them with a sparing hand. Were all, even then, prophets? Were all workers of miracles? Had all the gifts of healing? Did all speak with tongues? No; in no wise: perhaps not one in a thousand. Probably none but the teachers in the Church, and only some of them. It was, therefore, for a more excellent purpose than this, that *they were all filled with the Holy Ghost:* it was to give them—what none can deny to be essential to all Christians in all ages—those holy fruits of the Spirit which, whoever hath not, is none of His." i. 68. The *Laying on of Hands* for the gift of the Holy Ghost, Wesley held to be classed among those "principles of the doctrine of Christ" which are "*funda-*

mental," even " repentance" and " faith in God." "And when they believed, they were to be baptized with the Baptism of Christ, the next thing was to Lay Hands upon them, that they might receive the Holy Ghost; after which they were more fully instructed," &c. *Notes*, Heb. vi. 1, 2.

Against the argument entertained even by Bishops—the ministers of this Apostolic Ordinance—that not *the Holy Ghost*, but *a grace* of the Blessed Spirit, was what was given, he writes—

> "The grace, but not the Spirit of grace,
>   Their learned fools vouchsafe to allow;
> He might be given in ancient days,
>   But God, they teach, is needless now.
>
> But God we know is given indeed,
>   And still doth in His people dwell;
> And Him we every moment need,
>   And Him we every moment feel."
>
> (Hymn of Petition and Thanksgiving, "*For the Promise of the Father*.")

CHAPTER V.

OF THE HOLY COMMUNION.

1. THE REAL PRESENCE.

High Churchmen.

That Christ in His whole nature is really present in the consecrated elements is solemnly assured to us by His own words: "I am the living Bread which came down from Heaven. If any man eat of this Bread he shall live for ever, and the Bread which I will give is My Flesh, which I will give for the life of the world. Verily, verily, I say unto you, Except ye eat the Flesh of the Son of Man, and drink His Blood, ye have no life in you." "And Jesus took bread and blessed it, and said, Take, eat, *This is My Body;* and He took the cup, saying, *This is My Blood.*" And S. Paul, who "received of the Lord that which also he delivered," says, "The cup of blessing which we bless, is it not the communion of the Blood of Christ? The bread which we break, is it not the communion of the Body of Christ?" Of which, "He that eateth and drinketh unworthily" is "guilty of the Body and Blood of the Lord;" he "eateth and drinketh damnation to himself, not discerning the Lord's Body."

That so were these words understood by the Apostles, and by those who received Christ's teaching from them, is certain.

Wesley, 1745-1791.

"O Lord, in the simplicity of my heart, at Thy commandment I come unto Thee with hope and reverence, and do truly believe Thou art *present in this Sacrament.*" vol. viii. 16.

Three things "require that much more be contained therein than a bare *memorial* or *representation:*—1. The end of the Holy Communion, which is to make us partakers of Christ in another manner than when we only hear His Word. 2. The wants and desires of those who receive It; who seek not a bare representation or remembrance. I want and seek my Saviour Himself, and I haste to this Sacrament for the same purpose that SS. Peter and John hasted to His sepulchre—because I hope to find Him there. 3. The strength of other places of Scripture, which allow It a far greater virtue than that of representing only. 'The cup of blessing which we bless, is it not the communion of the Blood of Christ?'—a means of communicating the Blood, there represented and remembered, to every believing soul!"

"I come then to God's Altar with a full persuasion that these words, 'This is My Body,' pro-

High Churchmen.

While several of the Apostles were yet living, S. Ignatius was consecrated Bishop of Antioch, and thus wrote of certain heretics who denied that our Lord had come in the flesh: "They abstain from the Eucharist and from prayer, because they confess not *the Eucharist to be the Flesh* of our Saviour Jesus Christ, *which suffered* for our sins, and *which* the Father, of His goodness, *raised* up again." So also S. Justin the Martyr, "a disciple of Apostles," says:—"So likewise have we *been taught* that the food which is blessed by the prayer of His Word *is the Flesh and Blood* of that Jesus Who was made Flesh; for the Apostles, in their Memoirs composed by them, which are called Gospels, *have thus delivered unto us what was enjoined upon them.*" Ch. vii. *Ad. Smyr.*, and *1st Apol.* ch. lxvi., Clark's Translation.

It is a thing very much to be observed that this truth is never objected to as being un-Scriptural; Scripture is for it throughout, and has to be put aside by forcing upon its words a modern sense. It is rejected solely on the ground that its claim, though supported by the words of Scripture, is contrary to the evidence of our senses. But the falseness of such reasoning is evident; our senses testify only to the appear-

Wesley.

mise me more than a *figure;* that this Holy Banquet is not a bare *memorial* only, but may actually convey as many blessings to me as It brings curses on the profane receiver. Indeed, in what *manner* this is done, I know not; it is enough for me to admire." xxiii. 152-4.

Realizing this great truth himself, Wesley requires to know of his "Helpers" whether they also do: "Do you in communicating *discern* the Lord's Body?" xv. 316.

" We need not now go up to Heaven
  To bring the long-lost Saviour down;
Thou art to all already given,
  Thou dost e'en now Thy banquet crown;
To every faithful soul appear,
And shew Thy Real Presence here." *—H.* cxvi.

" Now on the sacred Table laid,
  Thy Flesh becomes our food;
Thy life is to our souls conveyed
  In Sacramental Blood."
  —*H.* lxv.

And draws attention to the following appropriate quotation from S. Justin the Martyr, who was born, if not during the life of the Apostle S. John, at latest not ten years after, and who, in giving an account of the public assemblies of the Christians in those first days, says, " We do not take This as common bread and com-

---

* Although these Hymns were published by John Wesley, a new edition being issued every fifth year after 1745, bearing the names of both John and C. Wesley on the title-page, there are Methodist writers who do not scruple to assert that C. Wesley alone is responsible for them. The assertion is unfortunate in every way. Speaking of these Hymns, a Methodist hymnologist says: "We have no means by which to distinguish between the compositions of the two brothers, and *therefore* fix upon Charles Wesley as the author of them all."

High Churchmen.	Wesley.
ance of a thing, not at all to its substance. For example, if I were told that a certain bread were a deadly poison, through some change or admixture, I must, as I valued my life, be guided by my faith, not by my senses—by the faithful testimony of the witness, not by the sight, touch, and taste. So when our Lord says, "This is My Body," we reverently believe, and the sufficient confirmation of our faith is, that so did the Early Christians—those taught by the Apostles—believe, and so has the Church, "the pillar and ground of the Truth," always held and everywhere taught unto this day.	mon wine, but as the *Flesh and Blood* of the *Incarnate Jesus*." ix. 28. "O the depth of love Divine, Th' unfathomable grace! Who shall say how bread and wine God into man conveys? How the bread His Flesh imparts, How the wine transmits His Blood, Fills His faithful people's hearts With all the life of God?" —*H.* lvii. As to searching out the mystery: "Ask the Father's Wisdom 'how?' Him that did the means ordain. Angels round our Altars bow To search it out—in vain." To presumptuous deniers, he says:— "Go, foolish worms, His Word deny; Go, tear those planets from the sky; But while the sun and moon endure, The Ordinance on earth is sure."—*H.* lxii.

2. THE EUCHARISTIC SACRIFICE.

High Churchmen.	Wesley, 1745-1791.
The Sacrament of the Altar is commemorative of the actual blood-shedding upon the Cross, and every celebration of It a "shewing forth the Lord's death till He come." But being "verily and indeed" "the Body and Blood of Christ," It is necessarily identical with, and inseparable from, the same glorified Offering in Heaven, where Christ now is,	"The main intention of Christ herein was not the bare *remembrance* of His Passion, but, over and above, to invite us to His Sacrifice, not as done and gone many years since, but, as to grace and mercy, still lasting. still *new*, still the same as when It was first offered for us. The Sacrifice of Christ being appointed by the Father for a propitiation that

High Churchmen.

shewing His Wounds and bearing His Blood within the Holy of Holies.

This, so far from being contrary to what S. Paul, in the Epistle to the Hebrews, says, is the only Eucharistic doctrine with which the whole of that Epistle entirely agrees. The Sacrifice is "once made," and "once offered," never more to be repeated, as respects the finished act of oblation on Calvary; but Christ having now "ascended into Heaven," It there continues to be offered by Him in glorified form, Who, by "abiding a priest for ever," must "of necessity have somewhat to offer:" and as being for ever pleaded before the Father, by Him Who "ever liveth to make intercession," It continues still of necessary efficacy for all them that believe.

Wesley.

should continue to all ages, and, withal, being everlasting by the privilege of its own *order*, which is *an unchangeable priesthood*, and by His worth Who offered It— that is, the Blessed Son of God— and by the power of the Eternal Spirit through Whom it was offered, it must in all respects stand eternal, the same yesterday, to-day, and for ever." xxiii. 145.

"Concerning the Sacrament, as it is a Sacrifice: There never was on earth a true religion without some kind of sacrifices. ... None of these sacrifices could ever take away sin, but in dependence on that of Jesus Christ. And no sacrifice under the Law could represent our service to God so fully as it is done under the Gospel. The Holy Communion alone brings together these two great ends, atonement of sins, and acceptable duty to God, of which all the sacrifices of old were no more than weak shadows."

"This Sacrifice (of Christ), which by a real oblation was not to be offered more than once, is by a devout and thankful commemoration to be offered up every day. This is what the Apostle calls 'To set forth the death of the Lord': to set it forth as well before the eyes of God His Father, as before the eyes of men: and what S. Austin explained when he said, The Holy Flesh of Jesus was offered in three manners—by *prefiguring sacrifices* under the Law before His coming into the world, in *real deed* upon His Cross, and by a *commemorative Sacrament* after He ascended into Heaven. All comes to this: 1. That the Sacrifice in itself can never be repeated; 2. That, nevertheless, this Sacrament, by our remembrance, becomes a kind of Sacrifice, whereby we present before God the Father that precious Oblation of His Son once offered. And thus do we every day offer unto God the meritorious sufferings of our Lord, as the only sure ground whereon God may give, and we obtain, the blessings we pray for." xxiii. 161-3.

Wesley.

"*The Holy Eucharist as It implies a Sacrifice.*"
Christ's Sacrifice still propitiatory, and offered alike in Heaven and on earth:—

> "He still respects Thy Sacrifice,
> Its savour sweet doth always please;
> The Offering smokes through earth and skies,
> Diffusing life and joy and peace.
> To these Thy lower Courts It comes,
> And fills them with Divine perfumes."
> —*H.* cxvi.

"A priest for ever," Christ still presents to the Father in Heaven the Offering once made, while we on earth "Do this" also, as He commanded:—

> "His Body, torn and rent,
> He doth to God present:
> In that dear Memorial shows
> Israel's chosen tribes imprest;
> All our names the Father knows,
> Reads them on our Aaron's breast.

> "He reads while we beneath
> Present our Saviour's death:
> Do as Jesus bids us do,
> Signify His Flesh and Blood;
> Him in a memorial show—
> Offer up the Lamb to God."—*H.* cxviii.

With careful accuracy, Wesley here states the Catholic doctrine of the Eucharistic Sacrifice: he makes It identical with That in glorified condition before the Throne, and commemorative of that Bloody Sacrifice and act of oblation once made on Calvary:—

> "The Cross on Calvary He bore,
> He suffered once to die no more;
> But left a sacred pledge behind—
> See here! It on Thy Altar lies,
> Memorial of the Sacrifice
> He offered once for all mankind."—*H.* cxxi.

In a few lines he sums up all—both the doctrine of the Eucharistic Sacrifice—

> "Thy Sacrifice is all-complete,
> The death Thou never canst repeat,
> Once offered up to die no more.

Wesley

" Yet may we celebrate below,
  And daily thus Thine Offering show,
    Exposed before Thy Father's eyes!
  In this tremendous Mystery,
  Present Thee bleeding on the Tree,
    Our Everlasting Sacrifice."—*H.* cxxiv.

And Its peculiar value—

" To Thee His Passion we present,
  Who for our ransom dies;
  We reach by this great Instrument
  The Eternal Sacrifice."—*H.* cxxvi.

" If the most Holy Sacrament was celebrated in one place only, and consecrated by one only person in the world, with how great desire would men be affected to that place, and to such a priest, that they might enjoy these Divine Mysteries!

" But now there are many priests, and Christ is offered in many places; that so the grace and love of God to men may appear greater, the more this sacred Communion is spread through the world." viii. 109.

" We believe there is, and always was, in every Christian Church (whether dependent on the Bishop of Rome or not) an *outward priesthood*, ordained by Jesus Christ, and an *outward Sacrifice* offered therein, by men authorized to act as *ambassadors of Christ, and stewards of the mysteries of God.*" xxviii. 348.

---

3. EUCHARISTIC ADORATION.

High Churchmen.

Were it not for faith in the Divine declaration, it would have been impossible for the first believers to have worshipped as God, the Son of Mary, Whose outward appearance was only that of a creature, weaker and more dependent on human succour than any one of themselves.

With the same Divine faith is Jesus to be worshipped, whether

Wesley, 1745-1791.

" Ought he not also to reverence and adore when he looks toward that good hand which has appointed for the use of the Church the memorial of these great things? As the Israelites, whenever they saw the Cloud on the temple—which God had hallowed to be the sign of His Presence—presently used to throw themselves on their faces, not to

Wesley.

present as the Babe of Bethlehem, or "in another form," or under the veils of Bread and Wine.

In the Sacrament of the Altar, we believe there is His Body and His Blood; the Divine declaration is the warrant of our faith, and wherever His Presence is, there also is He to be adored.

worship the Cloud, but God; so whenever I see these better signs of the glorious mercies of God, I will not fail both to remember my Lord, Who appointed them, and to worship Him Whom they represent." xxiii. 144.

"If so great devotion was there shown, and there was such celebrating of the Divine praise before the Ark of the Testament, what reverence is now to be performed in receiving the most precious Body and Blood of Christ?" viii. 108.

"We freely own that Christ is to be adored *in* the Lord's Supper; but that the elements are to be adored, we deny." xix. 87.

A call to an act of Eucharistic adoration:—

"Then let our faith *adore* the Lamb,
To-day as yesterday the same,
In Thy great Offering join;
Partake the sacrificial Food,
And eat Thy Flesh, and drink Thy Blood,
And live for ever Thine."—H. iii.

"Did Thine ancient Israel go
With solemn praise and prayer
To Thy hallowed courts below,
To meet and serve Thee there?
To Thy Body, Lord, we flee;
This the consecrated shrine,
Temple of the Deity,
The real House Divine."—H. cxxvii.

This (not to speak of intention) is strictly applicable only to the Reserved Host—a perpetual Presence calling for an unceasing worship.

---

4. BENEFIT AND GRACE OF THE HOLY EUCHARIST.

High Churchmen.

As our Sacrifice, commemorative of the finished act on Calvary, and one with the Pleading Victim in Heaven, the Holy Eucharist

Wesley, 1740-1791.

First, as our Sacrifice, procuring man favour with God; and, second, as our Feast, conveying Divine blessings to man.

High Churchmen.

is the Divinely-provided medium of approach to the Father. "One with Christ, and Christ with us," we can enter the Divine Presence certain of finding acceptance for ourselves and favour for our services. Joined to It our prayers are all-availing, for they are backed by the great Intercessor Himself. Asking thus in Christ's Name our suit can never be rejected. "As oft as we do this we do show the Lord's Death;" and pleading the merits of His Death, we obtain for ourselves, and for "all Christ's whole Church," the quick and the dead, every needed blessing.

For this sufficient reason, because, in Wesley's words—

"By this great Instrument we reach
The Eternal Sacrifice,"

all are exhorted to stay and join in faith and prayer, and holy worship, even though they do not at the time communicate. In ancient times, before love and faith had waxed cold, no one that was called a Christian ever thought of omitting on the Lord's Day to join in offering the Holy Sacrifice: for many hundred years after the command was given such a practice among Christians was a thing unknown.

As our *Feast*, conveying Divine blessings to man, there is given us in the Holy Eucharist the Body and Blood of Christ, to be verily and indeed taken and received by all the faithful. Being by Baptism grafted into Christ, and thus deriving the beginning of spiritual life from Him, we

Wesley.

"This great and Holy Mystery communicates to us the Death of our Blessed Lord, both as *offering Himself to God*, and as giving Himself to man. *As He offered Himself to God*, It enters me into that mystical body for which He died, and which is dead with Christ: yea, It sets me on the shoulders of that eternal Priest, while He offers up Himself, and intercedes for His spiritual Israel. And by this means It conveys to me the communion of His sufferings, which leads to a communion in all His graces and glories. *As He offers Himself to man*, the Holy Sacrament is, after the Sacrifice for sin, the true Sacrifice of peace-offerings, and the Table purposely set; to receive those mercies that are sent down from His Altar, *Take and eat; this is My Body, which is broken for you. And this is My Blood, which was shed for you.*" xxiii. 156.

"Now, there is no ordinance or mystery that is so blessed an Instrument to reach this everlasting Sacrifice, and to set It solemnly forth before the eyes of God, as the Holy Communion is. *To men* it is a *sacred Table*, where God's minister is ordered to represent from God his Master the Passion of His dear Son, as still fresh, and still powerful for their eternal salvation. And *to God* it is *an Altar*, whereon men mystically present to Him the same Sacrifice, as still bleeding and suing for mercy. And because it is the High Priest Himself, the true Anointed of the

High Churchmen.	*Wesley.*
are wholly dependent upon Him for the future sustentation, and further increase of it; this He, the True Vine, imparts to His branches by feeding them from the true source of all—His own Body. Having life in Himself, He grants to His members to have life in themselves; the ordained means is the Eucharistic Feast on His own Body and Blood. Such as worthily eat thereof have life; such as eat not have not life. In neglect of the means the disobedient perish; in the use of It the faithful live.	Lord, Who hath set up both this Table and the Altar for the communication of His Body and Blood to men, and for the representation of both to God, it cannot be doubted but that the one is most profitable to the penitent sinner, and the other most acceptable to His gracious Father." xxiii. 163.

"The Oblation sends as sweet a smell,
  E'en now It pleases God as well
As when It first was made;
The Blood doth now as freely flow
As when His Side received the blow
  That show'd Him newly dead."
—*H.* iii.

"Sat. 28.—I showed at large: 1. That the Lord's Supper was ordained by God to be a means of conveying to men either preventing, or justifying, or sanctifying grace, according to their several necessities." xxvii. 224.

"Yea, Thy Sacrament extends
  All the blessings of Thy Death
To the soul that here attends,
  Longs to feel Thy quick'ning breath."—*H.* lxiv.

"Memorial of Thy Sacrifice,
  This Eucharistic Mystery
The full atoning grace supplies,
  And sanctifies our gifts in Thee.
Our persons and performance please,
  While God in Thee looks down from Heaven;
Our acceptable Service sees,
  And whispers all our sins forgiven."—*H.* cxxiii.

Wesley records so many instances of the great efficacy of this Sacrament, that "He was made known to him [her] in the Breaking of Bread," has the appearance in his Journals of being a stereotyped phrase.

5. FITNESS AND PREPARATION FOR RECEPTION.

High Churchmen.

To the Children belongs "the Children's Bread." *All baptized into Christ* have a right of admission to the Holy Eucharist, however unworthy, however weak in grace, however fallen in sin. Repentance for sin past and a stedfast purpose of amendment is all the fitness God requires, all that even the best can bring. Wherefore all must obey Christ's command who have any desire to please Him. The privilege of joining in the Holy Communion is not *a reward* for grace gained, it is *a means* by which grace is given. As bread to the hungry, and medicine to the sick, so is the Holy Communion to him that is ready to perish.

Yet, while a right disposition of heart is alone "indispensably necessary," the benefit of Holy Communion is increased to us in proportion as we carefully prepare ourselves to receive It—by careful examination and Confession, by prayer for grace, by self-denial, by the deliberate surrender of our whole selves to God.

Wesley, 1740-1789.

"Sat. 28.—I showed at large: .... 2. That the persons for whom It was ordained are all those who know and feel that they *want* the *grace* of God, either to *restrain* them from sin, or to *shew their sins forgiven*, or to *renew their souls* in the image of God. 3. That inasmuch as we come to His Table, not to give Him anything, but to *receive* whatsoever He sees best for us, there is no previous preparation indispensably necessary, but a desire to receive whatsoever He pleases to give. And 4. That no fitness is required at the time of communicating but a sense of our state, of our utter sinfulness and helplessness: everyone who knows he is fit for hell being just fit to come to Christ, in this as well as all other ways of His appointment." xxvii. 224.

Yet ought everyone to come to the Holy Communion "with due preparation—that is, with solemn prayer, with careful examination, with deep repentance suited thereto, with earnest and deliberate self-devotion." xv. 316.

6. DAILY CELEBRATION.

High Churchmen.

By our Lord's own appointment the celebration of the Holy Eucharist is the one mode by which we plead before God the

Wesley, 1740-1791.

True to his principles, Mr. Wesley ever looked for direction to the Scriptures and the Primitive Church; and thence drew

High Churchmen.

merits of His Death. He appointed this and none other. This is the only Service which Christ instituted for general and continual observance. Psalms, and litanies, and sermons, and Scripture readings, are good; but these, in public worship, are of the Church's appointment and of human arrangement. The Holy Communion alone is the Service ordained by Christ Himself. Accordingly this is the very thing which the first Christians "continued stedfastly in"—"Breaking of Bread and in prayers," "daily in the Temple and Breaking Bread." (Acts ii. 42, 46.) This is the very purpose for which "Upon the first day of the week the Disciples came together—to Break Bread" (Acts xx. 7); and so it thenceforth continued. From the day of Pentecost, for fifteen hundred years, no such thing was ever known as for Christians to come together for worship on the Lord's Day *without* this Memorial of the Death of Christ. Even so impartial and competent a witness as Bingham, in his *Christian Antiquities*, says: "On the Lord's Day the Eucharist was celebrated in all the churches, and never omitted in any assembly of Christians whatever." Our present neglect is rightly attributed by Wesley to "coldness and want of love." A daily Celebration is still, however, the Church's standard. In the Book of Common Prayer she provides a Collect, Epistle, and Gospel for every Sunday in the year, "which shall

Wesley.

all that he believed and taught respecting the Holy Eucharist. In his "Instructions for Christians," Lesson 8, Question 4, he asks, and answers, "How often did the first Christians receive the Lord's Supper? Every day: it was their Daily Bread." This allusion to the Lord's Prayer—"Give us this day our daily bread"—he explains in his "Sixth Discourse on the Mount:" "It was the judgment of many of the ancient Fathers that we are here to understand the Sacramental Bread also, *daily received* in the beginning by the whole Church of Christ, and highly esteemed (till the love of many waxed cold) as the grand channel whereby the grace of the Spirit was conveyed to the souls of all the children of God." Priests, he reminds, that daily, or at least weekly, Celebrations are required in the judgment of the Church of England:—"The judgment of our own Church is quite in favour of constant Communion. She takes all possible care that the Sacrament be duly administered, wherever the Common Prayer is read, every Sunday and Holyday in the year." (*Ss.* ii. 429.) And to such teaching his own practice was always conformable. A Methodist writer, Mr. Jackson, bears witness that "they (John and his brother Charles) administered the Lord's Supper every Sabbath Day;" and Mr. Wesley's Journal shows that the Church's Festivals were his "*opportunities* of celebrating the solemn feast days according to

High Churchmen.	Wesley.

serve *all the week after;*" and expressly enacts, that " in Cathedral or Collegiate Churches and Colleges, where there are many priests and deacons," there shall be a Communion "every Sunday at *the least.*" This is *the least* that will satisfy her directions wherever there are three to communicate with the Priest; a *Daily Celebration* being what she provides for in all churches.

" According to the mind and order of our Church, as well as the Primitive, the Lord's Supper ought to be administered *every day*, that all who live as they ought in her communion may be daily partakers of It." *Bp. Beveridge.*

the design of their institution"— *i.e.*, by a Daily Eucharist. Journal, 1777—" Easter-day was a solemn and comfortable day, wherein God was remarkably present with His people. During the Octave I administered the Lord's Supper every morning, after the example of the Primitive Church." 1773 — " Dec. 25, and on the following days, we had many happy opportunities of celebrating the solemn feast days according to the design of their institution." Christmas, 1774—" During the twelve festival days" (from Christmas-day to Twelvth-day, or Epiphany) "we had the Lord's Supper daily; a little emblem of the Primitive Church. May we be followers of them in all things, as they were of Christ!"

In his Sacramental Hymns (of which he published the ninth edition shortly before his death) he attributes the spiritual deadness of the Church in his day to the ceasing of " the Daily Sacrifice," and prays earnestly for that restoration of It to its proper place, which by God's goodness we are now beginning to see:—

" Happy the Saints of former days
    Who first continued in the Word,
A simple, lowly, loving race,
    True followers of their Lamb-like Lord.

" In holy fellowship they lived,
    Nor would from the Commandment move,
But every joyful day received
    The tokens of expiring love.

" Why is the faithful Seed deceased,
    The life of God extinct and dead?
The Daily Sacrifice has ceased,
    And charity to Heaven is fled!

" Sad mutual causes of decay,
    Slackness and vice together move;
Grown cold, we cast the means away,
    And quenched the latest spark of love.

Wesley.

"O woulds't Thou to Thy Church return,
For which the faithful remnant sighs,
For which the drooping nations mourn,
Restore the Daily Sacrifice."—*H.* clxvi.

---

7. THE DUTY OF CONSTANT COMMUNION.

High Churchmen.

If any respect be paid to the example of the first disciples, who are rightly presumed to have known best what is the mind of Christ, then every faithful man will receive the Holy Communion "every Sunday at the least." Christ's command obliges us to "do this" "as often" as we can. To do this only now and then, or at long intervals, can never satisfy a command which is of *constant* obligation. "Daily," or weekly, are the only intervals which have Scriptural sanction. "Once a month" is "after the traditions of men," this having the sanction neither of Holy Scripture nor of the Church, either in ancient or modern times. "Three times a year at the least" is the lowest term of Church-membership—that which the Church absolutely requires of all; failing which she considers them *ipso facto* excommunicate—unworthy even to be called Christians.

Considered as a privilege, every opportunity of receiving the Holy Communion should be valued and responded to joyfully. "With gladness," the first Christians

Wesley, 1733-1788.

"In the ancient Church every one who was baptized communicated daily. So in the Acts we read, 'They all continued daily in the Breaking of Bread and in prayer.'" (xxvii. 223).
"Let every one therefore who has either any desire to please God, or any love for his own soul, obey God, and consult the good of his own soul, by communicating every time he can, like the first Christians, with whom the Christian Sacrifice was a constant part of the Service of the Lord's-day. And for several centuries they received It almost every day. Four times a week always, and every Saint's-day beside. Accordingly, those that joined in the prayers of the faithful never failed to partake of the Blessed Sacrament."

To the objection, "God does not command me to communicate *often*"—that is, the word "often" is not added to the command, "Do this"—he replies, "What then? Are we not to obey every command of God as often as we can? Are not all the promises of God made to those, and those only, who *give all diligence:* that

High Churchmen.	Wesley.
communicated "daily:" it was their "Daily Bread;" that for which they prayed and longed. He can scarcely be said to value the privilege of prayer, who prays only "once a month," or even once a week; and we, if we truly know our privilege and need, shall feast on our Lord's Body and Blood, and renew our spiritual strength, not once a month or once a week even, but at every opportunity.	is, to those who do all they can to obey His commandments? Our power is the one rule of our duty. Whatever we can do, that we ought. With respect either to this or any other command, he that, when he may obey it if he will, does not, will have no place in the Kingdom of Heaven."

Another "objection, which some have made against constant Communion is, that 'the Church enjoins it only three times a year.' The words of the Church are, 'Note, that every parishioner shall communicate, at the least, three times in the year.' To this I answer, first, What if the Church had not enjoined it at all, is it not enough that God enjoins it? We obey the Church only for God's sake. And shall we not obey God Himself? .... But, secondly, we cannot conclude from these words that the Church excuses him who receives only thrice a year. The plain sense of them is, that he who does not receive thrice at least, shall be cast out of the Church."

To the objection, "Constant Communion abates our reverence for the Sacrament," Wesley replies, "Reverence for the Sacrament may be of two sorts; either such as is owing purely to the newness of the thing, such as men naturally have for anything they are not used to; or such as is owing to our faith, or to the love and fear of God. Now, the former of these is not properly a religious reverence, but purely natural. And this sort of reverence for the Lord's Supper, the constantly receiving of It must lessen. But it will not lessen the true reverence, but rather confirm and increase it."

"I ask then, Why do you not accept of His mercy as often as ever you can? God now offers you His blessing; why do you refuse it? You have now an opportunity of receiving His mercy; why do you not receive it? You are weak; why do you not seize upon every opportunity of increasing your strength? In a word, considering this as a command of God, he that does not communicate—not once a month, but—as often as he can, has no piety; considering it as a mercy, he that does not communicate as often as he can, has no wisdom." *Ss*. ii. 424, 429.

Accordingly, Wesley required by the Rules of the Society "that all the members thereof (including Preachers, xv. 325) should constantly attend the Church and Sacrament" (and by the Rules of Bands bound every member thereof to communicate "every week"):

Wesley.

in one instance, after enforcing this rule, he says, "After this was done, out of 204 members 174 remained. And these points shall be carried if only 50 remain in the Society." *Jl.* xvii. 45.

In a note prefixed to the Sermon from which the foregoing paragraphs are taken, Wesley certifies that such was his teaching throughout the whole of his life:—" The following discourse was written above five-and-fifty years ago, for the use of my pupils at Oxford. But, I thank God, I have not yet seen cause to alter my sentiments in any point therein delivered.—1788. J. W."

8. ADMINISTRATION TO YOUNG CHILDREN.

High Churchmen.

"Little children" are not forbidden to receive God's grace by whatever means it is offered. And our authority for "suffering" them to receive the grace of Holy Communion is the same as it is for "bringing" them to Baptism:—(1) This command of Christ (S. Mark x. 13) which is general; (2) the practice of the Primitive Church, which received its direction from the Apostles; and (3) the declared necessity of these two Sacraments to salvation. That "these little ones" can and do receive Christ's blessing without "repentance and faith," "when by reason of their tender age they cannot perform them," is certain, because Christ *blessed* such. In Galilee "He could do no mighty work because of their unbelief;" but little children, who cannot place this bar against Christ, are so receptive of every grace which He offers, that they are specially mentioned by Him

Wesley, 1748-1784.

By the pious care of his excellent and good mother, "John Wesley was admitted as a communicant at the Lord's Table so early as his eighth year." And he never hesitated to admit children of six years old and upwards. Such were they (xv. 226) in Kingswood School:—" Sunday, 30—Eight of the children and the three maids received the Lord's Supper for the first time." (*Jl.* xvi. 9). And in Wardale:—" The children, about twenty of them, steady and consistent, both in their testimony and behaviour, desired to join with their elder brethren in the great Sacrifice of Thanksgiving." A few are mentioned by name: P. T., nine years and a half old; H. W., ten years old; A. R., not eleven years old; S. S., eight years and a half old. S. M., fourteen years of age, is as a *mother* among them. (*Jl.* xvi 69, 74.) Kingswood School again:— " Sunday, 5 — I ex-

High Churchmen.	Wesley.
as possessing the completest and most certain fitness of all. Their need arises from the Holy Sacrament being not only "daily food for daily waste," but also for the *increase* of life. How early children arrive at a knowledge of good and evil, and have also this need to "eat of the tree of life," that they may have strength to "refuse the evil and choose the good," cannot of course be determined: this at least is certain, that at six or seven years old they are capable of sin, and have a correlative capacity for repentance and faith, and in consequence have both need of and right to the Holy Sacrament. The Church of England allows their right to Holy Communion, when "ready and desirous of being Confirmed," which, as defined by herself, is "so soon as they can say the Creed, the Lord's Prayer, and the Ten Commandments," *i.e.*, at six or seven years old. If Bishops	amined sixteen of them (the children) who desired to partake of the Lord's Supper." (*Jl.* xvi. 117.) "Sunday, 12 (at Pensford)—Four of Miss Owen's children desired leave to partake of the Lord's Supper" (p. 118). "Once more ...... at Kingswood. Many of the children were much affected. I talked particularly with some, who desired to partake of the Lord's Supper. They did so the next morning."—"Out of the mouths of babes and sucklings God has perfected praise." *Jl.* xvi. 119, and xx. 73. Various abuses, so called, having been charged against the Church of the first three centuries by Dr. Middleton, amongst others the practice of infant Communion, Wesley pointedly excepts this from such a designation:—"That infant Communion was an abuse," "I call upon you," says he, "to prove." xviii. 154.

refuse then to Confirm them, priests are required to admit them to the Lord's Table. The Primitive Church regularly practised Infant Communion, and to this day the Eastern Church, which adheres most tenaciously to primitive custom, communicates infants twice every year.

The denial of Communion to infants proceeded from the same source as the denial of the Cup to the laity—the Church of Rome: it is now due to that rationalistic unbelief which makes Divine grace wait on intellectual apprehension.

9. THE MIXED CHALICE AND UNLEAVENED BREAD.

High Churchmen.

The simple fact that it was the *Mixed* Cup which our Saviour "took," and the *Unleavened* Bread which He "broke" in the first Celebration of the Eucharist, is sufficient to satisfy High Churchmen, whose "one desire and design is to be Bible-Christians," that it is not only right for them to desire both, but also that it would be wrong for them to be satisfied to be without either.

Nothing is of no account, or of small importance, which is a departure from the Divine Institution, and also contrary to the primitive custom of the Church.

Wesley, 1749-1791.

In the ix. vol. of his *Works*, Wesley transcribes for the instruction of his people S. Justin Martyr's account of the public assemblies of the Early Christians, of the generation next after the living Apostles, in which the holy Martyr testifies—" Prayers being over, bread, and a cup of *wine and water* are brought to the bishop, which he takes, and offers up praise and glory to the Father of all things, through the Name of His Son and Holy Spirit. The people answer with joyful acclamations, *Amen!* Then the consecrated elements, the Eucharistical Bread and Wine, are distributed to, and partaken by, all that are present, and sent to the absent by the hands of the deacons." p. 27.

In defence of the First Christians who thus used the Mixed Chalice, Wesley replies to Dr. Middleton—" In the Sacrament of the Eucharist, several abuses (you say) were introduced. You instance, first, in mixing the *wine with water.* But how does it appear that this was any abuse at all? Or, that 'Irenæus declared it to have been taught as well as practised by our Saviour'? The words you quote to prove this, do not prove it at all; they *simply relate a matter of fact:* 'Taking the Bread, He confessed it to be His Body, and the *Mixed Cup* He affirmed it was His Blood.' You cannot be ignorant of this fact, that the cup used after the Paschal Supper was *always mixed with water.*" xviii. 153.

And in a manuscript in Mr. Wesley's own handwriting, still preserved in an old Methodist family, he says—" I believe it a duty to observe, so far as I can, to use *water in the Eucharist.*" *Guardian*, Nov. 27, 1867.

In accordance with this, Wesley points out in his Sacramental Hymns that fact in the Sacred History which makes the Mixed Chalice so eminently proper:—

Wesley.

"See from His wounded side
 The *mingled* current flow!
The *Water and the Blood* applied,
 Shall wash us white as snow."—lxxiv.

And in like manner the use of *Unleavened Bread* (which his pupil and fellow-labourer, Dr. Adam Clarke, declared to be *necessary* to a *proper* Celebration of the Sacred Mystery):—

"Let us all with hearts sincere
 Eat the new *Unleavened Bread;*
To our Lord with faith draw near,
 And on His promise feed."—*H.* lxxxiv.

---

10. CHORAL CELEBRATION.

High Churchmen.   *Wesley,* 1762-1782.

To the unsophisticated Christian mind there is no time which so clearly calls for our lowliest adoration, and our highest strain of praise, as that in which the Divine Mysteries are being celebrated.

If we may not then, "with Angels and Archangels," make sweet melody and raise our voices in song—on that one only occasion on which we are ever told that our Blessed Lord "sung," an "authority and example" which even the Baptists, in 1722, declared to be "sufficient to *oblige* us to do likewise"—then we must take leave to deny that music has any right to a place in Christian worship at all. And just such is the judgment recently given by so moderate a Churchman as Dr. Goulburn, the present Dean of Norwich: "I hold that shutting up the organ, and dismissing the singers at the

Wesley was highly pleased with sweet, soft music during the Communion of the Lord's Body and Blood: a Service to which he would bring the highest triumphs of art, and also the simplest strains of the village choir. He composed and provided Hymns "on the tremendous Mystery," to be sung during the Celebration, and Hymns to be sung "after the Sacrament;" and by the same means provided also that the *Ter Sanctus,* and *Gloria in Excelsis Deo,* might be sung by every congregation; and in the spirit of "the sweet singer of Israel," thus invoked the Angels that "excel in strength" to join the song:—

"Ye that round our Altars throng,
Listening Angels, join the song;
Sing with us, ye heavenly powers,
Pardon, grace, and glory ours."
 —*H.* clxiv.

High Churchmen.

Celebration of Holy Communion, is a rank absurdity. Either music is an impertinence altogether, or it ought to adorn the chief Service."

Wesley.

The following evidence of the same kind is from his Journal:—
1782. "Sunday 18 (Exeter).— I was much pleased with the decent behaviour of the whole congregation at the Cathedral, as also with the solemn music at the post-Communion, one of the finest compositions I ever heard." (xix. 91.) 1762. "Sunday 29. At the Cathedral ...... the whole Service was performed with great seriousness and decency. Such an organ I never saw or heard before, so large, beautiful, and so finely toned. And the music of 'Glory be to God in the highest,' I think exceeded the 'Messiah' itself." (xii. 143.) "March 29 [1782], Macclesfield. I came to assist Mr. Simpson. While we were administering the Sacrament, I heard a low, soft, solemn sound, just like that of an Æolian harp. It continued five or six minutes, and so affected many that they could not refrain from tears. It then gradually died away. *Strange that no other organist* (that I know) *should think of this.*" *Jl.* xix. 77.

---

11. REPELLING EVIL-DOERS.

High Churchmen.

"*Stewards* of the *Mysteries of God*," priests must administer them according as they have received of the Lord, subject to no earthly power, save their own ecclesiastical superiors.

The charge of "spiritual tyranny and of usurping a new and illegal authority," they can bear unmoved; but in no case can they administer the Holy Communion to such as "testify against themselves" that they are ungodly in their lives, or heretical in their faith.

State laws may conflict with spiritual obligations, but the requirement of God is supreme. And while laws take their course, and faithful priests suffer "bonds

Wesley, 1737-1745.

"May not God complain...... 'they have put no difference between the holy and profane; therefore I am profaned among them.' For is it *not* so? Do *you* put a difference between the holy and profane, him that feareth God and him that feareth Him not? Do you put an effectual difference between them, even in the most solemn office of our religion? At the Table of the Lord, do you take care to *separate the precious from the vile?* to receive all those who (as you may reasonably believe) draw near with penitent hearts and lively faith, and utterly to reject those who testify against themselves that they are without

High Churchmen.	*Wesley.*
and imprisonment," or "take joyfully the spoiling of their goods," their only answer will be, "We ought to obey God rather than men."	hope and without God in the world?
Priests only of Wesley's stamp, who have faith in their office, can, as a recent case testifies (Birmingham *Papers*, Sep.-Dec., 1867), withstand the clamour, the threatenings, and Episcopal admonitions (in that case to the honour of the Bishop, be it said, withdrawn), and utterly refuse to give the Sacrament of the Lord's Body and Blood to the unholy and profane.	"Nay, who dares *repel* one of the greatest men in his parish from the Lord's Table, even though he be a drunkard or a common swearer? yea, though he openly deny the Lord that bought him? Mr. Stonehouse did this once. But what was the event? The gentleman brought an action against him, for the terror of all such insolent fellows in succeeding times."

John Wesley did: he *dared;* for he was no faint-hearted priest. "Sunday, 7, I repelled Mrs. Williamson from the Holy Communion. And Monday, 8, Mr. Recorder of Savannah issued out the warrant following: 'To all Constables,' &c. 'You and each of you are hereby required to take the body of John Wesley, clerk, and bring him,' &c. Mr. Joes, the constable, served the warrant, and carried me before Mr. Bailiff Parker and Mr. Recorder. My answer to them was, that 'The giving or refusing the Lord's Supper, being a matter purely ecclesiastical, I could not acknowledge their power to interrogate me upon it.'" The matter was brought before a grand jury, of which "one was a Papist, one a professed infidel, three Baptists, sixteen or seventeen others Dissenters, and several others who had personal quarrels against me, and had openly vowed revenge.

"To *this* grand jury, Mr. C. gave a long and earnest charge, '*To beware of spiritual tyranny, and to oppose the new, illegal authority which was usurped over their consciences,*'" &c.

It was then, as now,—The world against the Church: the one resisting, the other exercising, the authority inherent in the priestly office.

Besides this offending person, Mr. Wesley *repelled*, on several occasions, divers others, and stood on the Rubrics directing him so to act, and declared, that according to them, and not otherwise, "I will administer to you the Mysteries of God." xxvi. 199–208.

CHAPTER VI.
OF CONFESSION.

1. PRACTICE OF CONFESSION.

High Churchmen.

Of Confession to men,* as ministers or representatives of God, Scripture is full. Pharaoh confessed to Moses and Aaron, almost in the very words which have for ages been in use in the Christian Church, and in consequence was for the time forgiven. "I have sinned against the Lord and against you, now therefore *forgive, I pray thee, my sin*, and entreat the Lord that He may take away from me this death." In Leviticus and Numbers (v. 5, and v. 6) it is directed that "When a man or woman shall commit any sin .... then *they shall confess the sin* which they have done:" "and the priest shall make an atonement for him for the sin which he hath sinned, and it shall be forgiven him." Achan was moved to confession by Joshua :—" My son, give, I pray thee, glory to the Lord God of Israel, and make *confession unto Him*, and *tell me* now what thou hast done. And Achan answered Joshua, and said, Indeed I have sinned against the Lord God of Israel, and thus and thus have I done." Saul made confession

Wesley, 1738-1791.

Mr. Wesley had so high a sense of the value of this Ordinance that he commended it in its proper form—*i.e.*, to a priest; urged it in various forms—*e.g.*, to preachers, leaders, and "brethren like-minded:" and made it the chief feature of an Institution to which all members were earnestly requested to belong— viz., that of Bands. (*Minutes* i. 12, 79 ; ii. 347.)

In a confutation of Romish doctrine, he censures their making Confession to a priest *necessary to salvation*, or necessary *in all cases*, but adds thereto, "We grant Confession to men to be in many cases of use; public in case of public scandal, private to a spiritual guide for disburdening of the conscience, and as a help to repentance." (xix. 91.) And in pointing out the difference between Confession privately practised in Bands and Confession privately made to a priest, when the objection was urged, "All these Bands are mere Popery," he says, "Do not they yet know that the only Popish Confession is the Confession made by a single

---

* See two excellent essays (Nos. 7 and 11) in *The Church and the World*, 1867.

High Churchmen.

unto Samuel:—" I have sinned, for I have transgressed the commandment of the Lord and thy words. Now therefore, I pray thee, *pardon my sin*." That of David to Nathan may be said to be the type of the Christian practice, when, in consequence of the prophet's direct appeal to his conscience, the royal penitent confessed to him, "I have sinned against the Lord," and Nathan absolved him thus—" The Lord also hath put away thy sin," imposing, nevertheless, the penance, " The child that is born unto thee shall surely die."

And so does the course of Confession of sin and consequent remission continue when we come to the New Testament. The Jews came to John "*confessing their sins*," "and were baptized by him" " for the remission of sins." And so our Lord, as Son of Man, received Confession of sins, and having this power on earth as Sent of God, granted remission of sins. But on His earthly ministry ceasing, He delegated the office and power to His Apostles:— " As My Father hath sent Me, *even so* send I you:" " Whose soever sins *ye remit, they are remitted* unto them; and whose soever sins ye retain, they are retained." And henceforth, in measure befitting this high source, ministers, as delegates of Christ, forgave sins "in the person of Christ," acting "in Christ's stead."

From the time of the Apostles downwards until the Reforma-

Wesley.

person to a priest? And *this itself* is *in no wise* condemned by our Church; nay, she recommends it in some cases. But the truth is, this is a stale objection, which many people make against anything they do not like." xv. 214.

In *Thoughts on a Single Life*, he says, " It may be of infinite service to disclose to these the very secrets of your hearts: especially the weaknesses springing from your natural constitution, or education, or long-contracted habit, and the temptations which from time to time most easily beset you." (xxiv. 259.) Here is Confession encouraged to " brethren like-minded;" and if " it may be of infinite service" when made to men of our own age and standing, it cannot with any reason be discouraged, nor have less said for it. when made to a spiritual guide and director who has received the charge by Divine appointment, and is furnished with all the means and opportunies requisite thereto. And such was the judgment of the early Methodists :—" Mr. Baxter, after long experience and the maturest reflection, was so persuaded of the necessity of such assistance as to recommend it to all penitents in the most pressing terms. ' Never,' says he, ' expect that all thy books or sermons, thy prayers or meditations, should serve thy turn without the advice and counsel of thy pastor; for that were devising to prove God's officers needless to His Church.' An expression of the celebrated

High Churchmen.

tion, the case is so clear as to the continued exercise of this power, that when the Reformation set men feeling afresh for the old foundations, they " all, with one consent," bore witness to the practice and need of such Confession. Luther, " the father of the Reformation," in his own strong words, said, " he would rather lose a thousand worlds than suffer private Confession to be thrust out of the Church." Calvin, the head of the Swiss and French Reformers, bids " every faithful man remember that it is his duty (if inwardly he be vexed and afflicted with the sense of his sins) not to neglect that remedy which is offered him by the Lord, to wit, that for the easing of his conscience he make private Confession of his sins unto his pastor." " By means of private confession pardon is obtained from those to whom Christ said, 'All that you shall have loosed and remitted in earth shall be loosed and remitted in Heaven.' "

"The Anglican Fathers" of the Reformation, Cranmer, Latimer, and Ridley, also held and taught the same with one voice. Cranmer says, " God doth not speak to us with a voice sounding out of Heaven, but He hath given the keys of the Kingdom of Heaven, and the authority to forgive sins, to the ministers of the Church; wherefore, let him that is a sinner go to one of them, let him acknowledge and confess his sin, and pray him that, according to God's commandment,

Wesley.

Ostervald is somewhat stronger. 'It is certain,' says he, 'that multitudes perish for want of laying themselves open to their spiritual physician.'" *Mag.* xix. 130.

Answering thereto, Wesley, " as a wise master-builder," urges his preachers to make sure their groundwork. " In doing this it may be well, after a few loving words spoken to all in the house, to take each person singly into another room, where you may deal closely with them about their sin and misery and duty. Set these home, or you lose all your labour." Anticipating the objection of those who shrink:— "But should not tenderness hinder us from giving pain? Yes, from giving unnecessary pain. But what manner of tenderness is this? It is like that of a surgeon who lets his patient be lost because he is too compassionate to probe his wounds. Cruel compassion! Let me give pain so I may save life. Let me probe that God may heal." xv. 291; x. 138.

Call this Confession, or whatever you will, it is the Church's work in the Ordinance of Confession. The world, *The Times*, will call it "pumping," and " priestcraft:" and priestcraft it is in its proper sense; it is the priest showing a knowledge of his proper craft or calling, and faithfully applying it.

Institution of Bands. " The design is to obey that command of God, 'Confess your faults one to another, and pray one for another, that you may be healed.'

High Churchmen.

he will give him Absolution ...... and when the minister doth so, I ought stedfastly to believe that my sins are truly forgiven in Heaven." Bishop Latimer says, "To speak of right and true confession, I would to God it were kept in England; for it is a good thing." And Bishop Ridley, the other of this famous trio, says, "Confession unto the minister which is able to instruct, correct, and inform the weak, wounded, and ignorant conscience, indeed I ever thought might do much good to Christ's congregation, and so, I assure you, I think to this day."

And as by Protestants of all kinds abroad, so by Protestants of all kinds at home was private Confession maintained and practised. Dr. Reynolds, the representative of the Presbyterians; Dr. Owen, the leader of the Independents; Richard Baxter, the spiritual guide of the Puritans; and Cecil, the light of the Evangelicals, all defended, or as ministers received, private Confessions.

And in the English Church whoever obtained honour above his fellows—Jewel, "the jewel of Bishops," as Evangelicals delight to call him; "the judicious Hooker," "the pious Bishop Ken," "the saintly George Herbert," "the Apostolic Bishop Wilson,"—was also an upholder and firm maintainer of the use and need of private Confession of sin to a priest.

And that these represented not only the theory of Confession as

Wesley.

"The chief rules are:—
"1. To meet once a week.
"2. To come punctually.
"3. To begin with singing or prayer.
"4. To speak each of us in order, freely and plainly, the true state of our soul, with the faults we have committed in thought, word, or deed, and the temptations we have felt, since our last meeting.
"5. To desire some person among us (thence called a leader) to speak his own state first, and then to ask the rest in order, as many and as searching questions as may be, concerning their state, sins, and temptations."

"Some of the questions proposed to every one before he is admitted among us may be to this effect:—

"Do you desire we should come as close as possible, that we should cut to the quick, and search your heart to the bottom?

"Is it your desire and design to be on this and all other occasions entirely open, so as to speak everything that is in your heart, without exception, without disguise, and without reserve?

"The preceding questions [these two and others] may be asked as often as occasion offers; the four following at every meeting:—

"1. What known sins have you committed since our last meeting?
"2. What temptations have you met with?
"3. How were you delivered?
"4. What have you thought, said, or done, of which you doubt

High Churchmen.

it is set forth in the Book of Common Prayer, but also the existent practice of the Church, is at once evident from the Visitation Articles issued from time to time by the Bishops, directing and regulating the practice. And the Canons of the Church, both English and Irish, clench the evidence and remove the last possibility of honest doubt. By the XIX. Canon of the Irish Church it was ordered that a bell should be tolled before the administration of Holy Communion, for the purpose of enabling penitents to avail themselves of the *Special Ministry of Reconciliation*—i.e., "the benefit of Absolution by the power of the Keys, which Christ has committed to the ministers for that purpose." And by the CXIII. Canon of the Church of England it is ordered:—"If any man confess his secret and hidden sins to the minister for the unburdening of his conscience, and to receive spiritual consolation and ease of mind from him; we do straitly charge and admonish him that he do not reveal and make known to any person whatsoever any crime or offence so committed to his trust and secresy under pain of irregularity."

So that the motto which emblazoned every Protestant standard in the sixteenth century, "Diligenter retinemus in Ecclesia Confessionem," is equally ours also—Diligently do we retain in the Church the *Ordinance of Confession*.

Wesley.

whether it be a sin or not?" xv. 212, and *Rules of the Band Societies*.

Here is *Compulsory Confession*, or Protestants must sacrifice their charge of *Compulsory Celibacy* against Roman Catholics—i.e., compulsory with a limitation—on all who enter Bands or Orders respectively, and not otherwise. That it is Confession proper, and Confession to man, none can doubt: that what is lawful when made to many, is lawful when made to one, none can deny. Whether it be attended with as great spiritual advantages when the Confession is made to one Divinely appointed for this very thing—to direct, to instruct, to assist; and be liable to fewer abuses when breathed into his ear alone, remain the only questions: the former Wesley admits (xix. 91); the latter his Journals prove (xxi. 16); and the present disuse amongst Methodists of this Ordinance, which at first they regarded as of Divine obligation (page 31), shows that the one only way of still observing it, and still satisfying all spiritual needs, is the one Wesley first points out and approves, "private to a spiritual guide."

2. BENEFIT OF CONFESSION.

High Churchmen.

As a means of *Holy Living*, no less than of *Holy Dying*, Private Confession is commended not only by the author of these golden treatises, Bishop Jeremy Taylor, but even in such books of Puritan writers, Abbott's *Young Christian*, for example, as receive a ready welcome into every dissenting family. Jacob Abbott therein instructs the young Christian, "The first step to break the chains of any sinful habit is to *confess it* fully and freely. That single act will do more to give your fault its death-blow than anything else you can do. If you are a child, you can derive great assistance from confessing to your parents; or confess, and express your determination to amend, to some confidential friend of your own age." And the reason why we may confess to a friend, because burdened and entangled by sin, is the reason why we should confess to a priest, because he bears the Ministry of Reconciliation. We may disclose our wounds to a friend, but we seek out a physician to obtain a cure. "Multitudes perish," says a writer quoted with approval in the *Methodist Magazine*, "for want of laying themselves open to their spiritual physician." Never, indeed, can we neglect what is of Christ's appointment, save to our own loss. "Never expect," says Richard Baxter, "that all thy books or sermons, thy prayers

Wesley, 1748-1764
(*post obit.* 1796).

"We grant Private Confession to a spiritual guide to be in many cases of use for *disburdening of the conscience and as a help to repentance.*" xix. 91.

"It may be of infinite service to disclose to these (brethren like-minded) the very secrets of your hearts: especially the weaknesses springing from your natural constitution, or education, or long contracted habit, and the temptations which from time to time most easily beset you. By this means a thousand devices of Satan will be brought to nought, innumerable snares will be prevented, or you will pass through them without being hurt." xxiv. 259.

His judgment was justified by his experience. Speaking of the Bands, he says, "They prayed for one another that they might be healed of the faults they had confessed: and it was so; the bands were burst in sunder, and sin had no more dominion over them. Many were delivered from the temptations, out of which, till then, they found no way to escape. They were built up in the most holy faith. They rejoiced in the Lord more abundantly. They were strengthened in love, and more effectually provoked to abound in every good work." xv. 213.

Closely allied to the Band-meeting is the Class-meeting, offering the same opportunity for Confession, but not like the Bands, making it a matter of obligation,

High Churchmen.

or meditations, should serve thy turn without the advice and counsel of thy pastor; for that were devising to prove God's officers needless to His Church." Also many who do truly repent of their sins, are yet unrelieved of their distress; they can receive no assurance of sins forgiven, nor make further progress in the spiritual life, until they hear the absolving voice: but, says Archbishop Cranmer, "God doth not speak to us with a voice sounding *out of Heaven*," this voice we can hear only through His ministers; and when a truly penitent man hears it, he has Divine assurance that sins remitted on earth are remitted in Heaven. Nothing is so presumptuously contrary to God's law of giving grace as that power of self-appropriation, often fatally deceptive, which is worked up by the *subjective* influence of spiritual exercises. Some men choose to be their own physicians, their own lawyers, their own advisers (not, as all but themselves can see, to their own advantage), but no man may safely dispense with the services of a spiritual confessor. Thus speaks even the Evangelical Richard Cecil. "Incalculable injuries to health and property must be sustained for want of proper advisers. This applies in a very high sense to a minister, considered as a confessor, a director of the conscience." And in nothing is the well-intentioned effort of those who dissent from what the Church requires in the case of

Wesley.

to be elicited if necessary by a course of questioning. Methodists of Wesley's generation, in 1796, quote approvingly testimonies to the value of Private Confession, and take it as a matter which needs no proof that the Class-meeting is so similiar thereto, in nature and design, as to share in the commendation: they speak of Class-meetings as affording "such assistance" as penitents obtain by going to their minister when in spiritual distress, and "laying themselves open to their spiritual physician:" they find Scriptural confirmation of such means in that the penitent Jews "confessed their sins" to John, "and each received advice as his case required." (*Mag.* xix. 126, 130.) And the early Methodists were right: such private communications to Wesley, as a physician of souls, were the seed out of which the Class-meeting grew:—"Several persons who had been awakened by his sermons came to him for advice and comfort. At length he judged it most convenient for him, and profitable for them," to have a fixed time, and to join together all that came in singing and prayer; then "he enquired into the state of their minds, and gave them advice one by one. This is the simple form of a Methodist Class, which has continued invariably the same to the present day." (*Id.* 128.) And the Class-meeting was reasonably expected to show fruit after the same kind as the seed. All the Societies were everywhere

| *High Churchmen.* | *Wesley.* |

those spiritually "troubled" so fatally mischievous as in offering an easy cure — "healing the wound slightly"—instead of inducing, what a physician would term, a healthy suppuration; and a priest, a cleansing confession; for to this, and this only, is attached, by Christ's ordinance and promise, the remission of post-baptismal sins.

But as a means of *Holy Dying* it is that the necessity of Confession appears in the strongest light. Whilst in health, there is an inner reserve—a barrier never yet broken down—and the pulpit ministrations of the priest, though ever so faithful, have been, as Hammond observes in his eulogy on Confession, an attempt to fill narrow-mouthed bottles by setting them together, and throwing never so many buckets of water on them. Hence, real work cannot end there; in many cases it is not even consciously begun; and too often, howsoever great that work is, it is relegated by that same reserve to the bed of sickness or death. Then, if ever, there must be a leading of the soul from sin unto repentance, and through the narrow gate of repentance to reparation, and on to the full restoration of God's favour and sense of sins forgiven. But how can the priest attempt this unless he knows the state of the sick man's mind? And how is he to know his state unless it be laid open by Confession? Without Confession, in whatever form, or under whatever name, this is by all admitted to be im-

told, "we wish to hear of the depravity of the old man as well as the grace of the new:" they were expressly warned against any concealment arising from the temptation, that "if we discover the whole of our unfaithfulness and depravity, we shall be considered as the pests of religious society, and as the vilest of human characters;" and very justly is it intimated in the following lament, that the speaking fluently of mercies received, and the concealment of sins committed, is a species of deception calculated to make hypocrites rather than saints:—"Many of our brethren are so frequently induced to give us a very unfair and partial account of their experience. They speak freely enough of the goodness and mercy of God; but they hide, or only hint in an obscure manner, whatever is disagreeable and worthy of blame; and their testimony amounts to no more than an illusive fragment, instead of a plain and just account." *Id.* 180, 181.

It is in the unreserved, full disclosure, to which all are invited, that the whole benefit of the Class-meeting is placed:— "In order that the weekly classes may be edifying and profitable, it is essentially requisite that the people speak their experience with the utmost freedom and simplicity: where this method is attended to, the utility of these meetings is found to exceed everything that can be said in their favour. We must acknowledge, indeed, that when people are de-

High Churchmen.	Wesley
possible. "We cannot," says a writer in a Methodist publication, "as the Blessed Jesus, reply to the secret cases of our auditors; it is solely by the use of this means that the spiritual pastor is enabled to make a proper selection of subjects, and to apply the promises and direct the threatenings as their cases may require." As completely fast as a physician would be, who, on being called in, was suffered to ask no questions, and make no examination, is the pastor without Confession; and the priest who is satisfied without it is as great an empiric, and his visits are as worthless, as that physician and his services who should be satisfied to render them so debarred from the knowledge requisite to the due discharge of his office. Professional help implies a previous disclosure of the case, and without this—Confession—the pastoral office is, and must be, a painful distressing nullity. Take an every-day instance. A priest is called to see one in sickness, of whom as to the inner workings of sin or grace in his soul he knows nothing. All appears satisfactory, and he hopes well; or otherwise, he is perplexed and in fear, but has no clue: days pass on, and with them a soul is being hurried into eternity and the presence of its Judge. It then comes to his knowledge that up to the time of sickness, this one, of whom he has been hoping well, or otherwise, knew not how to treat, was living in deadly sin—that	fective in either of these virtues, and discover an unwillingness to open their state, the true end of these social means is subverted, and the devotion rendered both tedious and unprofitable." *Id.* 179. When persons are brought to make confession of their sins as well as to speak of the goodness and the love of God, many are the benefits which ensue:—"Mutual communion is further recommended by its being a most powerful preservative to all young professors, against a relapse into any of their former sins. And, indeed, the far greater part of those who have resolved to quit their vain and wicked course, and to dedicate the subsequent part of their life to God, have found upon trial that their feeble resolutions were, at first, unequal to the force of temptation. Their vows in the morning were violated in the evening, because they were not the offspring of virtuous habits, but the result of chagrin and fear, or of remorse for recent guilt. Seldom, therefore, did they survive the assault of repeated temptation. And even the strongest of those who stand alone, and are indifferent as to the counsel and communion of saints, seem to be strangely insensible of the dangers to which they are exposed. Were any pleasing or lucrative vice to present itself, they are destitute of all restraint and admonition from the Church of God. And as their relapse would be supported by innumerable examples in the world, they are the more easily

High Churchmen.

even now there exists an unrepaired wrong. Thus furnished, he hurries at once to the dying man's side, and if he be sufficiently heedless of popular clamour, how easy henceforth is his task; like Nathan, he points out the sin, and its enormity; he hears a confession of guilt; he probes the sick man's heart to the bottom, and thereout brings to the light other transgressions; quickened by the sight of a soul on the very edge and border of another world, he directs reparation to whatever extent it is possible; he assures him of a free and full forgiveness on his sincere repentance; now he can pray, and pray in faith, and "the prayer of a righteous man," when faults are confessed, "availeth much;" he is encouraged with evidence of contrition; he rises with his office, and on a profession of hearty repentance and true faith, he gives him Absolution, and the man is saved, though "scarcely," and, as it were, "by the skin of his teeth." And who is he that dare condemn? As God liveth, is there not a cause? This is not a time for trusting to random shots, in hope that some one will hit the mark! And these are not the cases that can be served by Scripture readings and general prayers; and in their light, before which outside clamour pales into absolute insignificance, the direction of the Church—that the sick man, after he has been brought into spiritual distress, "shall be moved to make a special Confession"—is

Wesley.

beguiled by that fatal sophism of fleshly wisdom, 'I may sin to-day and repent to-morrow.' So then they fall in heart before they have the opportunity to enjoy either the emolument or pleasure of their favourite vice: they fall alone, and they have none to lift them up. Now, it is *impossible* for these men to make much progress in religion while they keep at a distance from God's people, and *hide the corruptions of their heart, as a secret disease.* The eye of a spiritual leader, the affectionate care of their brethren, and the consideration that they have *disclosed their case* to the faithful, and openly espoused their cause before the world, would be powerful motives against their besetting sins, and strengthen them against the force of future temptations." *Id.* 177.

Nor does the benefit end here. The "hearing experience," or confession, whether by preacher or priest, "is infinitely advantageous to our public ministry:" "It is finally observed that mutual communion is infinitely advantageous to our public ministry, by giving us every necessary information concerning the people's state and experience. We are not endowed with the powers of omniscience; we cannot, as the Blessed Jesus, reply to the secret cases and thoughts of our auditors; but by frequently meeting the classes, and visiting from house to house, we shall be enabled to make a proper selection of subjects, and to apply

High Churchmen.	Wesley.
seen to be not only a commendable counsel, but even *a pressing necessity to save a soul from death.*	the promises, or direct the threatenings, as the cases may require. Here it is worthy of remark that a minister, whose abilities are cultivated by hearing

experience, and advising in cases of conscience, by removing objections and supporting the tempted, acquires a habit of preaching much more pertinent and useful than one who improves them merely by the efforts of reading and study. The latter may judiciously explain and beautifully illustrate the sacred writings; he may instruct and edify the ignorant, and acquire much applause as an orthodox and popular speaker; but the former opens and exposes the conscience, and addresses the sinner in the striking language of his own heart." *Id.* 179.

3. SHAME: A HINDRANCE TO CONFESSION.

High Churchmen.	Wesley, 1756 (*post obit.* 1796).
It has been well said that "the devil makes restitution; having taken from men the fear of shame in committing sin, he gives it back to prevent them from confessing it." Wherefore, "not to confess sin is shame;" that shame which comes not from above, but is a giving place to the devil. For he who shrinks from confessing his sin, shrinks from what many have found the only way of escape from it. Confession, though it be as abhorrent to the mind as a painful operation is to the body, is remedial, and should gladly be endured for the sake of the spiritual health it offers. "Be not ashamed," says the author of the Book of Ecclesiasticus, "when it concerneth thy soul—be not ashamed to confess thy sins, for there is a shame which	"Now, when Satan has tempted us to any particular sin, or overcome us by any of the aforesaid evils, he tempts us also to conceal it; because he is well aware that the works of darkness are unable to bear the light, and that speaking of our temptations is the surest way to subdue them. He suggests that our distresses are the more deplorable, and our sins more heinous, than those of other men. He suggests, again, that if we discover the whole of our unfaithfulness and depravity, we shall be considered as the pests of religious society, and as the vilest of human characters. And, as every man is better acquainted with the corruption of his own heart than with any other, we are but too apt to believe him. It is partly, there-

High Churchmen.

bringeth sin, and there is a shame which is glory and grace." iv. 20, 21, 26. induced to give us a very unfair account of their experience."

"Never, therefore, let us entertain the thought that we shall be despised for telling the truth; for however wise and holy those may now be to whom we speak, their minds were once as ignorant, and their hearts as much depraved, as our own; and the numerous conflicts they have had in obtaining the victory have taught them to be the more compassionate towards the weak." *Mag.* xix. 180, 181.

To this Wesley need only add, "Be not ashamed when it concerneth thy soul." x. 138.

Wesley.

fore, through temptation, and partly through the prevalence of haughty reason, that many of our brethren are so frequently induced to give us a very unfair and partial

---

4. SECRECY IN CONFESSION.

High Churchmen.

Richard Cecil, speaking as an "Evangelical," from his own sense of what is right, says, "Professional men—a minister, a lawyer, a medical man—have an official secrecy imposed on them. If this were not the case, a distressed conscience could never unburthen itself to its confessors." Touching this, the Church has always held that what the priest hears under the seal of confession, he hears only as a minister of God; and that the highest sacrilege would be committed by discovering it to men. One such instance occurred during the Decian persecution (A.D. 250) and was immediately followed by deposition from the ministry. The Church of England, in the CXIII. Canon, threatens the same punishment

Wesley, 1748 (*post obit.* 1796).

Wesley knew how essential to any system of Confession is *inviolable secrecy*. And amongst the few directions needed, laid down —"First, let nothing spoken in this Society be spoken again. (Hereby we had the more full confidence in each other.)" xv. 217.

And the early Methodists knew how to turn this rule to account in urging the less-established members of the Society to a full disclosure of their state, sins, and temptations:—"As the conversation is confined to the state of the soul, and no one allowed to divulge it elsewhere; as nothing is said with regard to private or family concerns, there can be no just cause for our restraint and want of freedom." *Mag.* xix. 281.

High Churchmen.

for the same offence:—"If any man confess his secret hidden sins to the minister ... we do straitly charge and admonish him that he do not at any time reveal and make known, to any person whatsoever, any crime or offence so committed to his trust and secrecy (except they be such crimes as by the laws of this realm his own life may be called in question for concealing the same), under pain of irregularity." The "pain of irregularity" is the heaviest punishment of an ecclesiastical offence that can be inflicted—involving a deprivation of any present office, and rendering a person incapable of holding any thereafter. It is true that these Canons have not Parliamentary authority, but they serve equally well without, and, indeed, better, to show what the mind of the Church is. Accordingly Bishops have from time to time made formal inquiry in their Visitation Articles addressed to the Churchwardens, "Whether the minister has ever revealed the secret and hidden sins committed to his trust?" But so inviolable is the secrecy that even an *apostate* priest has never been known to divulge a confession.

5. OBJECTIONS AGAINST CONFESSION.

High Churchmen.

An accepted argument against the practice of Confession is, that it is *polluting*, both to the confessor and also to those who confess. Weak, foolish babbling! The polluting details of the worst breaches of the Seventh Commandment are drawn out in public in courts of law; are published daily in a thousand newspapers, and lie under the eye of every youth and maiden in this realm! How stupidly ignorant—or worse—then, must those be who behold this sink of corruption laid bare to all eyes, and yet find no protest except for the penitent that comes weeping for a cure, and the priest of God who brings and applies a remedy! Who is not aware that there are, lying beneath the outer polish of

Wesley, 1748-1750.

The practice of the Methodists was assailed with the usual objections:—" Your fifth argument is, 'That they use Private Confession in which everyone is to speak the state of his heart, with his several temptations and deliverances, and answer as many searching questions as may be. And what scene, say you, is hereby disclosed; what a *filthy jakes* opened, when the most searching questions are answered without reserve?'" (xvi. 345.) Wesley hints pretty plainly that the ready supposition of the objector, and his forwardness to condemn, make it not unlikely that his own heart is "a very filthy jakes" indeed, and bids him not to measure others by that same measure.

High Churchmen.

modern society, festering sores which no other hand can reach? Freely is any of these disclosed to the lawyer when it touches any temporal interest; to the physician when it affects the bodily health; but to confess it before the priest of God is pollution, forsooth! The body may command the man skilled in physical ailments; earthly interests may have the services of the man learned in law; in neither case is any necessary disclosure shrunk from; but the soul must be left without help and given over to corruption and death! And with entire accuracy did Wesley indicate—very generally it is the case that those who cry out the most against them on whom the office to remedy is laid, are they who most of all delight to dabble in those disgusting details which the newspapers furnish.

High Churchmen.	Wesley.
Obj. 2. "But there is *no Scripture* for it." The key to the objection hangs beside the door — what people never look for they are never likely to find. A Unitarian reads Scripture all through without finding proof for our Lord's Divinity, but does find many passages which he interprets as inconsistent therewith. No man who *wishes* to accept Confession, if agreeable to Scripture, will find the slightest difficulty on the score of want of Scripture sanction. He will see the principle enjoined in the Old Testament, and the practice of Confession both to priest and prophet. As a link between the two dispensations he will see that Confession of sins was made to	Obj. 2. "But it was soon objected, 'There is *no Scripture* for them.'" None is needed, concludes Wesley. "They are prudential helps, grounded in reason and experience in order to apply the general rules given in Holy Scripture according to particular circumstances." But Scripture there is: even "that command of God, 'Confess your faults one to another, and pray one for another, that you may be healed.'" Again, "The penitent Jews who were admitted to the Baptism of John *confessed their sins*, and each received advice as his case required." xv. 214; *Band Rules*; and *Mag.* xix. 126.

S. John the Baptist. To the Apostles under the New, he will see that "those who believed came and confessed and showed their deeds;" and that to them was committed the power to remit or retain sins, according as the conditions of Absolution were, or were not, fulfilled. As he passes on to the General Epistles he will see in close connection, one command to "send for the elders of the Church," and one to "confess," with the assurance that "the prayers of a righteous man availeth much." Scripture evidence immeasureably greater than can be produced for the Baptism of Infants, or the sacred observance of the First Day of the week.

High Churchmen.	Wesley.
Obj. 3. "It is all *Popery*." The witty Dean Swift says that brother Jack has discovered "a short and easy method" of settling all controversies—If brother Peter says "Aye," then brother Jack says "No;" but if brother Peter says "Nay," then brother Jack says "Yea." It is known amongst Protestants as the *Rule of Contrary*:—that is right which Papists say is wrong, and that is wrong which Papists say is right. Unfortunately this ready rule of faith and practice labours under two slight defects: the	Obj. 3. "An objection much more boldly and frequently urged is, 'All these Bands are mere *Popery*.'" A very stale objection, retorts Wesley, which many people make against anything they do not like;" and which betrays the gross ignorance of those who make it, in two respects: the Confession we practise (in Bands) Papists do not; the Confession they hold (*i.e.*, private to a priest) our Church holds also. xv. 214.

first is, they cannot get *others* to accept it; sensible men are not content thus to supersede Scripture and to silence reason, but maintain with Wesley (xvi. 288) that against a sentiment or practice, just in itself, it is an objection of no weight that it is also to be found amongst the Papists; the other is, they do not accept it *themselves*; they use the Lord's Prayer, recite the Creed, preach from a pulpit, and beg for money; which leaves them open to Wesley's retort, that they follow the Papists so far as they feel inclined, and cry out "Popery" against whatever they do not like.

6. OF PENANCE.

High Churchmen.	Wesley, 1733-1790.
Repentance, like every other Christian grace, has of necessity an inward power and an outward form. These two are Scripturally expressed in Prayer-Book language by Penitence and Penance. And as faith is made perfect only by obedience, and charity by acts of Christian love; so is penitence, the inward sorrow, made perfect and manifest only by "works that are meet" for it—viz., confession, reparation, "revenge,"	Wesley earnestly lamented the present abeyance of the Church's discipline in an Office which he used and highly valued:—"Brethren, in the Primitive Church there was a godly discipline, that, at the beginning of Lent, such persons as stood convicted of notorious sin were put to open Penance, and punished in this world, that their souls might be saved in the day of the Lord; and that others, admonished by

High Churchmen.

mortification of flesh or spirit. Without these (acts of Penance) Penitence "is dead, being alone." The right to impose Penance flows naturally from the relation which the Church bears to the offender. Every Society has a recognized right to protect itself and the interests of its members by imposing appropriate punishments on those who act injuriously to them. This right the Church exercises, to the manifest benefit of all, but especially of him who submits to her discipline. Thus avarice is appropriately combatted by almsgiving; tale-bearing, by the imposition of silence; uncleanness, by fasting and bodily rigour; unwatchfulness, by prayers at specified times; fraud, by liberal restitution: justice might be satisfied with measure for measure, but spiritual discipline may require four-fold. Men ease themselves of these burdens, and flatter themselves that the inward emotion of sorrow is sufficient, but the spiritual necessities of the individual and the well-being of the Church alike bear witness that the imposition of Penance is a very useful part of ecclesiastical discipline.

Wesley.

their example, might be the more afraid to offend. Instead whereof (until the said discipline may be restored again, which is much to be wished)," &c.: and as earnestly prayed for its revival— a *desideratum* which corruptions in the Catholic Church and ensuing divisions and heresies have rendered well-nigh impossible—"Reform the corruptions of Thy Catholic Church, heal her divisions, and restore to her her ancient discipline."—"Give to all heretics humility and grace to *make amends to Thy Church* by the public acknowledgment of an holy faith." x. 64, 79.

Even in a popular review of Romish errors Wesley freely concedes that "The giving satisfaction to the Church in case of scandal, and the imposing penances upon notorious offenders, is an useful part of ecclesiastical discipline." (xix. 93). And in a declaration of conformity to the Anglican Church, the year before his death, he says, "I hold all the doctrines of the Church of England, I love her Liturgy, *I approve her plan of discipline and only wish it could be put in execution.*" Mag., 1790. p. 287.

---

7. OF SACERDOTAL ABSOLUTION.

High Churchmen.

If our Lord's words, "Whosesoever sins ye remit, they are remitted unto them," have not from the first been misunder-

Wesley, 1746-1790.

The Church's Doctrine of Absolution she has embodied in an Office:—"Our Lord Jesus Christ, Who hath left power to

High Churchmen.

stood, and Christians in all ages been acting under a mistake, then the Ordinance of Absolution is a means of grace established by Divine promise; and as such, should by all Christian people be thankfully received; then, every objection commonly urged against it is of like force as when urged against other means of grace. "Who can forgive sins but God alone?" True. But who shall tie God in forgiving sins to one way? God uses the ministry of man "for the remission of sins" in Baptism, and He has equally promised remission of sins by the ministry of man in Absolution. (S. John xx. 21-23.) The need is the same and the ministry the same whether for sin before Baptism or for sin after Baptism. Repentance and Faith on our part do not alone suffice to put us *in possession* of the grace offered through sacramental means, but only entitle us to their use, and infallibly secure to us their whole benefit. Following therefore God's Holy Word, and the teaching and practice of the Church from the first ages, High Churchmen confidently believe that the penitent and believing man receives the forgiveness of all his sins when the words are pronounced over him by the priest as certainly, and may be as comfortably assured thereof, as if he heard the same voice direct from Heaven. The priest authoritatively declares, the penitent conditionally receives, and God judicially bestows, that pardon, which being thus offered is to be thus obtained.

Wesley.

His Church to absolve all sinners who truly repent and believe in Him, of His great mercy forgive thee thine offences: And by His authority committed to me, I absolve thee from all thy sins, In the Name of the Father, and of the Son, and of the Holy Ghost. Amen." And to this Wesley gave his whole *ex animo* assent: he both taught the Doctrine and used the Office—ministering at her Altar, he knew nothing of denying the one and of contemning the other—"As a minister, I teach her doctrines; I use her offices." (1746. xvi. 158.) And from this, if his oft-repeated declarations of unvarying belief in "*all* the doctrines of the Church of England" (1790) are to be credited, he never to the end of his life departed. In illustration: A condensed statement of Mr. Wesley's views, conveying his whole meaning, in his own words, stands thus: "In the forgiveness of sins men show a ministry;" the priest authoritatively declares; the penitent conditionally receives; and God judicially bestows. "The authority of the priest," and the efficacy of the Absolution, are both recognized by him. Limitations and cautions he dwells upon as against those (the Papists) who may be supposed to require them. xix. 91.

CHAPTER VII.

OF ANOINTING THE SICK WITH CONSECRATED OIL.

High Churchmen.

Never, while the Epistle of S. James stands where it does, can it be denied that the Unction of the Sick is enjoined upon Christians by Divine authority. Wholly disconnecting it from the Apostles and their exercise of extraordinary powers, S. James gives a *general* direction that whosoever is sick shall send, not for those so specially gifted, but, for the *ordinary* presbyters or priests of the Church, and they shall anoint him with oil, and pray over him, and the prayer of faith shall save the sick. A direction which God thus distinctly gave with the promise of restoration from the two-fold malady, sin and sickness, it can never be wise or reverent to omit, because, as to the less important of the two, the promise is not now expected to be fulfilled. Nor was it uni-

Wesley, 1749.

Wesley rescues this from the catalogue of abuses which Dr. Middleton, more zealous than wise, brings against the teaching and practice of the Christian Fathers during the third century—"As to the Consecrated Oil, you seem entirely to forget, that it was neither S. Jerome, nor S. Chrysostom, but S. James, who said, 'Is any sick among you? Let him send for the elders of the Church. And let them pray over him, anointing him with oil, in the name of the Lord. And the prayer of faith shall save the sick, and the Lord shall raise him up.'"

"Anointing the sick with oil, you will not easily prove to be any corruption at all." xviii. 154, 155.

formly fulfilled in those days; but that did not set aside the obligation of the command. Furthermore, on this ground the *prayer* also should be omitted, since the promise "the prayer of faith shall save the sick" is not ordinarily fulfilled. So clear is the Scripture authority, and so invariable continued the Church's practice for fifteen hundred years after the command was given, that "Bible Christians," to use Mr. Wesley's words, "taking the Bible as interpreted by the Primitive Church," can do no other than earnestly contend for the entire restoration of this sacramental rite wherever now it is unhappily omitted.

CHAPTER VIII.

OF HOLY ORDERS.

1. THE VIRTUE OF ORDINATION.

High Churchmen.

Ordination is a Divine Institution, and by it is conveyed a commission to minister in God's Name. There is not a single instance, anywhere to be found in the New Testament, of any man ministering the Sacraments who had not received this outward ordination as well as the inward call: there is not a verse to be found therein which justifies the assumption. And for fifteen hundred years after our Blessed Lord had given this commission to the Apostles, the requirement and practice of the Church everywhere continued so uniform, that there is not so much as a single instance producible, of any man being accounted a lawful minister in Holy Things, who had not received this commission, by the solemn laying on of hands of those who had so received it in like manner before him. On the contrary, by all Christians, in every age, from the Apostles' time until the Reformation, this assumption was denounced as being substantially the sin of Korah, Dathan, and Abiram, for for whose signal punishment God prepared a new and speedy judgment in token of His high dis-

Wesley, 1745-1762.

" We account Ordination to be of Divine institution, and that by it a ministerial commission is conveyed." xix. 97.

The *sacerdotal* character of the *priest* is *indelible*:—" Before those words which, you suppose, ' limit the exercise of the *sacerdotal* powers to that congregation whereunto each *priest* shall be appointed,' were those spoken without any restraint or limitation at all, which I apprehend to convey an *indelible* character, ' Receive the Holy Ghost, for the office and work of a priest in the Church of God, now committed unto thee, by the imposition of our hands.' " (xvi. 150, 3.) So far from shrinking from the literal sense of these words, Wesley solemnly reaffirms it, even in the case of unpriestly recipients, and extends their application through even their ministry:—" The Bishop said, when you were ordained, ' Receive thou the Holy Ghost.' But that was the least of your care. Let who will receive this, so you receive the money, the revenue of a good benefice. While you minister the Word and Sacraments before God, He

High Churchmen.

pleasure. Wherefore, if there be any truth in God's Word, if any knowledge of His Will in Christ's Church, then, to minister in Holy Things, without this outward call, by those who are Divinely empowered to give it, is, as Wesley says, *a sin*.

The people cannot give this commission; for the priest acts as the minister *of God, in the things of God*. Personal fitness is not sufficient; a man may be chosen because he is fit, but fitness, even amongst men, never *confers* an office. And as authority to act is determined by no question of fitness, so personal unfitness, simply of itself, does not invalidate this authority when given. Peter, who fell and rose again, and Judas, who fell and went to his own place, each received the same commission, each exercised the same power in the execution of it. (S. Matt. x. 1-8.) In like manner at this day, some receive the Divine commission worthily, some unworthily; to both it is equally conveyed, and to none beside them. Once received, the sacerdotal character is indelible; no priest can rid himself of it, any more than a baptized man can free himself from his Baptism and the obligations which it imposes upon him. Such priests in the Christian Church there are, and have always been, offering the Holy Sacrifice, acting as ambassadors of Christ and stewards of the Mysteries of God.

Wesley.

gives the Holy Ghost to those who duly receive them: so that *through your hands* likewise *the Holy Ghost is* in this sense *given*." (x. 147.) An affirmation which stands on the sound principle at all times so familiar to Wesley:—
"The validity of the ordinance does not depend on the goodness of him who administers, but on the faithfulness of Him that ordained it, Who will and doth meet us in His appointed ways." *Ss.* i. 369.

"We believe there is, and always was, in every Christian Church (whether dependent upon the Bishop of Rome or not), an outward priesthood ordained by Jesus Christ, and an outward Sacrifice offered therein, by men authorized to act as ambassadors of Christ, and stewards of the Mysteries of God." (xxviii. 348.) "They are authorized to exercise that office by those who are empowered to convey that authority: I believe Bishops are empowered to do this, and have been so from the Apostolic age." xvi. 250.

Accordingly, when asked in 1762, "By what authority I did these things, I replied, 'By the authority of Jesus Christ, conveyed to me by the Archbishop of Canterbury when he laid his hands upon me, &c." xxvii. 88.

In the same year Charles Wesley, expressing the sentiments of his brother, also of Dr. Coke, Asbury, Averell, and a host of Methodist worthies, wrote, anent the lay-preachers, on Numbers xvi. 10, "And seek ye the priesthood also?"—

Wesley.

"Raised from the people's lowest lees,
Guard, Lord, Thy preaching witnesses;
Nor let their pride the honour claim
Of sealing cov'nants in Thy Name:
Rather than suffer them to dare
Usurp the priestly character,
Save from the arrogant offence,
And snatch them, uncorrupted, hence."

And, satirically exposing such a combination of ignorance and presumption as has had no parallel since the world began, on 1 Kings xii. 31, "Jeroboam made priests of the lowest of the people:"—

"But kings may spare their labour vain,
For in such happy times as these
The vulgar can themselves ordain,
And priests commence, whoever please."

The truth is stated calmly and well, in the *Arminian Methodist Magazine*, under Conference direction, the year after Mr. Wesley's death:—"There is a call to service as well as a capacity for it. It is a mistake that mere gifts oblige us to do those things which are not peculiar to our office. *This is an usurpation, whatever usefulness men may pretend to.* That there be magistrates, God hath enjoined; how they should be qualified, and their power executed, He doth also appoint. But what particular persons shall be magistrates, and the extent of their power, He hath left to rules adjusted by the community whereto they belong. In like manner, Christ hath enacted that there be Ministers of the Gospel; their qualifications, authority, and work, He hath also described, which He permits not men to alter or limit. But He hath made other ministers judges whether this or that proposed man be so qualified, and being found so, to ordain him; and among them so approved, He hath made members of the Church the ordinary electors who shall be *their* particular minister. Nothing but confusion proceeds from men's running before they are sent; and ordinarily, as a proud conceit of their own gifts puts them out of their place, where alone God accepts their service, and they might have been truly useful to the utmost of their gifts: thus mischief to the public, and prejudice to their own spiritual state, proves at length the effect of their usurpation."

"Serve your generation as you can in your lower place: to which end beg God's direction, that you may not mistake your place or work, nor be left to yourself in the meanest service. Go not out of your calling; for God will neither accept nor bless encroachments on other men's work, *nor your usurpation of power; no, nor at their*

Wesley.

pleasure who are not authorized to give it." (pp. 298, 572.) An expression in weighty words, which none can condemn, of the sentiments contained in Mr. Wesley's address to the Rev. G. Whitfield:—

> "Brother in Christ, and well beloved,
> Attend, and add thy prayer to mine;
> *As Aaron called* and *inly moved*
> To minister in things Divine.
> Faithful and often owned of God,
> Vessel of grace by Jesus used,
> Stir up the gift on thee bestowed—
> The gift, *through hallowed hands* transfus'd."

---

2. THE APOSTOLIC SUCCESSION.

High Churchmen.

That Christ appointed ministers is never denied: did He intend them to be a standing order, and empower them to appoint their successors? or, did He withhold such power, and leave it for congregations in future to make and appoint their own? If the former be maintained, then the *principle* of *Apostolic Succession* is affirmed; if the latter be maintained and proven, then is Apostolic Succession that unscriptural figment which its opponents say it is. The former has all the sanction and authority which Holy Scripture can give it: it was commenced by Christ, continued by the Apostles, and perpetuated by those whom they set over the Churches. The latter has *none:* there is in Holy Scripture not a single intimation of congregations having a power to make and appoint their own, nor a single case in which ordi-

Wesley, 1745–1789.

In 1745 Wesley said, "We believe it would not be right for us to administer either Baptism or the Lord's Supper unless we had a commission so to do from those Bishops whom we apprehend to be in a succession from the Apostles." xxviii. 348. And prays that Bishops may not flinch from asserting the Divine right of their office before the world:—

> "The worthy successors of those
> Who first adorned the sacred line;
> Bold let them stand before their foes,
> And dare assert their Right Divine."
> (*Hymns* by J. and C. Wesley.)

To which we devoutly add, "Amen." These two specimens out of many to the same effect sufficiently show what Wesley's teaching on this subject was.

High Churchmen.

nary ministers were appointed otherwise than they are now: (1) the Deacons, (2) the Presbyters, (3) the Bishops, such as S. Timothy at Ephesus, S. Titus at Crete, and the seven Angels of the seven Churches, were all ordained by the Apostolic Laying-on-of-Hands; and these same Bishops, Timothy, Titus, &c., commanded to transmit the ministerial commission by ordaining others in the same way. (2 Tim. i. 6, ii. 2, and 1 Tim. v. 22.)

This is what is upheld as "Apostolic Succession." The ministerial commission which the Apostles received from Christ, was by them transmitted, as need required, to those who succeeded them in their ordinary ministry, by prayer and the Laying-on-of Hands. This is the only mode of perpetuating the ministerial office which has Scripture sanction, and the promise of Christ's blessing. This the Church has always maintained, and in consequence enjoys a ministry which is not of man but of God. This the various bodies of separatists from the Church have discarded, and instead thereof, have originated ministries which are of themselves.

It is never contended that Priests or Presbyters are not Bishops, in the single sense in which Scripture calls them Bishops, viz., *Overseers* of their respective flocks over which they have been appointed by one superior in authority to themselves: they are, however, not *such*

Wesley.

Two others, susceptible of an opposite interpretation, must in fairness be noticed; and in fairness, also, must if possible, be understood in harmony with, not in opposition to, previous and also *subsequent* avowals.

On one occasion, in controversy with a Romish priest, he declares (xxxi. 77, and afterwards repeats, *Mag*. ix. 50) "*uninterrupted* succession to be a fable which no man ever did or can prove." This *uninterrupted* succession (so italicised by Wesley) is explained by what is exhibited as evidence of it—a list of the Bishops of any see drawn out from the Apostles' time to the present. But such lists show on the contrary that *interruptions* have been frequent and are a sufficient warranty for saying that "*uninterrupted* succession no man ever did or can prove." Even were there no vacancies extending over lengthened periods, every time a Bishop does not himself ordain his successor, he is succeeded by one who has not necessarily any other connection with him than the Archbishop of Canterbury has with the Patriarch of Constantinople. And this is not all: Wesley expressly says that he meets his Roman antagonist on his own grounds; who, in requiring such an uninterrupted succession is convicted of requiring that which his own Church cannot show, and which records cannot prove: he speaks, as he confesses, "*ad hominem*," and not, "*ad rem*." To conclude, each line of succession has

High Churchmen.

Bishops, or Officers entrusted with this superior authority, as were SS. Timothy, Titus, &c. Their oversight at Ephesus was over *their flocks*; S. Timothy's at the same place was over *themselves*.

Whether Bishops and Priests are substantially of one order, is a question not necessary to be determined: they are, and always have been, sufficiently distinguished by the power of ordination being reserved (by the usage of the Apostles and the invariable practice of the Church) to the former alone. Hooker's oft-quoted challenge on this point has never been met—"No man is able to show either Deacon or Presbyter, ordained by Presbyters only, and his ordination lawful, in any ancient part of the Church; everywhere examples being found both of Deacons and Presbyters ordained by Bishops alone."

It is as idle to ask for *direct* proof of the Succession, as it would be to require for the child last born direct proof that it has by successive generations been regularly derived from Adam. No child is born without a father; and no Bishop is made but by Bishops before him. Families may have died out; long ancestral lines may be shown broken, but from the law of *kind succeeding kind*, it is certain that the present generation are derived from their first progenitor. Of such a nature is the certainty, arising from the Church's invariable law of requiring of neces-

Wesley.

been interrupted, again and again: but all that Wesley wrote, both before and after, requires the belief that the Christian Ministry is continuous, in prescribed succession, from the Apostles, and that the grace of Orders is to be conveyed as oil from vessel to vessel till the completion of all things and the end of all days.

The other instance does not touch the doctrine of Apostolic Succession at all, but only raises the question as to whether the grace of Orders of which it is the guarantee is transmitted through Bishops only or through Priests as well as Bishops. Wesley, yielding to the arguments of Lord King, in faith that his was "a *fair and impartial* draught," decided for the latter, and, in a case of admitted necessity, ordained Dr. Coke to execute the office of Bishop in British North America; the English Bishops being, as Wesley complained, too timorous and time-serving to send out any. For this act he got severely satirized by his brother Charles:—

"How easy now are Bishops made
    By man or woman's whim;
Wesley his hands on Coke hath laid,
    But who laid hands on him?"

And what is more; Dr. Coke distrusted this foolish assumption of Episcopal power and sought a better ordination. And what is most of all: Lord King, on reading Sclater's reply to his arguments, declared their unsoundness and withdrew them.

High Churchmen.	Wesley.

High Churchmen.

sity a Bishop to be made by Bishops, that the present generation of Bishops are the actual successors of those to whom the Divine Commission was first given. The operation of this law in the present age is matter of observation: if any man can show, either in the Apostles' age, or in any age subsequent, a time when it was inoperative, he will have established what would be beyond doubt an insuperable obstacle to the truth of Apostolic Succession.

Some, impatient of the obscure yet certain proof of Apostolic Succession which the necessary operation of this law affords, have attempted to prove it by the direct method: *i.e.*, by lists of Bishops of the principal sees of Christendom, as they have succeeded each other, from the Apostles' days to the present. But these are lists of successive *occupation* merely, not of *consecration*; and such "proofs" with their many intermissions and interruptions only give occasion to Wesley's just retort, that "*uninterrupted* succession" "no man ever did or can prove:" his own concurrent concession being far more adequate, containing as it does, all which the fact of Apostolic Succession of necessity requires—"*Bishops* are, and have been *from the Apostolic age* empowered to convey the requisite authority for the exercise of the priestly office."

Every new instance of succession to the Episcopate being united by "a threefold cord" to

Wesley.

Two years after yielding his judgment to King's fallacious book, Wesley repeats his belief "that Bishops are, and have been from the Apostolic age empowered to convey the requisite authority for the exercise of the priestly office (xvi. 250); and never ceases to his life's end (as the next following paragraphs will clearly show) to insist that those who would exercise it require to be authorized by those who are empowered to convey that authority.

This requirement constantly acted upon in all ages *is Apostolic Succession*, and therefore Wesley may be allowed, without any violation of its essential truth, to impugn that which is at most only an evidence of it, and which would, if unduly weighted, by being weak, betray.

In 1756 (more than ten years after reading King's book) Wesley writes, "Some of our preachers who are not ordained think it quite right to administer the Lord's Supper, and believe it would do much good. I think it quite wrong, and believe it would do much hurt. You believe it is a duty to administer. I verily believe it is a sin; which consequently I dare not tolerate." *Mag.* 1779, p. 649.

What he had said in 1745, in defending his lay-preachers— "But does not the Scripture say, 'No man taketh this honour to himself: but he that is called of God as was Aaron'? Nor do these. The honour here mentioned is the priesthood. But

High Churchmen.	*Wesley.*
all which have preceded it, as it in turn unites and becomes one with all that follow it; any one acquainted with the progression of numbers will see that it would be impossible to give the proof commonly asked for, since it would be impossible to *complete* it. It is sufficient that the requirement in all cases of a Bishop to be made by Bishops, is, and has been from the beginning, the Church's invariable law.	they no more take upon them to be priests than to be kings (anticipating the plea sometimes urged from Rev. i. 6). They take not upon them to administer the Sacraments, an honour *peculiar* to the *priests of God*. Only according to their power they exhort their brethren to continue in the grace of God." (xv. 154.)— He repeats in 1789, the year but one before his death; addressing at this time some of these same preachers who were ambitious of exercising the functions of the

priesthood:—" You never dreamed," he says, " of this, for ten or twenty years after ye began to preach. Ye did not then like Korah, Dathan, and Abiram, seek the priesthood also. Ye knew, no man taketh this honour to himself: but he that is called of God as was Aaron. O contain yourselves within your own bounds. Be content with preaching the Gospel ... in God's Name stop there." (*Mag.* 1790.) This is final and decisive. It is, as the Irish Methodists have called it, "The dying testimony which he was resolved to leave"—*i.e.*, two years before his decease John Wesley on a public occasion in Ireland thus solemnly declared his unflinching adherence to what he had all his life held and taught: that none but Priests could administer the Sacraments without sin; and that the power and appointment of the Methodist Preachers was solely to preach the Gospel. So memorable a testimony to the necessity of receiving the Sacerdotal Office through those who have been duly invested with the authority requisite to convey it (Apostolic Succession) has, since then, been met, as might be expected, with every effort to weaken its force.*

* The author of *The Relations of John Wesley and of Wesleyan Methodism to the Church of England* has insinuated (p. 26) that Wesley in proclaiming this truth was influenced by the honour which his Church friends paid him. We could even afford to grant this; and should then ask, Was John Wesley less himself when amongst those to whom " his sympathy and his taste inclined him," than when amongst his Preachers, who, he confessed, were " too much for him"? Moreover, Wesley returned to London, and thirteen months passed away: here there was time for re-consideration; here he was surrounded by his Preachers, suggestions were offered, plans were reviewed, last instructions were received; yet again, this time nine months only before his death, he gave the sermon to his Societies afresh, and placed it on permanent record—a testimony which should remain when

he was no more seen—in the pages of the *Arminian Methodist Magazine*. But we will now take the matter on a perfectly sure ground. Mr. Wesley's testimony was in this respect *uniform*. He did not now announce it for the first time, as if it was the fruit of the honour in which his Church friends began once more to hold him. Wesley *founded* his Society in the assertion of this principle. A member of the little Society in London, Mr. Shaw, " began to sow the seeds of discord among his brethren, by affirming that there is no order of men in the Christian ministry that, properly speaking, are commissioned to exercise the functions of the priesthood; and that he himself, though a layman, had as good a right to baptize and administer the Lord's Supper as any of those who had been formally ordained to the sacred office;" and " he was quickly expelled for his heterodoxy." (*Centenary of Methodism*, Dublin, p. 38.) And his (Wesley's) connection with it *closed* with an equally firm protest against any violation of it, as we have seen: whilst at every intermediate stage of his course, 1745, 1756, 1762, 1779, 1789, it was deliberately and solemnly re-affirmed.

Dr. Rigg advances another plea: Wesley's "faculties were beginning to fail;" his "judgment was enfeebled." So also have Churchmen said, when wishful to find for Wesley some excuse for the ordinations in which he took part. This, if true, only weakens the case which Dr. Rigg is anxious to make out, whilst it yields an important accession of strength to our own. For whereas this famous sermon is only the *last* of a series of similar utterances which fairly cover the whole of Wesley's mature life, the *first* act of ordination in which he took part was not until his judgment had become "enfeebled by the weight of fourscore years and two." In any case Wesley was perfectly consistent with himself. So early as 1746 he had become persuaded that Bishops and Priests are substantially of one order: but forbore from exercising his supposed inherent power " as a priest of the Catholic Church" till cases arose which, to his mind, imperatively demanded it; and, on the other hand, proclaimed with no uncertain voice to the very end of his life, that none but those who have been duly admitted into this order can execute its functions without sin.

On both these points the recognized leaders of modern Methodism are at issue with those who in Wesley's day stood highest in honour and esteem, as well as with those (a large body in Ireland) who have throughout adhered to Methodism on its *primitive* plan. As to the Priest's assumption of the power of ordination, Coke, the Xavier of Methodism, "doubted;" Asbury, a man of Apostolic character, who was nominated as Coke's colleague, "expressed strong doubts about it;" Charles Wesley, the poet of Methodism, and second only to John Wesley himself, was overwhelmed with grief, and denounced it in the strongest terms; Dr. Whitehead, to whom John Wesley by his will entrusted his papers, questioned, along with Charles Wesley, how far his judgment remained unimpaired by his years; and bears witness that to the " uninfected itinerants" this error of judgment was " amazing and confounding;" whilst the Methodists in Ireland, they, who alone maintained Methodism as its Founder left it, candidly avowed, even after the lapse of half a century, that " in their judgment the position (on which alone the act proceeded) is much easier assumed than proved." (*Centenary*, p. 203.) So much for an aberration which, however grave in itself, was simply without effect on Mr. Wesley's Sacerdotal and general High Church principles, except in leading him the more to magnify his office.

Of the utter unlawfulness, in Wesley's mind, of lay-preachers assuming the priestly office and administering Sacraments, no stronger proof indeed could be given than that he thus encountered every species of opposition and obloquy from both friend and foe, rather than suffer the Sacraments to be administered by them even in the most extreme cases. Such a thing as the possibility of Sacraments being thus administered without sin, as afterwards he declared, never entered into his mind. And with the exception of a few discontented preachers, the Methodists so long as he lived were in accord with him. This was the reason that Wesley was "repeatedly importuned" to exercise his supposed inherent right to ordain. In America after the War of Independence "for some hundreds of miles together there was none either to Baptize or to administer the Lord's Supper." All the clergy being driven out of the country, the Methodists went for years without the Sacrament of Holy Communion, and their children grew up and hundreds of them died unbaptized. With tears and entreaties they sent, again and again, a representation of their sad case to England. By the Bishops these moving appeals were unheeded: a fatal Erastianism held them in bonds; and in consequence thereof Wesley did for the Methodists, what even American Churchmen were on the point of doing *provisionally* for themselves, and what in their despair the Methodists had already attempted:—"Seeing no mode by which their want might be supplied," the preachers "elected three of their senior brethren to ordain others by the imposition of hands, to administer the Sacraments of Baptism and the Lord's Supper to such persons as *under these circumstances* were willing to receive them." (*Centenary*, p. 199). This is important: it shows that the Methodists, like John Wesley, knew no way by which valid Sacraments could be obtained, even in the extremest cases, except by ordained men. But the sequel proves more: this Ordination (of which the first English Ordination in 1836 was the exact counterpart) was by their American brethren "at a subsequent Conference declared to be unscriptural and invalid." *Id.* p. 200.

In Ireland, also, these principles were affirmed by the Methodists in Conference assembled, even after Mr. Wesley's death:—"When the British Conference adopted the principle of Sacramental administration" by the *lay*-preachers, the subject was discussed in the Irish Conference of 1792 "whether the plan pursued by their English brethren should be adopted in this country or not, and it was *unanimously* rejected by the preachers assembled on that occasion." (*Id.*, p. 276). Some of the junior preachers however commenced an agitation amongst the Societies, and at length, in 1816, permission to administer Sacraments was carried by vote, and Methodism in Ireland became divided between those who continued "on the primitive plan," and those who began on the "new." The former must have been a sharp thorn in the sides of the innovators, both Irish and English, whom they charged, and truly, with being "*self-appointed*," having *by their own vote* admitted "themselves into an order to which they had no previous pretensions" (*Id.*, pp. 267, 273), especially as they continue to this day an organized body of living witnesses to the plan of *Wesley's* Methodism.

CHAPTER IX.

OF THE CELIBATE STATE.

High Churchmen.

Blessed, blessed of their Lord are they (called by whatever name) who abjure things lawful in themselves, and for the Kingdom of Heaven's sake, forsake home, house, and lands in order to be without carefulness for the things of this world, and to be more devoted to their Lord in the service of His Church and poor, and to be holy both in body and soul: great is their reward, now in this life, and in the world to come. Not all can receive this saying, but he that is able, "*Let* him receive it." Specially true is this of those called to the priestly office: "No man that warreth entangleth himself with the affairs of this life;"

"A Virgin Priest the Altar best attends
Our Lord that state commands not, yet commends."

In nothing perhaps are Protestant ideas more directly at variance with God's Word and the Will of Christ than on this article. The high estate of those "blessed" ones, who, at Christ's call "forsook all, and followed Him;" of those women who daily attended Him, forgetful of all, save in ministering to Him of their substance; of those in early times, who acting on His

Wesley, 1751-1764.

"Blessed are they who have made themselves eunuchs for the Kingdom of Heaven's sake: who abstain from things lawful in themselves, in order to be more devoted to God. Let these never forget those remarkable words: 'Peter said, Lo we have left all and followed Thee.' And Jesus answered and said, 'Verily I say unto you,' a preface denoting the certainty and importance of what is spoken, 'There is no man that hath left' (either by giving them up, or by not accepting them) 'house, or brethren, or sisters, or father, or mother, or wife, or children, or lands, for My sake and the Gospel's, but he shall receive an hundred-fold—now, in this time; and, in the world to come, eternal life.'"

"When the Apostles said, 'If the case be so, it is good not to marry, He said unto them, All men cannot receive this saying ... He that is able to receive it, *let* him receive it.'" "To this happy few I say. Know the advantages you enjoy; many of which are pointed out by the Apostle himself: You may be *without carefulness*. You are under no necessity of *caring for the things of the world.* You have only to *care for the things of the Lord, how you may please the*

High Churchmen.

counsel, sold all, and laid their money at the Church's feet; of those in each succeeding age, who have contracted no family ties in order to spend and be spent alone for Christ: this is what the Protestant world hates and seizes every opportunity of calumniating.

That state of celibacy for the Kingdom of Heaven's sake which Christ commended and commands all who are able to embrace, the "religious world" in its wisdom has condemned and opposes any acceptance of.

A woman may leave a widowed mother to marry a godless man, and this the world approves: "Marriage is woman's vocation;" no tongue is raised against it. But for one who in obedience to a higher call leaves the house of her father, where she might save a housekeeper's wages, to follow a holy spiritual vocation, there are no reproaches too bitter. Lessons of holy poverty, of abstraction from worldly cares, of abnegation of things lawful for Christ's sake and the Gospel, these the world sneers at and condemns; these Christ gives, and promises His blessing to all who receive them.

Wesley, 1751-1764.

Lord. One care alone lies upon you, how you *may be holy both in body and spirit.*"

"And let it be matter of daily thanksgiving to God that He has made you a partaker of these benefits. Indeed the more full and explicit you are herein, the more sensible you will be of the cause you have to be thankful, the more lively conviction you will have of the greatness of the blessing." xxiv. 252.

Celibacy "for the Kingdom of Heaven's sake," though not of *general* obligation, is, Wesley points out, a *Divine Command:* "' He that is able to receive it, let him receive it.' This gracious command (for such it is unquestionably) ... is not designed for all men; but only for those few who are able to receive it. O let those receive it joyfully:" And also one of the *Evangelical counsels:* "' I would,' says the Apostle, 'that all men were herein even as I'—I would that all believers who are now unmarried, would remain ' eunuchs for the Kingdom of Heaven's sake.' But every one hath his proper gift from God—According to our Lord's declaration, ' All men cannot receive this saying save they,' the happy few, 'to whom it is given.'"

And further, Wesley is careful to expose the falseness of that Protestant gloss which would make void the command of Christ, as well as limit the Apostle's counsels in their application to "the present distress," or time of persecution: "' It is good for them if they remain even as I,' *i.e.* single. It does not appear that this declaration (any more than v. i.) hath any reference at all to a state of persecution:" "vs. 26, 27. *This* is good for the present distress—while any Church is under persecu-

Wesley.

tion—'for a man *to continue as he is*,' whether married or unmarried. S. Paul does not here urge 'the present distress' as a reason for celibacy, any more than for marriage, but for a man's not seeking to alter his state, whatever it be, but making the best of it." No: the "difference," which is the measure of the superiority of celibacy over marriage is a *standing* one, "whether the Church be under persecution or not:" "the unmarried man, if he understand and use the advantage he enjoys careth only for the things of the Lord, how he may please the Lord. The unmarried woman—if she know and use her privilege careth only for the things of the Lord. All her time, care, and thoughts centre in this, how she may be holy both in body and spirit. This is the *standing* advantage of a single life, in all ages and nations." *Notes on the New Test.*, in loco.

" Wednesday 6.—I met (in Society) the single men, and showed them, on how many accounts it was good for those who had received that gift from God to remain single for the Kingdom of Heaven's sake." *Jl.* viii. 92.

For the Society which received such teaching from John Wesley, he appointed a formal " Covenant," which he recommended should after a solemn fast be renewed every year. The form, which was sold at all the Methodist preaching-houses, contains, after suitable instructions and directions for earnest prayer that they might " promise unto the Lord and keep it," the following solemn profession which is to be said aloud, the people all kneeling: " ... And since Thou hast appointed the Lord Jesus Christ the only means of coming unto Thee, I do here, upon the bended knees of my soul, accept of Him as the only new and living way ... and do here solemnly join myself in a marriage covenant to Him. O Blessed Jesus! I come to Thee hungry, wretched, miserable, blind, and naked; a most loathsome, polluted wretch, a guilty condemned malefactor, unworthy to wash the feet of the servants of my Lord, much more to be solemnly married to the King of Glory; but since such is Thine unparalleled love, I do here, with all my power, accept Thee, and take Thee for my Head and Husband, for better for worse, for richer for poorer, for all times and conditions, to love, honour, and obey Thee, before all others, and this to the death, &c." " Amen, so be it; and the Covenant which I have made on earth, let it be ratified in Heaven." "Tremendous Blasphemy!" did men of a worldly temper exclaim. But these early Methodists with their midnight vigils, their daily morning five o'clock services, their weekly and at times daily Eucharists, were in too marked contrast with the closed churches, the chilling services, the unheeded fasts and unkept festivals, and the quarterly Communions, of that age, to *please men*.

Wesley.

How Wesley and his Celibates would enter with peculiar spirit into such a service we are not left to imagine only:—

"I have no sharer of my heart
To rob my Saviour of a part
And desecrate the whole:
Only betrothed to Christ am I,
And wait His coming from the sky
To wed my happy soul."
(*Hymn* 68 *in the Methodist Collection—a verse now omitted.*)

It is a note-worthy fact, for which Mr. Myles in his *Chronological History* vouches, that in 1780, of the whole body of Itinerant Preachers in Great Britain and Ireland more than two-thirds were Celibates.

His brother-in-law, "who 14 or 15 years ago was holy and unblamable in all manner of conversation," he reproaches for marrying, "being well assured" says Wesley, "that you were *able to receive* the Lord's saying, (so you had continually testified) and be an eunuch for the Kingdom of Heaven's sake." "Hence I date your fall." (xxix. 70.) And for those who can and do receive their Lord's saying, he expresses his sense of their high estate thus:—

"Thousands of Virgins chaste and clean
From love's pleasing witchcrafts free,
Fairer than the sons of men
Consecrate their hearts to Thee."
(Hymn *The Saviour Glorified by All.*)

"Monday, 5. [1764.]—My scraps of time this week I employed in setting down my present *Thoughts upon a single life*, which indeed are just the same they have been these thirty years. And the same they must be, unless I give up my Bible." xxxi. 346.

In vol. xxii. p. 103 the question is asked and answered: "Why then did Mr. Wesley marry?—For reasons best known to himself."

CHAPTER X.
OF FASTING.

1. OBLIGATION OF FASTING.

High Churchmen.

Protestantism either makes our Lord a false prophet, or our Lord makes it a false religion, and excludes its adherents from being of the number of the children of the Bridegroom:—" the days will come, when the Bridegroom shall be taken away from them, and then shall they fast." Either our Lord's words *have passed away*, or His directions, ' How to fast,' though of perpetual obligation, are by Protestant traditions made of none effect. Either His Saints were chargeable with works of supererogation for being "in fastings often," or Protestants in their neglect of fasting, are chargeable with leaving undone that which God requires.

A spiritual exercise which was by God prescribed for His people under the Old Dispensation (Joel ii. 12), and which has been re-inforced by our Lord and practised by His Apostles and all the faithful in every age under the New, none can omit, without thereby imperilling their salvation.

Wesley, 1762-1789.

"God hath, in all ages, appointed this, to be a means of averting His wrath, and obtaining whatever blessings we from time to time stand in need of. How powerful a means this is, to avert the wrath of God, we may learn from the remarkable instance of Ahab;" (and from other instances cited from the Old Testament).

"And it is a means not only of turning away the wrath of God, but also of obtaining whatever blessings we stand in need of;"—(as shown by many cited instances.)

"In like manner the Apostles always joined fasting with prayer, when they desired the blessing of God, on any important undertaking;" (as shown by several instances which Wesley cites.)

"Yea, that blessings are to be obtained in the use of this means, which are no otherwise attainable, our Lord expressly declares, in His answer to His disciples, asking, ' Why could not we cast him out ? ... if ye have faith, nothing shall be impossible unto you. Howbeit this kind goeth not out, but by prayer and fasting.'"

"There were the *appointed* means. For it was not merely by the light of reason, or of natural conscience, (as it is called), that the people of God have been in all ages directed, to use fasting as a means to these ends. But they have been from time to time taught

Wesley.

it of God Himself, by clear and open revelations of His will. Such is that remarkable one by the prophet Joel (ii. 12), &c."

"Now whatever reasons there were to quicken those of old in the zealous and constant discharge of this duty, they are of equal force still to quicken us. But above all these we have a peculiar reason for being 'in fastings often,' namely, the Command of Him by Whose Name we are called. He does not indeed in this place *expressly* enjoin, either fasting, giving of alms, or prayer. But His directions how to fast, to give alms, and to pray, are of the same force, with such injunctions. For the commanding us, to do anything *thus*, is an unquestionable command, to do that thing; seeing it is impossible to perform it *thus*, if it be not performed *at all*. Consequently, the saying, give alms, pray, fast, in *such a manner*, is a clear command to *perform* all those duties, as well as to perform them in that *manner*, which shall in no wise lose its reward." "'Tis possible, either to fast or pray, in such a manner, as to make you much worse than before; more unhappy, and more unholy. Yet the fault does not lie in the means itself; but in the *manner* of using it. Use it still; but use it in a different manner. Do what God commands *as* He commands it, and then doubtless His promise shall not fail." ii. 260-8

"If we were to fast without praying, would not this be a way of worship of our own invention? And if we pray and neglect fasting, is it not equally choosing a worship of our own? For He that has taught us the use and advantage of prayer, has also taught us the use and advantage of fasting: and has likewise joined them together, as having the same power with God." iv. 300.

---

2. NEED OF FASTING.

High Churchmen

If the Prophets did not err in attributing spiritual declension to "fulness of bread," and the Apostles imagine a vain thing in considering severe bodily-denial to be essential to the soul's health, then is the necessity of being "in fastings often" greater now than it was in any former age.

If anyone can be imagined as having been safely exempt from voluntary fastings and the strictest self-discipline, that man was S.

Wesley, 1762-1789.

"Here then is the natural ground of fasting. One who is under deep affliction, overwhelmed with sorrow for sin, and a strong apprehension of the wrath of God, would without any rule, without knowing or considering, whether it were a command of God or not. *forget to eat his bread*, abstain not only from pleasant, but even from needful food."

"We abstain from food with

High Churchmen.

Paul, who lived "in infirmities, in reproaches, in necessities, in persecutions, in distresses for Christ's sake;" yet he disciplined himself by fasting, and laboured to "keep under" his body, not only as a good and advisable thing, but as of the last necessity—lest finally he "should be a cast-away:" he counted all his virtues as insecure, and his salvation in danger, without this constantly exercised discipline of the body, which so-called Christians now flee from, and even contemn.

Wesley.

this view, that by the grace of God, conveyed into our souls through this outward means, in conjunction with all the other channels of His grace, which He hath appointed, we may be enabled to abstain from every passion and temper which is not pleasing in His sight."

"Another reason or ground of fasting is this. Many of those who now fear God, are deeply sensible how often they have sinned against Him, by the abuse of these lawful things ... how they have indulged their sensual appetites, perhaps to the impairing even their bodily health; certainly to the no small hurt of their soul. For hereby they continually fed and increased that sprightly folly, that airiness of mind, that levity of temper, that gay inattention to things of the deepest concern, that giddiness and carelessness of spirit, which were no other than drunkenness of soul. ... To remove, therefore, the effect, they remove the cause. ... They often wholly refrain; always take care to be sparing and temperate in all things.

"They likewise well remember how fulness of bread, increased not only carelessness and levity of spirit, but also foolish and unholy desires, yea, unclean and vile affections. And this experience puts beyond all doubt. Even a genteel, regular sensuality, is continually sensualizing the soul, and sinking it into a level with the beasts that perish. It cannot be expressed what an effect variety and delicacy of food have on the mind as well as the body: making it just ripe for every pleasure of sense, as soon as opportunity shall invite. Therefore, on this ground also, every wise man will refrain his soul and keep it low. ... Here is another perpetual reason for fasting."

Nor does Wesley omit to include "Another reason for fasting, which some good men have largely insisted on: namely, the punishing themselves for having abused the good gifts of God, by sometimes wholly refraining from them: thus exercising a kind of holy revenge upon themselves, for their past folly and ingratitude, in turning the things which should have been for their health, into an occasion of falling." So David "when he said, I wept and *chastened* or punished my soul with fasting: and S. Paul, when he mentions 'what *revenge*' godly sorrow occasioned in the Corinthians."

"A fifth, and more weighty reason for fasting, is, that it is a help to prayer ... And it is chiefly as it is a help to prayer, that it has so

Wesley.

frequently been found a means in the hand of God, of confirming and increasing not one virtue, not chastity only, but also seriousness of spirit, earnestness, sensibility, and tenderness of conscience; deadness to the world, and consequently the love of God and every holy and heavenly affection." ii. 256-260, 267.

And how evidently does Wesley, in Law's words, teach us the need of fasting in order to a worthy participation in the Holy Communion—an omission which he severely condemned in the case of the Presbyterians: whose practice herein was not comformable to their profession—" The difference between the same man full and fasting, is often almost the difference of two persons; a man that in the morning finds himself fit for any meditation, is after a full meal changed into another creature, fit only for idle amusements or the yawnings of an animal." " He has no more feeling of sin than he has of hunger, and can no more perceive himself to be miserable fallen creature, than he can perceive himself to be a beggar."* iv. 294, 7.

3. TIMES OF FASTING.

High Churchmen.

Stated duties require stated times. And the proper times for fasting are those which the Church points out and imposes upon all her members :—" The Forty Days of Lent; the Ember Days at the Four Seasons; the Three Rogation Days, and all the Fridays in the Year, except Christmas-Day." To these are added, "The Evens or Vigils before" certain Festivals of our Blessed Lord, of His Virgin Mother, and of His Saints: a Table of which is given.

Wesley, 1762-1789.

Stated duties require stated times. "Any time," observes Wesley, "is no time." "It is not the day that makes the duty to be necessary: but the day happens to be a proper occasion of exercising a necessary duty."

"In the Jewish Church, there were some stated fasts ... appointed by God Himself to be observed by all Israel, under the severest penalty." " In the ancient Christian Church there were likewise stated fasts, and those both annual and weekly. Of the former sort was that before Easter; observed by some

---

* But chief amongst reasons for Communicating Fasting is that given in the words of S. Augustine :—" For the *honour* of so great a Sacrament, the Lord's Body and Blood should enter the Christian's mouth before other food."

The Original Institution is confirmatory of the Church's law; the Paschal Supper with the Holy Eucharist formed on that occasion one Sacrificial meal, in which the Old Rite passed away into the New, and to it all the faithful in Israel were bound to come *fasting*.

for eight and forty hours; by others, for an entire week; by many for two weeks, taking no sustenance till the evening of each day. Of the latter, those of the fourth and sixth days of the week (Wednesday and Friday) observed (as Epiphanius writes, remarking it as an undeniable fact) *in the whole habitable earth*, at least, in every place where any Christians made their abode;"—"'half-fasts' (as Tertullian styles them) on which they took no sustenance till three in the afternoon, the time when they returned from the public service." "The Annual fasts in our church are, the forty days of Lent, the Ember days at the four seasons, the Rogation days, and the vigils or eves of several solemn festivals: the weekly, all Fridays in the year except Christmas-Day." (ii. 252-4.) These, Wesley strictly observed himself; gave public notice of in obedience to the Rubric; and enforced so far as he could on all his people by the Rules of his Societies. His last words are strong; not stronger however than he was accustomed to use on this subject: addressing his own people, a little more than a year before his death, on spiritual declension, he says, " While we were at Oxford, the rule of every Methodist was (unless in case of sickness) to fast every Wednesday and Friday in the year, in imitation of the Primitive Church, for which we had the highest reverence. Now this practice of the Primitive Church is universally allowed: 'Who does not know (says Epiphanius, an ancient writer) that the fasts of the fourth and sixth days of the week (Wednesday and Friday) are observed by the Christians throughout the whole world?' So they were by the Methodists for several years; by them all, without any exception. But *afterwards*, some in *London* carried them to excess, and fasted so as to impair their health. It was not long before others made this a pretence for not fasting at all. And I fear there are now thousands of Methodists so called, both in England and Ireland, who, following the same bad example, have entirely left off fasting: who are so far from fasting twice in the week, that they do not fast twice in the month. Yea, are there not some of you who do not fast one day from the beginning of the year to the end? But what excuse can there be for this? I do not say for those that call themselves members of the Church of England; but for any who profess to believe the Scripture to be the Word of God: since, according to this, *the man that never fasts is no more in the way to Heaven, than the man that never prays.*—1789." *Ss.* ii. 522.

F

CHAPTER XI.

OF JUSTIFICATION BY FAITH.*

High Churchmen.	*Wesley,* 1738–1770.

High Churchmen: Our Justification (or Pardon) comes of God's free favour and love, "only for the merit of our Lord and Saviour Jesus Christ by faith, and not for our own works or deservings." The instrumental means of our Justification are the Sacraments by which God ordinarily conveys it. The conditions are faith and repentance on which we receive it. Faith alone does not suffice to put us *in possession* of this gift of God; it must be sought for in the means which God hath appointed: "to which," as Wesley well says, "God hath tied us, though He may not have tied Himself." In disregard of these means, or of Good Works so far as opportunity is given, it would be sought in vain.

Wesley, 1738–1770: In 1738, the date of his "conversion," John Wesley was for a short time greatly enamoured of the doctrine of Justification by Faith into which he had been schooled by the Moravians. His views at this period on this important point are clearly and concisely set down in his *Journal* (iv. 14, 15)—these, writes he, "I cannot but maintain (at least till I have a clearer light)." The "clearer light" soon came: and in 1740 he expressly and distinctly repudiated, so far as they are exceptionable, the very notions respecting Justification which he had avowed in 1738; and taught a doctrine which all High Churchmen acknowledge to be "much agreeable to the mind of the ancient Fathers:"—"I believe Justification by Faith alone. But *let it be observed*, the *true sense* of those words 'We are justified by faith in Christ only,' is not, that this our own act, To believe in Christ, or this our faith which is within us, justifies us, (for that were to account ourselves to be justified by some act or virtue that is within us,) but that although we have faith, hope and love within us, and do never so many good works, yet we must renounce the merit of all, of faith, hope, love, and all other virtues and good works, which we either have done, shall do, or can do, as far too weak to deserve our

---

* As our Methodist friends are disposed to make *everything turn* on this Article—for a typical instance see *Relations of John Wesley, &c., to the Church of England, investigated and determined*—it has been thought suitable to devote a chapter to its special consideration.

Wesley.

justification: for which therefore we must trust only in God's mercy, and the merits of Christ. For it is He alone that taketh away our sins. To Him alone are we to go for this; forsaking all other virtues, good words, thoughts and works, and putting our trust in Christ only.

In strictness therefore, neither our faith nor our works justify us, *i.e.*, deserve the remission of our sins. But God Himself justifies us of His own mercy, through the merits of His Son only. Nevertheless, because by faith we embrace the promise of God's mercy and of the remission of our sins, therefore the Scripture says, that faith does justify, yea, faith without works. And it is all one to say, faith without works, and faith alone justifies us, therefore the ancient Fathers from time to time speak thus: Faith alone justifies . us." xvi. 22.

These two years (1738-1740), were silently and surely establishing the incompatibility between the *Lutheran* doctrine of Justification by Faith and John Wesley's deep and ever-undisturbed faith in God's Holy Ordinances. Returning from Germany in September, 1738, he says, " I exhorted all I could to follow after that great salvation, which is through faith in the Blood of Christ; waiting for it in all the ordinances of God, and in doing good, as they had opportunity, to all men." (*Jl.* ii. 82.) But the new leaven introduced by the Moravian teachers had spread, and was everywhere corrupting:—
" I observed every day more and more," writes Wesley in 1739, " the advantage Satan had gained over us ... almost all these had left off the means of grace, saying, ' They must now cease from their own works: they must now trust in Christ alone: they were poor sinners, and had nothing to do but to lie at His feet.'" (xxvii. 170.) In January, 1740, he writes, " I earnestly besought them all, To stand in the old paths:" " to go to church; to communicate; to fast; to use as much private prayer as they can; to read the Scripture: Because I believe, these are *means of grace*, *i.e.*, do ordinarily convey God's grace to unbelievers" [who have not the faith "that overcometh"]. (*Id.* pp. 187, 189.) But the old Oxford teaching now found slight favour:—" Many censured;" some " scoffed:" on all sides the two Wesleys were accused of " laying too much stress upon the ordinances"—of preaching up the Sacraments "instead of Christ;" of " preaching up the works of the law," and " man's faithfulness and not the faithfulness of God:" meanwhile, the Moravian Methodists waited for salvation *not* " in the means of grace ordained of God, and in all the ways of His holy law and the works of His commandments;" but in the exercise of " faith alone." " In flat opposition"—" I began," says Wesley, " to expound the Epistle of S. James, the great antidote against this poison." (*Id.* 213.) By the " enlightened " brethren Wesley was

Wesley.

declared to be "unawakened," and "not fit" to instruct the Societies: a spurious *revivalism* was on the spread: one, a specimen of many more. "was," says Wesley, "on a sudden so much wiser than her teachers, that I could neither understand her, nor she me." Another, also one of his members, roundly told him to his face, "she had been hitherto taught of men, but now she was taught of God only." Sick at heart, Wesley went to Oxford; but everywhere disappointment awaited him: "I found," says he, "a great change among the poor people here. Out of twenty-five or thirty weekly communicants, only two were left. Not one continued to attend the Daily Prayers of the Church. And those few that were once united together were now torn asunder and scattered abroad." Wesley earnestly called for a return to the old paths:—June 27, 1740. "I preached on 'Do this in remembrance of Me.' In the Ancient Church, everyone who was baptized, communicated daily. So in the Acts we read, "They all continued 'daily' in the Breaking of Bread, and in Prayer." (*Id.* 223.) The next day "Saturday, 28. I shewed at large, That the Lord's Supper was ordained by God, to be a *means of conveying* to men, either preventing, or justifying, or sanctifying grace." *Id.* 224.

Having once laid down (viz., in 1740) the doctrine of Justification by Faith in "the *true sense* of those words," Wesley went on from step to step, ever making it more and more manifest that he had no part or share in the Protestant "by faith alone" heresy, and its hideous distortions of the Scriptural and Primitive doctrine. Already, on this ground, he had withdrawn himself from the Moravians, and the year after (1741) saw him part company with Luther: June, 1741. "I read over Martin Luther's Comment on the Epistle to the Galatians. I was utterly ashamed. How have I esteemed this book ... how blasphemously does he speak of Good Works and of the law of God! ... Here (I apprehend) is the real spring of the grand error of the Moravians. They follow Luther, for better for worse." Again, (same date,) "In the evening I preached on those words, 'In Christ Jesus neither circumcision availeth anything, nor uncircumcision, but faith which worketh by love.' After reading Luther's miserable comment upon the text, I thought it my bounden duty openly to warn the congregation against that dangerous treatise, and to retract whatever recommendation I might ignorantly have given of it." (*Id.* 285-7.) "Aug. 1 (same year). I had a long conversation with Mr. Ingham (Moravian Methodist). We both agreed, 1. That none shall finally be saved, who have not, as they had opportunity, done all good works; and 2. That if a justified person does not do good, as he has opportunity, he will lose the grace he has received, and if he 'repent' not and 'do the former works,' will perish eternally. But with regard to the unjus-

Wesley.

tified, (if I understand him,) we wholly disagreed. He believed, it is not the will of God, that they should wait for faith *in doing good.* I believe, this is the will of God, and that they will never find Him, unless they seek Him in this way." (*Id* 295.) Three years later, namely in 1744, Wesley lays down in the first Methodist Conference the following "*Minutes*":—"*Q*. 1. What is it to be justified? *A*. To be pardoned. *Q*. 2. Is faith the condition of Justification? *A*. Yes. *Q*. 3. But must not repentance and works meet for repentance go before this faith? *A*. Without doubt: if by repentance you mean conviction of sin; and by works meet for repentance, obeying God as far as we can, forgiving our brother, leaving off from evil, doing good, and using His ordinances according to the power we have received." xv. 238.

Ten years later still (1754), in his *Notes on the New Testament*, and in all succeeding editions, on Acts v. 16, "Be baptized and wash away thy sins," Wesley says, "Baptism administered to real penitents, is both a means and seal of pardon. Nor did God ordinarily in the Primitive Church bestow this on any unless through this means." Two years later than this (1756), Wesley wrote *A Treatise on Baptism*, in which he sets forth as his own the ordinary High-Church doctrine of Baptismal Regeneration, and calls "Baptism *the ordinary instrument* of our Justification."* xix. 280. This "sacramental Justification," as modern Methodists derisively call it, Wesley taught also in respect of the Lord's Supper (as has already appeared):—"I showed at large," writes Wesley, "that the Lord's Supper was ordained by God to be *a means of conveying* to men ... justifying grace."

In 1767 Wesley threw overboard the watchword of all Protestant communities—Justification by Faith, *as* the Article by which a Church stands or falls. After showing, what to him "appeared clear as the day," that the Gospel plan of salvation does not require any such belief, he drives home the wedge:—"But if so, what becomes of *Articulus stantis vel cadentis ecclesiæ?* If so, is it not high time for us, Projicere ampullas et sesquipedalia verba—to lay aside big words that have no determinate meaning—and to *return* to the plain word, 'He that feareth God and worketh righteousness is accepted with Him'!"

The wave of re-action swept further, and in 1770, when Wesley was of the ripe age of 67, there appeared the famous "*Large Minutes*," to which Mr. Wesley ever afterwards constantly pointed, as expressing his matured conclusions on the subject: the last edition of which he prepared eighteen months only before his death: in them he says, "We have received it as a maxim, that 'a man is to

---

* "Wesley, up to 1738, had been a High Church sacramentalist; all his life afterwards he taught the Evangelical doctrine of salvation by faith." (!) Dr. Rigg—*The Relations of John Wesley, &c.*, p. 40.

Wesley.

do nothing, *in order to* Justification:' nothing can be more false. Whoever desires to find favour with God, should 'cease from evil and learn to do well.' Whoever repents, should do 'works meet for repentance.' And if this is not *in order* to find favour, what does he do them for? Is not this 'salvation by works'? Not by the *merit* of works, but by works as a *condition*. What have we then been disputing about for these thirty years? I am afraid, *about words.* As to *merit* itself, of which we have been so dreadfully afraid: we are rewarded 'according to our works,' yea, *because* of our works. How does this differ from 'for the sake of our works'? And how differs this from '*secundum merita operum*'?— As our works *deserve?* Can you split this hair? I doubt, I cannot." xv. 356, 357.

This was the last straw which broke the Protestant camel's back. This "advanced re-actionary" could no further go:[*] and if in these passages which determine what Wesley's view of Justification by Faith was, throughout every decade of his life after 1738, there be anything which the *highest* High-Churchman does not accept, it is only that John Wesley in this last passage goes further than he.

The storm which followed the publication of these *Minutes*—raised by those who styled themselves, in contradistinction from Wesley, "*real* Protestants"—has nothing to compare with it, save certain recent popular exhibitions against High-Churchmen of Wesley's stamp. A furious agitation was got up. A Circular Letter was despatched "through the Three Kingdoms;" in which it is proposed to all "Christian friends," and "real Protestants," "that they go in a body to the said Methodist Conference, and insist upon a formal Recantation" of such "dreadful heresy." These were his friends: others published at length parallels between Mr. Wesley's teaching on Justification, Works, &c., and the decrees laid down by the Holy Synod of Trent, and maintained, that "whoever has leisure and opportunity of consulting Jewel, Hall, Downham, against Cardinal Bellarmine, and others, will find the whole system of Mr. Wesley's divinity strenuously contended for by the Papists, and fully and satisfactorily confuted by the above able champions for the Protestant faith." Wesley defended himself and the *Minutes* from the charge these zealots had fastened on them —Justification by Works—by declaring with the same dying Cardinal (*Ss.* ii. 49), "We have no trust or confidence but in the alone merits of our Lord and Saviour Jesus Christ for justification or salvation, either in life, death, or the day of judgment." It was admitted that the language of the *Minutes* was "unguarded"—as doubtless had been designed: a truth to take hold must not be over-

---

[*] This is the only subject in which years wrought a progressive change in Mr Wesley's views after 1738: it is the one exception which proves the rule.

Wesley.

shadowed by qualifications—but of "Recantation" Wesley would not hear one word; of the *Minutes* as they stood, he would not abate one jot: and to this day they stand, the foremost exponent of the doctrines and principles of Wesleyan Methodism.

Wesley's agreement with himself, and with High-Churchmen, is apparent throughout. He held, as they do, that Justification (pardon) and salvation are of the grace and love of God alone. Faith, along with repentance and works meet for repentance, is the *condition* of salvation; the Sacraments the *means or instruments* of it: (Two things perfectly distinct.) And, "That we are justified by faith alone, is spoken to take away clearly all merit of our works, and wholly to ascribe the merit and deserving of our justification to Christ only." (1766. *Ss.* ii. 49.) The doctrine of "faith only," in any other sense and connection, he expressly disavowed, and with all his heart repudiated. Throughout his long life he waged one unceasing warfare against solifidianism in every shape. And with this, his deep and reverent faith in all Christian Ordinances, especially the two Greater Sacraments—Baptism and the Holy Eucharist—was in perfect and closest consistency.

CHAPTER XII.

OF THE COMMUNION OF SAINTS.

High Churchmen.

Christ's Body the Church is the exclusive heritage of no generation of Christians: all the faithful, in every age, have equal share and part in it: all true believers, who have been, who are, and who shall be, belong to it. Our union with Christ, in His Body the Church, does not begin with life, it does not end with it; this is a *spiritual* relationship over which Death hath no power. Our communion with each other depends only on union with our Head: if we have union with Him we have fellowship one with another. Therefore the Communion of Saints extends beyond the grave. Death being nothing else than the separation, for a season, of the soul from the body, not the separation of the soul from Christ, there is truth as well as poetry in the lines:

"Can death's interposing tide
 Spirits one in Christ divide?"

The living have communion with the dead, in faith, in prayer, in hope, in patience: the dead have communion with the living, in faith, in prayer, and in the highest act of all intercessory worship—the Offering of the Holy Sacrifice. They pray for the hastening of Christ's Kingdom, and wait for "the redemption of the body:" we also pray for the coming of Christ's Kingdom, and the com-

Wesley, 1756-1791.

Under this heading, Wesley writes:—

" Happy souls whose course is run,
 Who the fight of faith have won,
 Parted by an earlier death
 Think ye of your friends beneath?

" Have ye your own flesh forgot
 By a common ransom bought?
 Can death's interposing tide
 Spirits one in Christ divide?

" No: for us ye ever wait
 'Till we make your bliss complete;
 'Till your fellow-servants come,
 'Till your brethren hasten home.

" You in Paradise remain
 For your testimony slain,
 Nobly who for Jesus stood
 Bold to seal the truth with blood.

" Ever now your speaking cries
 From beneath the altar rise:
 Loudly call for vengeance due,
 ' Come, Thou Holy Lord, and True.'

Then, in response, Wesley represents those who are on this side the flood as (1) saying to those who have crossed it 'that they should rest yet for a little season':—

" Wait, ye righteous spirits, wait,
 Soon arrives your glorious state;
 Robed in white, a season rest,
 Blest, if not completely blest.

" When the number is fulfilled,
 When the witnesses are killed,
 When we all from earth are driven,
 Then with us ye mount to Heaven."

And (2) as uniting with them in fervent prayers:—

OF THE COMMUNION OF SAINTS. 73

High Churchmen.	*Wesley.*
pletion of the number of God's elect: that "all His whole Church" may have "perfect consummation and bliss both in body and soul." And these, our joint prayers, ascend to the common Father of all, and bring down blessings upon them and upon us.	"Jesu, hear, and bow the skies, Hark! we all unite our cries, Take us to our heavenly home, Quickly let *Thy Kingdom come.* "Jesu come, the Spirit cries, Jesu come, the Bride replies, One triumphant Church above, Join us all in perfect love." *(Hymns and Sacred Poems* by J. and C. Wesley. 1756.)

Will this be called a "poetic effusion," and fathered on Charles Wesley? John Wesley expressed the same in sober prose, in a sermon, six weeks only before his death: speaking on the Intermediate State, he says:—" May we not probably suppose, that the spirits of the just, though generally lodged in Paradise, may yet sometimes, in conjunction with the holy angels, minister to the heirs of salvation? May they not

'Sometimes on errands of love
Revisit their brethren below?'

It is a pleasing thought, that some of these human spirits, attending us with, or in the room of angels, are of the number of those that were dear to us while they were in the body. So that there is no absurdity in the question,

'Have ye your own flesh forgot
By a common ransom bought?
Can death's interposing tide
Spirits one in Christ divide?'

But be this as it may, it is certain human spirits (after death) swiftly increase in knowledge, in holiness and in happiness." "All those holy souls who have been discharged from the body, from the beginning of the world unto this day, will be continually ripening for Heaven, will be perpetually holier and happier, till they are received into 'the Kingdom prepared for them from the foundation of the world.'" *Ss.* ii. 554, 5.

Here is, as Wesley has pointed out, the sure ground of acceptable prayer for each other, for those above by those below, and for those below by those above, viz.,—Our common union with Christ and with each other, our like capacities for further growth in grace, and our joint participation in hopes and blessings not yet realized.

The transcendent nature of the union between Christ and His Church is felicitously set forth by Wesley, thus—

"With Him the Corner Stone
The living stones conjoin;
Christ and *His Church* are ONE,
One Body and One Vine."

CHAPTER XIII.
OF PRAYERS FOR THE DEAD.

High Churchmen.

Prayer for the Faithful Departed is rooted in the fact that we are members of a community deathless, indissoluble, and labouring under imperfection, in different degrees, in all its parts. No special need, therefore, for express texts authorizing us to do that which, if we pray at all, we cannot fail to do—who, subjects of grace, cannot forego praying God to hasten that work of grace, which, having begun, He is completing in all, and therefore in the departed, "till the Day of Christ." We cannot even say the Lord's Prayer without using a petition for the Faithful Departed: "Thy Kingdom come"—an event which manifestly concerns them as much as it does us; since on that they wait for the perfecting of their bliss, and "the redemption of the body." Their present state admits also, as Wesley observes (chap. xii.), of an *increase of holiness*, as well as of happiness—a further fact establishing the propriety of prayer.

God's people under both Dispensations have, with one consent, continued in Prayers for the Dead. This was the "holy and good thought" of Judas Maccabeus for his brethren that were slain. (2 Mac. xii. 44, 45.) This was the character of S.

Wesley, 1733-1772.

Wesley taught the propriety of Praying for the Dead, practised it himself, and provided *forms* that others might. These forms, for daily use, he put forth, not tentatively or apologetically, but as considering such prayer a settled matter of Christian practice, with all who believe that the Faithful, living and dead, are one Body in Christ, in equal need and like expectation of those blessings which they will together enjoy, when both see Him in His Kingdom. Two or three examples, out of many, may be given:—"O grant that we, with those who are already dead in Thy faith and fear may together partake of a joyful resurrection." (x. 40.) "... that we all together with those that now sleep in Thee, may awake to life everlasting." (p. 48.) "Bring us, with all those who have pleased Thee from the beginning of the world, into the glories of Thy Son's Kingdom." (p. 73.) "By Thy infinite mercies, vouchsafe to bring us, with those that are dead in Thee, to rejoice together before Thee," &c. (p. 77.) The Prayers passed through many editions, and were in common use among thousands of Methodists of every degree, who, without scruple or doubtfulness, prayed for those who sleep in

High Churchmen.

Paul's petition for his deceased convert Onesiphorus. (2 S. Tim. i. 18.) This was a marked feature in all the early Christian Liturgies. Never was there a church upon earth which did not keep up this interest in their departed members: even in those remnants of the afflicted Israelites, or of decayed Apostolic churches, which have been isolated from the rest of the world for seventeen hundred years, whatever the other variations, this one feature has been found uniformly preserved.

"The Lord grant unto him that he may find mercy of the Lord in that day." All competent textuarists say that every reference which can be brought to bear points wholly to one conclusion—that at this time Onesiphorus was dead, and the continual use in that age, and all ages succeeding, of these very words as a Prayer for the Faithful Departed, places it beyond reasonable doubt. If, then, Onesiphorus was dead—and all evidence both internal and external proclaims it—the practice has direct Scripture authority, given by the most favoured Apostle.

No one need retort that the Apocryphal Scriptures are not received as canonical by the Church of England. The Apocrypha is history—unimpeachable testimony to the customs and beliefs of the Jews: the Jews in the time of the Maccabees used Prayer for the Dead; they did so in our Lord's time; they do so still. And, what is

Wesley.

Jesus every day that they prayed to the common Father of all. Insomuch that there are Methodists of the old school (still abiding in the Ship by Wesley's advice), who use them night and morning to this day, entirely undisturbed by the doubts which modern disputers have sought to cast upon the practice.

One such disputer (Bishop Lavington) did Wesley encounter, and notices him thus: — " Your fourth argument is, That in a collection of Prayers, I cite the words of an ancient Liturgy—'for the Faithful Departed.' Sir, whenever I use those words in the Burial Service, I pray to the same effect: ' That we, with all those who are departed in Thy faith and fear, may have our perfect consummation of bliss, both in body and soul.' Yea, and whenever I say, 'Thy Kingdom come;' for I mean both the kingdom of grace and glory. In this kind of general prayer, therefore, for the Faithful Departed, I conceive myself to be clearly justified, both by the earliest Antiquity, by the Church of England, and by the Lord's Prayer." (1750.) xvi. 345.

Dr. Middleton, who was afflicted with that peculiar belief that everything in the early Church which did not exactly square with his own views was thereby convicted of being wrong, also urged, "'Tis certain, Praying for the Dead was common in the second century:' you might have said, and in the first also

High Churchmen.	*Wesley.*

High Churchmen.

striking confirmation of the rightfulness of the practice, our Blessed Lord when on earth joined regularly in that worship of which those prayers formed a part: and no warning on the point ever came from Him. And S. Paul also, "a Hebrew of the Hebrews," knew well that it was accounted, not a "superfluous and vain" thing, but "an holy and good thought," "to pray for the dead," and was perfectly aware of its regular practice amongst his brethren, in their public worship, in which he also joined, yet he utters no word of condemnation, but directly sanctions it by his own Christian petition:— "The Lord grant unto him that he may find mercy of the Lord in that day."

How such prayers should have a place given them in all the early Liturgies—some of which bear the names of Apostles, and were in use before parts of the New Testament were written—without Apostolic sanction, it is impossible to conceive.

Valuable remnants of these early prayers are contained in our present Liturgy: a Commemoration of the Faithful Departed in the Prayer for the Church Militant; a petition for "all Thy whole Church"—words as inclusive of every member, as the petition is inclusive of every blessing, "remission of our sins and all other benefits of His Passion"—in the Prayer for Acceptance; besides one clear and indubitable Prayer for the Faithful Departed in the Burial

Wesley.

(replied Wesley); seeing that petition 'Thy Kingdom come,' manifestly concerns the saints in Paradise, as well as those upon earth." "Praying thus far for the dead, 'That God would shortly accomplish the number of His elect, and hasten His Kingdom,' you will not easily prove to be any corruption at all." xviii. 154, 155.

Having thus silenced these clerical disputants, Wesley republished the above Prayers and continued the sale of them at all his preaching-houses as long as he lived. And in those Sermons which he made the legal standard, to which, after his death, the doctrinal teaching in his Society should always remain conformable, he shows more fully the nature of the sanction given to the Church's practice of Praying for the Dead by the Lord's Prayer, and also by the Anglican Burial Service:—"in these words, 'Thy Kingdom come,' we pray for the coming of His everlasting kingdom, the kingdom of glory in Heaven, which is the continuation and perfection of the kingdom of grace on earth; consequently this, (as well as the preceding petition,) is *offered up for the whole intelligent creation*, who are all interested in this grand event, the final restoration of all things, by God's putting an end to misery and sin, to infirmity and death, taking all things into His own hands, and 'setting up the Kingdom which endureth throughout all ages.' Exactly answerable to all this

High Churchmen.

Service:—"that it may please Thee, of Thy gracious goodness, shortly to accomplish the number of Thine elect, and to hasten Thy Kingdom; that we, with all those that are departed in the true faith of Thy Holy Name, may have our perfect consummation and bliss, both in body and soul, in Thy eternal and everlasting glory." This can mean only one of two things: we pray either that we may have our perfect consummation and bliss both in body and soul with those who *have obtained* it by departing this life in the true faith of God's Holy Name; or, that we and all those that have departed, &c., *may have* our perfect consummation and bliss both in body and soul." Now, it cannot mean the former for a very evident reason: they do not yet enjoy their "perfect consummation and bliss both in body and soul:" nor will they till God has accomplished the number of His elect, and the resurrection of the body has taken place: this being *the very thing that is prayed for.*

Wesley.

are those awful words, in the prayer at the burial of the dead—'Beseeching Thee, that it may please Thee of Thy gracious goodness shortly to accomplish the number of Thine elect, and to hasten Thy Kingdom; that we, with all those that are departed in the true faith of Thy Holy Name, may have our perfect consummation and bliss, both in body and soul, in Thy everlasting glory.'" *Ss.* i. 298.

On visiting "the venerable tomb" of Bp. Bedel in 1787, Wesley's comment is, "a plain flat stone inscribed, 'Depositum Gulielmi Bedel, quandam Episcopi Kilmorensis:' over whom ever the rebel army [Puritans as they were] sung, '*Requiescat in pace* ultimus Anglorum.' 'Let the last of the Englishmen rest in peace.'" *Jl.* xxi. 52.

And in a Manuscript of Mr. Wesley's, recently published for the first time; without date, but expressing the sentiment of his whole life as the above citations from his several works sufficiently show; he says, "I believe it to be a duty to observe to pray for the Faithful Departed."

CHAPTER XIV.

OF THE ORDER OF PUBLIC SERVICES AND OF CHURCH ARRANGEMENTS.

Here, the practice of Wesley and other early Methodists might, concisely stated, stand permanently on the notice-board of some of our most advanced "*Ritualistic* Churches:"—1. Daily Service throughout the year, Morning and Evening. 2. Holy Communion every Lord's-Day, and Daily during the Octaves of the Great Festivals. 3. The Morning Services divided "according to the original appointment of the Church." 4. Baptisms and Catechizing after the Second Lesson. 5. A Weekly Offertory. 6. No pews: but benches —free alike for rich and poor—and "the first comers to sit down first." 7. The Men and Women to Sit Apart, on their respective Sides, "as they always did in the Primitive Church."

1. DAILY SERVICE.

High Churchmen.

Until an "*unsparing* revision" of both Bible and Prayer-Book has taken place in the interest of an emasculated and devotionless religion, both will continue to enjoin the duty of Daily Prayers in the Church: the former by every example which it can afford, the latter by express enactment:—"*All* Priests, and Deacons, *are to say daily* the Morning and Evening Prayer, either privately or openly, not being let by sickness, or some other urgent cause. And the *Curate that ministereth in every Parish Church* or Chapel, being at home, and not being otherwise reasonably hindered, *shall say the same in the Parish Church* or Chapel where he ministereth." This is a duty to which every clergyman in the English Church

Wesley, 1730-1788.

To the Ordinance of Daily Prayer Mr. Wesley was always warmly attached. He accounted it as one of his choicest blessings that whilst he remained in Oxford the constant opportunity was afforded him of joining, morning by morning, and evening by evening, in the Church's daily sacrifice of prayer and praise; and he laboured diligently, and not unsuccessfully, in making others—the poor people of the city—sharers in the same benefit. (xxvi. 95.) On being removed to Georgia in 1735, he "immediately began" to say Morning and Evening Prayer "daily throughout the year." The ready objection, that a Daily Service interferes with the hours of labour, was of course soon heard; but was excellently forestalled by

High Churchmen.

has. by solemn oath, in the most solemn moment of his life, bound himself. Allowing as wide a margin for "sickness or other urgent cause" as it is possible to maintain, it plainly was never intended that what is allowed as the exception should be proclaimed as the rule. No one can imagine that the Church's direction is satisfied in its fulfilment by one clergyman out of twenty, or in one parish church out of ten.

The present general neglect is equally in violation of all that is read in the Bible. God's people have in all ages been taught by Himself the duty of a daily public worship. In the Tabernacle, and in the Temple, He daily received from them that honour which is His due. The Apostles, first ministers of Christ, upon whom more was laid, and for whom less provided than any who bear the name of ministers now, were never sparing in this service, but served Him "daily in the Temple and [in] Breaking Bread from house to house." All the first Christians "continued stedfastly in the Breaking of Bread and in Prayers;" and for a thousand years, in every Church, as often as the sun rose and set, the Offering of prayer and praise was duly given.

All objections are based on

Wesley.

Wesley, in his fixing the time of Service out of ordinary working hours:—"The Morning Service began at five, the Evening Service began at seven." (xiv. 319.) "The same rule I follow now,"—wrote he in 1744. seven years after his return to England—"at every place, winter and summer." (xiv. 320.) This early hour, five, was fixed for Sundays also, Wesley pertinently asking, "Why should we make God's Day the shortest of the seven?" Forty-four years later, Wesley says—speaking of the daily practice of the Methodists—"Their public Service is at five in the morning, and six or seven in the evening, that their temporal business may not be hindered." (Ss. ii. 473.) Wesley testifies that a sufficient attendance was always secured, and in warning words towards the end of his life says, "if they will not attend now, they have lost their zeal, and then it cannot be denied, *they are a fallen people.*"* Jl. xx. 46.

Then, as now, were seen the companion pictures of "*Sloth*" and "*Diligence*," in close proximity:—(1) Wesley admonishes "all calm and impartial men," "not to censure" those who, in acts of Divine worship, do what "seems to have been practised by the primitive Christians; and when, alas! there are so many

---

* Full of sad significance, is the attitude, which Methodists of the present generation have taken up towards the revival in our churches of the service of Daily Prayer; and one, which separates them by a wide interval, which nothing can bridge over, from him whom they fondly claim as their *Father*.

If they will not themselves return to their first faith and love, this, his deliberate judgment recorded against them, should at least withhold them from contemning us, because we follow their former and better example.

High Churchmen.	Wesley.
the most transparent of fallacies. Because there is not a considerable number *to whom* the prayers might be *read* (!)*, is no reason why the faithful "two or three," to whom the promise is given, should defraud God of the honour which is His due; those who have been taught the barest rudiments of religion need not to be informed that prayers are not for *their edification*, but for the *glory of God*. No one can imagine the Apostles and early disciples, instead of meeting "daily with one accord" for *common* worship, each substituting a *family* worship in his own home, after his own way; the very idea violently outrages all our religious feelings. No one need to be told that in the New Testament there is not the slightest trace of any such practice: "in the Temple," in the	parishes, where a person piously disposed has no opportunity of joining in the public Service of our Church more than *one hour and a half in a week*." (xxvii. 119.) (2) The other, Wesley exhibits, in delineating the life of an early Methodist:—" He read prayers *twice a-day*, early in the morning, and in the evening after the people came from work. He also daily catechized the children, and visited from house to house." (Ss. i. 589, 590.) " *Look on this picture and on that*." How pertinent, also, is Mr. Wesley's reflection—"How much easier it is for our brethren in the ministry to find fault with such a labourer in our Lord's vineyard than to tread in his steps."

house" — wherever means were afforded for joining in common worship—there were they gathered together. The idea of staying at home, and there offering *apart* "the prayers," as "a more excellent way," had not yet dawned upon Christian people. And as indefensible is such a custom, except from necessity, on six days of the week, as it would be on the first. " Forsake not the assembling of yourselves together," is a command, taken by common consent to mean—meet together for the joint worship of God; but is this command in force on Sundays only? Certainly it was not to S. Paul, by whom it was given, and to those, to whom it was first addressed; Christians, then, as often as opportunity was offered, met daily, with one accord, in one place: and no one was accounted a Christian who neglected so to do.

If more is needed; let it be, in Wesley's words, "an appeal to men of reason and religion:"—If a private individual, in earnest for his own salvation, and the salvation of those around him, were to

---

* The present Bishop of Chester lately urged upon all his clergy the duty of obeying the Church's directions. In reply, Dr. McN——, as the spokesman of the so-called Evangelical party, begged to know whether he, and others, could be desired to devote time, which otherwise might be *usefully* employed, "in order to *read* the Church Service *to a congregation* of three, four, or half-a-dozen persons?" !!!

High Churchmen.

throw open his own house, evening by evening, and invite his neighbours to come in for united prayer, what praise or encouragement would be thought too great? but if this person should be a priest, whose calling and duty it is to do this very thing; and if this house should have been built for this especial purpose, and for this end devoted solemnly to God; how does it follow that *he* does a vain thing—a thing rather to be discouraged than commended? Hence it undeniably appears that either in unreasoning prejudice, or, in some secret unbelief in the efficacy of prayer, is to be found the true spring of all current objections against the Church's standing requirement of Morning and Evening Prayer.

---

2. WEEKLY OR DAILY COMMUNION.

High Churchmen.

As a step towards what is imperatively required High Churchmen have never ceased to insist upon the necessity of a Weekly Communion on the Lord's Day: a necessity, which is now becoming recognized and acknowledged by all who wish to retain or establish for themselves the character of being "Bible Christians." Even amongst Nonconformists, tracts are appearing, urging on Scripture grounds, the adoption of the practice of Weekly Communion. A significant utterance of this kind is imputed to the famous Baptist preacher Mr. Spurgeon:—" The Tractarians held very erroneous notions about the Holy Communion, but, notwithstanding that, they had shown the Christian world where they had been lacking, and he hoped the time would come when they (the Nonconformists) would Break Bread on the first day of *every week.*"

G

Wesley, 1730-1790.

Preaching before the University, in S. Mary's, Oxford, on *Scriptural Christianity*, and portraying the early Christian, he says— " And as he was deeply sensible of the truth of that word, ' Without Me ye can do nothing,' and consequently, of the need he had to be watered of God every moment; so he *continued daily* in all the Ordinances of God— the stated channels of His grace to man:—' In the Apostles' doctrine,' or teaching, receiving that food of the soul with all readiness of mind; ' in the Breaking of Bread,' which he found to be the communion of the Body of Christ;' and in the prayers and praises offered up by the great congregation. And thus he daily grew in grace, increasing in strength and in the knowledge and love of God." (i. 73.) This explains everything. It was because Wesley believed that these Daily Ordinances were re-

High Churchmen.	*Wesley.*
What is imperatively required is the restoration of the Daily Sacrifice—a daily shewing forth the Lord's Death in intercession for all men—offering a daily opportunity for any of the faithful to communicate. This is the first of all needful things and the greatest of all blessings: and never until It be secured, shall we have established our claim to be faithful followers of the first believers, and a sound part of Christ's Church. *See* Chap. V. § 6 and 7.	quired alike by Scripture, by the Church, and by our own daily spiritual necessities, that he taught his people to use them, and provided the opportunities. Similarly in his *Instructions for Christians*, intended for general use as a Catechism, he asks and answers—" How often did the first Christians receive the Lord's Supper? Every day: it was their 'Daily Bread.' How often did they join in public prayers? Twice a-day, as many of them as could. How did they search the Scriptures? They heard or read them every day, and meditated therein day and night.

How long is every Christian to use these means of grace? To his life's end." xxiv. 127.

Also, in his *Forms of Prayer for every day in the Week*, he takes for granted that all who use them and are in earnest about their salvation, are constant in their use of the means of grace and duly sensible of their privileges: "Hear the Daily Prayers of the Catholic Church:" "I thank Thee for blessing me with ... frequent returns of Thy ever Blessed Sacrament:" "And for so often feeding my soul with Thy most precious Body and Blood." x. 33, 61, 107.

At Oxford, Wesley and his companions were constant in the use of these means—" Communicating as often as we had opportunity, which is here once-a-week;" (xxvi. 93) and spent a part of every day in visiting the poor, "enforcing upon them more especially the necessity of private prayer, and of frequenting the Church and the Sacrament." (*Id.* 95.) In 1735, Wesley accepted a call to go as Mission Priest to Georgia. On arriving there, he writes, "I immediately began reading Prayers, and expounded the Second Lesson both morning and evening. The morning service began at five; the evening service began at seven. Every communicant, *i.e.*, every serious person in the town constantly attended, unless in case of sickness, throughout the year." (xiv. 319. *Jl.* xx. 46.) On Sundays, "the morning service began at five, and office of Holy Communion with a sermon at eleven." (xxvi. 130.) This was done so long as Wesley was in Georgia. On his return to England, the same practice was everywhere established. Visiting about this time his poor people at Oxford, he laments, "I find a great change among the poor people here: out of twenty-five or thirty weekly com-

Wesley.

municants only two were left. Not one continued to attend the Daily Prayers of the Church." (xxvii. 287.) By the Rules of the Society he required that every preacher, leader, and member, "should constantly attend the Church and Sacrament" (xv. 325), and enforced compliance on refractory members or expelled them. (*Jl.* xvii. 45.) Their own ordinary service, he showed, pre-supposed a further service by its obvious incompleteness. Any service which was not consummated by the Holy Eucharist, he regarded as being essentially defective:—" If it were designed to be instead of Church Service," to give his own words on this important point, "it would be essentially defective: for it seldom has the four grand parts of public prayer; neither is it, *even on the Lord's Day*, concluded with the Lord's Supper." (xv. 313.) But when the defect was not supplied at Church, it was, as often as possible, specially met, by Wesley providing for his own society an early Celebration. What he had done abroad, he did, when occasion required, at home:—he made Holy Communion a separate service; only now he assigned to it an earlier hour. " Norwich. Sunday, 19. At seven I administered the Lord's Supper to about 170 serious communicants" (xxxii. 230); " I administered the Lord's Supper at eight, and afterwards attended our parish church" (*Jl.* xxi. 24)—example thus attending precept—" Let every preacher go always on Sunday morning, and when he can in the afternoon; God will bless those who go on week-days too as often as they have opportunity " *given*. (*Min.* 1768, xxvi. 93.) Wherever he went, he made it his business pointedly to interrogate his people on both these heads: (1) " Do you join in prayer with the great congregation? *Daily*, if you have opportunity? (2) Do you neglect no opportunity of attending and partaking of the Christian Sacrifice?" (*Ss.* i. 287, *circ.* 1762.) Suitable Altar Manuals were brought into the service: *Thomas à Kempis*, and Dr. Brevint's *Treatise on the Christian Sacrifice* bound up with J. and C. Wesley's Sacramental *Hymns* (166 in number) to form a complete manual, were put into the hands of every preacher and leader, and sold at "all his preaching houses, in town and country." " Few of the works which they published passed through so many editions; for the writers," remarks Mr. Jackson, (himself a Methodist of note,) " had succeeded in impressing upon the minds of their societies the great importance of frequent Communion. They administered the Lord's Supper in London every Sabbath day; and urged the people *everywhere, at all opportunities*, to eat of This Bread and drink of This Cup." Wherever Methodism obtained a footing, whether in Georgia, in England, Ireland, British North America, or in Scotland, there also were established the Daily Prayer and the Weekly Eucharist: the former by the preachers, in all places, after their manner; the first and second by Dr. Coke and

Wesley.

his colleagues in the New World, in a new state of society (*Min.* 1785); both, duly and regularly, by the Wesleys themselves and their clerical associates, in London, Bristol, Dublin, and all other centres where the services of a priest could be secured. And glorious and abundant were the fruits. God's blessing was unmistakably manifest from the numbers which were led to Holy Communion. Here are a few illustrations, taken from the fifth volume of Mr. Wesley's *Journal*, extending over the last ten years of his life (1780-1790):—Leake—" Easter Day. I preached in the church morning and evening, when we had about 800 communicants;" " at the Communion was such a sight as I am persuaded was never seen at Manchester before, 11 or 12,00 communicants at once;" " Leeds—We were ten clergymen and 7 or 8,00 communicants;" " I found it work enough to read prayers and preach, and administer the Sacrament to several hundred people;" " Macclesfield—We administered the Sacrament to about 13,00 persons;" Manchester again, " Mr. Baily came very opportunely to assist me, it was supposed there were 13 or 14,00 communicants;" " Easter Day, near 1000 communicants;" " Leeds—Having five clergymen to assist me, we administered the Lord's Supper to 16 or 17,00 persons;" " Bristol—It was supposed we had 1000 communicants, and I believe none went empty away;" " Manchester—We had 12,00 communicants;" " Kingswood—I read prayers and preached and administered the Sacrament to above 500 communicants;" " Old Church, Leeds—We had eighteen clergymen and about 11,00 communicants;" " Sheffield—I read prayers, preached, and administered the Sacrament to 6 or 7,00;" Birmingham—" Mr. Heath read prayers and assisted me in delivering the Sacrament to 7 or 8,00 communicants;" Bolton—" We had five clergymen and 12 or 13,00 communicants. The Master of the Feast was with us, as many found to their unspeakable comfort;" " London—The number of communicants was so great that I was obliged to consecrate thrice;" " I preached, and with Dr. Coke's assistance administered the Sacrament to 11 or 12,00 communicants;" " Birstall—With the assistance of three other clergymen I administered the Sacrament to 15 or 16,00 persons;" Bath—" I know not that ever I had so large a number of communicants before." * Manchester—" Easter Day, I think we had about 16,00 communicants;" Plymouth—" In the morning I believe we had not less than 600 communicants: they were

---

* More than a fear is justified that some of these received the Holy Communion without that due preparation which should always attend so great an act. But with this at present we have nothing to do. These accounts show, unmistakably, what the *character* of Wesley's teaching was, in the last years of his life. Thousands baptized in a day, or made partakers of Christ in the Eucharistic Feast, we do read of in the Catholic Church; but in Protestant annals such accounts have no place: all low-church teachers look for other results.

Wesley.

all admirably behaved, as if they indeed *discerned* the Lord's Body."
Dublin—"I preached in the new room at 7, at 11 I went to the Cathedral. I desired those of our Society, who did not go to their parish Churches, would go with me to S. Patrick's. Many of them did so. It was said the number of communicants was about 500: more than went there in the whole year before Methodists were known in Ireland."

These figures are startling: even now that we are happily again accustomed to hear of the lesser numbers. They speak eloquently for the soundness of Wesley's work, and have even no distant parallel, except in the large crowds which by like influences are brought to the Altars of our more advanced "high churches."

In two things, Wesley's judgment and public teaching were absolutely uniform, throughout the whole of his long life:—(1st) That the restoration of "The Daily Sacrifice" is very much to be wished and ardently to be prayed for. (2) That the early Christians, those taught by Christ and the Apostles, communicated daily; and that it is our bounden duty to follow them herein, so far as opportunity is given. *H.* clxvi. xxiv. 127. *Ss. II.* No. cvi.

The Church's Festivals with their Octaves, and her solemn seasons were Wesley's *opportunities;* these he observed according to the desire of his heart, and the Church's design in their institution, *i.e.*, by a *Daily Eucharist.* See Chap. V. § 6 & 7.

3. SEPARATION OF THE MORNING SERVICES.

High Churchmen.

Matter of accusation is sometimes found against the High Church Clergy, by casual church attenders, in that they depart from the ordinary custom of saying the whole Morning Service at 11 a.m. *Ans.* (1) The "ordinary custom" is itself a *departure* from the original design and institution of the Church; and one which is not conformable to the nature of the Services themselves. In the Matin Office, *e.g.*, it makes

Wesley, 1736-1786.

As with all true Reformers, Wesley's daily aspiration was— Conformity to the Church in her best estate: hence he *must* go contrary to corrupt customs, and in their place restore what they have too long supplanted — so long, that they, the original usages, re-appear under the reproach of being "innovations." Instances of this are seen in the present and four following sections.

"Sunday, 9. [1736, in Geor-

High Churchmen.	Wesley.
us defer thanking God that He "hath safely brought us to the *beginning* of this day" until it is near noon, and summons us only three hours later to pray God to "defend us from all perils and dangers of *this night*"! A yet more serious objection is, that it gives the faithful no opportunity of receiving the Holy Communion before breaking their fast. (2) Matins, Litany, and Holy Communion being three distinct offices, have each only what is proper to it, but the *repetitions* created by running these three offices together are intolerable— Our Father five times repeated, Confessions of Faith and Confessions of Sin twice made, and Absolution twice given. This cannot be conducive either to reverence or to edification: to all it is a weariness more than sufficient, to invalids and children a weariness too great to be borne. (3) Herein, also, occasion is given to the many loud demands	gia.] I began dividing the Public Prayers according to the original appointment of the Church (still observed in a few places in England)." Service of Holy Communion, with sermon at 11; Matins at an earlier hour. (xxvi. 130.) Raked up by Wesley's opponents as matter of accusation against him, it being "asserted upon oath 'that John Wesley, Clerk, had broken the laws of the realm, contrary to the peace of our Sovereign Lord the King his crown and dignity— by *dividing* the Morning Service on Sundays.'" *Id.* 205. Wesley, nothing daunted, continued to give occasion for the same charge on his return to England — by celebrating the Holy Eucharist as a separate and independent Service, at an early hour—*e.g.*, "at seven," or "at eight." xxxii. 230, *Jl.* Dec. 3, 1786.

for revision, &c., by persons who are strangely unmindful that these repetitions are occasioned by the very changes which have been made for their special accommodation. The true remedy is obvious— Revert to the Church's original practice: let each office begin and consecrate its own portion of the day: then with services shorter and more frequent, there will be opportunities appropriate for all, and for none either weariness or repetition.

4. BAPTISMS AND CATECHIZING OPENLY IN CHURCH.

High Churchmen.	Wesley, 1736-1744.
1. The Church has taken the utmost care, (having made it the special subject of no less than three	1. The Direction — "'The Children to be Baptized must be ready at the Font, immediately

BAPTISMS AND CATECHIZING OPENLY IN CHURCH. 87

High Churchmen.

Rubrics,) that none be Baptized otherwise than openly in the Church after the Second Lesson; and even thus, on no day, (unless "necessity so require,") "but upon Sundays and other Holydays, *when the most number of people come together;*" to this intent—(1) That all there present "may testify the receiving of them that be newly Baptized into the number of Christ's Church." (2) "That every man present may be put in remembrance of his own profession made to God in his Baptism." (3) That those who are present may, with the Minister, call upon God in prayer, "that of His bounteous mercy He will grant to that child (to be Baptized) that thing which by nature he cannot have; that he may be Baptized with Water and the Holy Ghost," and "receive remission of his sins by spiritual regeneration." (4) That they all may "give thanks to Almighty God for these benefits" which (being Baptized) "he is made partaker of." *Office of Baptism.*

The "Private Baptism of children in houses," "without great cause and necessity," is unallowed.

2. Sermons for the adult members and Catechizing for the Children, has always been one of the Church's statutes. Both are imposed by the same authority; both are of like obligation: the morning being assigned to the former, the afternoon to the latter. "The Curate of *every*

Wesley.

after the Second Lesson,' I have observed punctually." xiv. 156, 157. (1744.)

Another *direction* commanded Mr. Wesley's obedience and respect, as the two following paragraphs from his *Journal* show:— " Sat. 21. Mary Welsh, aged eleven days, was baptized according to the custom of the first Church, and the rule of the Church of England, by immersion. The child was ill then, but recovered from that hour." (xxvi. 121.) "Wed. May 5. I was asked to baptize a child of Mr. Parker's, second bailiff of Savannah. But Mrs. Parker told me, ' Neither Mr. P. nor I will consent to its being dipped.' I answered, 'If you *certify that your child is weak, it will suffice* (the Rubric says) *to pour water upon it.*' She replied, ' Nay, the child is not weak; but *I am resolved* it shall not be dipped.' This argument I could not confute. So I went home; and the child was baptized by another person." *Id.* 130.

2. " On Saturday in the afternoon I catechize all the children. The same I do on Sunday before the Evening Service (*Canon* 59). And in the church immediately after the Second Lesson, a select number of them having repeated the Catechism and been examined in some part of it, I endeavour to explain at large, and to enforce that part, both on them and the congregation. xxvi. 155.

Practised by the early Methodist Preachers with success.—" Sun-

High Churchmen.	Wesley.
Parish shall diligently upon Sundays and Holy-days after the Second Lesson at Evening Prayer, openly in the Church instruct and examine" the "Children of his parish ... in some part of this Catechism." The present general neglect of the Church's order to Catechize is full of sad results:—the Children are uninterested, unedified,	day, 11. I met about a hundred children who are Catechized publicly twice a week. Thomas Walsh began this some months ago, and the fruit of it appears already. What a pity that all our preachers, in every place, have not the zeal and wisdom to follow his example." xxx. 70.

and—in the exclusive thought that is shown for their elders—unconscious that any provision for them is made; the adult members of the congregation often are, and often remain through life, (notwithstanding Sermons*) ignorant to the last degree.

That the oral delivery of a Sermon is the one mode of Preaching, is a pure fabrication, without either Scripture or reason as its warrant.

---

5. A WEEKLY OFFERTORY.

High Churchmen.	Wesley, 1739-1790.
There has never been an acceptable worship without a material Offering. "None shall appear before Me empty" is the expression of an obligation which existed from the beginning, and which in Christian times has been enforced by the Apostolic direction—" Upon the first day of the week let every one of you lay by him in store as God hath	Another "regulation" of Mr. Wesley's was the revival amongst his own people of the Weekly Offertory. Each member of his Society was expected to bring a weekly offering. Each week the alms-dish was passed round, and the brother of low degree cast in his penny, the poor widow her two mites, and the richer brother his gift according as God had

---

* Wesley asks, "What avails public *preaching* alone, though we could preach like angels?" And gives several instances of the general inaptitude of the bucolic mind to take in what is addressed to it in *sermons*.

"I heard Dr. Lupton say [that] my father, visiting one of his parishioners, who had never missed going to church for forty years, then lying on his death-bed, asked him, 'Thomas, where do you think your soul will go?' 'Soul! soul!' said Thomas. 'Yes: do you not know what your soul is?' 'Aye surely,' said he; 'why, it is a little bone in the back, that lives longer than the rest of the body.' So much Thomas had learned by constantly hearing sermons, yea and exceeding good sermons, for forty years!" "After all our preaching, many of our people are almost as ignorant as if they had never heard the Gospel." xv. 284, 286.

High Churchmen.

prospered him," and the appropriate opportunity of discharging it, is given by the Church's weekly practice of collecting alms in the highest office of Christian worship.

In bringing our gifts to the Altar, we "honour the Lord with our substance," and obtain the sanctification to our own use of that which remains. And herein is its special value:—what otherwise must "*of necessity*" be extracted, by fixed charges, by importunate begging, by human interest, by bazaars, by balls, &c.; is "*willingly offered*" to the *honour of God*, and becomes, instead of a money-payment for value received, an act of acceptable worship. And never may it be forgotten that the poor widow's offering of two mites, which obtained from our Lord such imperishable praise, was a casting into the *Church's* treasury.

Wesley.

prospered him. "Let none be excluded from giving something; be it a penny, a halfpenny, a farthing. Remember the widow's two mites. And let those who are able to give shillings, crowns, and pounds do it willingly." It is the pence that make the pounds; the many givers that swell the sum given; but above all, the *frequent* giving which yields the unfailing supply. And to this—the Weekly Offertory—Mr. Wesley trusted, as a sound principle of church finance having direct Scripture sanction.

This formed the Sustentation Fund of the Preachers; easily gathered, willingly offered, it was the chief pecuniary support of early Methodism. And to this day it remains the main channel through which there flows to the Methodist ministers an average income one hundred per cent. larger than half the clerical incomes within the Church of England.

To almsgiving, in general, Wesley assigns the highest obligation, "namely, the command of Him by Whose Name we are called." (ii. 265.) To give "alms, in the [Holy] Eucharist," in particular, he says "I believe it to be a duty to observe:" (Memoranda, *Guardian* Newspaper, Nov. 27, 1867.) on the principle, familiar to all Bible students, that Bringing to the Altar is one ordained means of making us Partakers of the Altar.

---

6. NO PEWS, BUT BENCHES FREE ALIKE FOR RICH AND POOR.

High Churchmen.
If there be one point on which Holy Scripture is emphatic, and express beyond a doubt, it is that

Wesley, 1737–1787.
"The Committee proposed to me, (1) That families of men and women should sit together in both

High Churchmen.

it is wrong and contrary to God's will, to show respect to worldly distinction in that House which is His—it is that the assignment of good places to the rich in goodly apparel, while the poor are relegated to the worst and most distant places, is sinful and unbrotherly. How any one can read S. James ii. 1-9, and yet doubt this, is incomprehensible to men of *ordinary* understanding, and has never been explained.

As respects the practice in Parish Churches, it is contrary to English Law and was unknown even to custom until that dark age of the Church—the latter half of the 17th and the whole of the 18th centuries—an age which for its gross spiritual neglect, its sheer worldliness, and its unmitigated selfishness is without a parallel. Indeed, in almost every village there are men yet living who remember the time when the old open seats, free alike to rich and poor, were torn out to make way for the Pews, which have since then become generally appropriated by the rich and middle classes to the grievous injury of their poorer, and in every respect more needy brethren. Wherefore, on every ground, but especially as "Bible Christians," High Churchmen must wage an unceasing war against that abomination in God's House—the modern pew system.

Wesley.

chapels; (2) That every one who took a pew should have it as his own: thus overthrowing at one blow *the discipline which I have been establishing for fifty years!*" *Jl.* Dec. 21, 1787.

"From the beginning [of Methodism] the men and women sat apart, as they always did in the Primitive Church: and none were suffered to call any place their own, but the first comers sat down first. They had no pews; and all the benches for rich and poor were of the same construction." *Mag.* 1787, p. 101.

In full accord with this, the only community which can claim Mr. Wesley's name—through adherence to his plan—the Primitive Wesleyan Methodists, in Ireland, have stedfastly maintained the freedom of sitting in all their preaching-houses:—" In all of them the *sittings are free*, the Conference being determined in this respect, as well as in all others, to adhere to the arrangements of Mr. Wesley. Under no circumstances are pews permitted to be erected, and, though the income derivable from pewrent might, in a pecuniary way, be useful to the Connexion, they are resolved to sacrifice this, rather than throw any impediment in the way of the poorest person's having an opportunity of hearing the glad tidings of salvation, *without money and without price.*" *Centenary of Methodism*, p. 347.

7. SEPARATION OF THE SEXES.

High Churchmen.

One half of the objections against the whole body of the church being kept for the joint use of the parishioners in common had no existence so long as it continued the unbroken rule: then men and women by immemorial usage took their respective sides therein, and to this day there remains evidence of this, in those numerous parish churches where a portion of the *old* seats have been left undisturbed for the use of the poor. Then it was impossible for a lady to find herself seated next a man objectionable in his personal habits, or for a girl to be seated by a youth intent upon paying her improper attentions. This also the low and open seats would have prevented, just as the high close pews favour, and directly incite it.

The other half—instead of being valid objections—turn out, on due consideration, manifest proprieties:—*God's* House is not a place for family parties and an exhibition of family religion; for that we have houses of *our own*. In *God's* House, at least, there should be visible manifestation of the truth that we all are One Body in Christ and members one of another;—that, as the Family of God, we assemble there at His invitation, to render Him a common worship. Hence, as the highest exhibition of this oneness, the most beautiful sight to be seen on earth is, young and old, "rich

Wesley, 1737-1787.

"I likewise insisted upon another 'strange' regulation—That the men and women should sit *apart*." (xxx. 257.) "Should the men and women sit apart everywhere? By all means. Every preacher should look to this." (*Min.* 1765.) Directions to Building Committees.—"Engage that the men and women shall sit apart, both above and below." (*Min.* 1782.) "Is there any exception to the rule—'Let the men and women sit apart'? In those galleries where they have always sat together, they may do so still. But let them sit apart everywhere below, and in all newly erected galleries." (xv. 332.) "Shall we insist on the observance of this direction for the time to come, or not? We will permit none to collect for any future building unless security be first given." (*Min.* 1786.) "From the beginning the men and women sat apart, as they always did in the Primitive Church." *Mag.* 1787, p. 101

"Rich Methodists," since Wesley's death, have succeeded in "overthrowing" their Founder's discipline. Still, for the *poor*, this separation of the sexes is still insisted upon:—"The places in each chapel which are free, are divided, one part for the men, and another part for the women, who always sit separate in those places." Myles' *Chronological History.* 1813.

High Churchmen.

and poor, one with another," kneeling in *common* worship side by side: all other ties and bonds of union being, for the time, overshadowed by *that* which is highest of all—our spiritual kinship one to another in our Blessed Lord.

No one, whose knowledge of human nature is even moderate, can ignore the existence, in most families, of those private feelings, and oftentimes special circumstances, which render the family-circle system the *least* favourable of any, to that Worship which is Divine, only as it is in forgetfulness of all save the Divine Presence. Those who urge on behalf of their own personal preferences an exemption from the rule, will do well to remember, that the sacrifice of even a private good is a bounden duty as well as an acceptable offering when it can be made for the common good of all.

CHAPTER XV.
OF RITUAL.

High Churchmen.

All our knowledge of Worship, as to its forms and proprieties, is derived from three sources: — (1) Worship prescribed by God under the Old Dispensation; (2) Worship in Heaven revealed to S. John under the New; and (3) Worship practised by the Church on earth. If we could, for a moment, dissociate from our minds all ideas derived from these three sources we should be quite at a loss to understand in what way, and with what accessories, God willed worship to be offered. And if from these three sources there issues *one* stream of clear direction, scarcely so much as a doubt can arise, whether we may accept it, or whether of our own mere will we may set it aside. Here, then, we are met by the great fact that with Forms of Prayer and Praise, and Bodily Prostrations; Incense, Lights, Music, Vestments, and a splendid Ritual, have always been associated in the offering of Worship, and this by the Will of God Himself.

In God's first Revelation to man this Ceremonial Worship was *prescribed and enjoined*; in His second Revelation it was shown to be *still in accordance* with His Will, and consistent with the highest spirituality

Wesley, 1733-1782.

Curiously enough, Wesley has by some been called, "a Pharisaic institutor of forms and ceremonies," while others have represented him as the enemy of forms and ceremonies. In truth he was neither. Between outward form and inward life Wesley acknowledged no opposition. Himself the emphatic teacher of the necessity of inward and spiritual religion, and of the utter worthlessness of all forms and faiths standing in place of it; he was at the same time the emphatic teacher of our necessity of forms as means and helps, against those who disparaged them under the plea of promoting a purer and more spiritual religion. With a sounder and more discriminative judgment, one who knew him well, and was the intimate friend of his riper years—Alexander Knox—has testified of him thus:—"In his prevalent tastes and likings, as an individual, he was a Church of England man of the highest tone: not only did he value and love that pure spirit of faith and piety which the Church of England inherits from Catholic Antiquity; but even in the more circumstantial part, *there was not a service or a ceremony, a gesture, or a habit, for which he had not an unfeigned*

| *High Churchmen.* | *Wesley.* |

attainable—being the pure worship of pure spirits in Heaven; and the Church—properly guided by all that God has at any time revealed—has *in every age* and *every place* worshipped with this same Holy Worship. For 15,00 years before Christ and 15,00 years after, whether in earth or Heaven, worship with incense and lights, music and song, has been by God's people offered, and by God accepted, as the homage which is required and is His due. Such was the worship in which our Blessed Lord as Son of Man constantly joined, and in which His chosen Apostles and the first believers so long as the Temple stood took part: and such has it ever since remained; excepting in times of persecution, when, the Christians being driven to hide in caves of the earth, it was necessarily presented without the gold and the sweet frankincense in a less costly shrine: on the cessation of persecution, jewelled plate for the Altar, "holy garments" "for glory and for beauty," for the priest, "goodly buildings" for the worshippers, and lights and incense for the service, immediately resumed their use. From East to West, and from North to South, a Church was never to be found which withheld this honour from "the *Lord's* House" and Service, and bestowed it in ungodly preference upon *their own.* Even when the Reformation violently upturned old traditions, God's Service in its outward form and beauty re-

predilection. He was not only free from every puritanical leaning, but the aversion for those early enemies of the established Church which he had imbibed in his youth, though repressed and counteracted, was by no means wholly subdued, even in the last stage of his life." Wesley *could* not have been an "Anti-Ritualist." His impatience against those puritanical and not over-scrupulous zealots, who, in a former age strove to abridge the Church's Ceremonial, breaks out again and again: "Indeed, many of the Reformers themselves complained, that 'The Reformation was not carried far enough.' But what did they mean? Why, that they did not sufficiently reform the *rites* and *ceremonies* of the Church. Ye fools and blind! To fix your whole attention on the circumstantials of religion! Your complaint ought to have been, The essentials of religion were not carried far enough. You ought vehemently to have insisted on an entire change of men's *tempers* and *lives*—on their showing, they had 'the mind that was in Christ,' by 'walking, as He also walked.' Without this, how exquisitely trifling was the reformation of opinions, and rites, and ceremonies." *Ss.* ii. 74. And even in jealously guarding heart-religion from being supposed to consist in any outward thing *whatsoever*, whether "forms," or "actions," or "opinions,"—he assigns no mean place to correct forms and ceremonies, as without doubt he does

High Churchmen.

mained nearly undisturbed. It continued the law in the Anglican Communion, the rule amongst the Protestants of Germany and Sweden and other countries professing the Lutheran faith; whilst to the followers of one man alone was it left to abridge God's Worship, and rob it of those meet adornments which God Himself had sanctioned, under plea of bringing in a more spiritual religion.

To say, that the tendency of these accessories of Divine Worship is to unspiritualize the mind, is directly to impeach the goodness of God in prescribing them for His ancient people. To say that they were for this people alone, and enjoined upon them for temporary reasons, is directly contrary to God's Revelation that such is the unceasing worship in Heaven—the pattern of all acceptable worship, and in which "all nations and kindreds and people" must hereafter join. Whilst to declare that such worship is not pure enough for mortal men, is in strange opposition to the fact, that it is the fitting worship of pure spirits round the Heavenly Throne, and the highest homage they can bring to Him that sitteth thereupon. There, whilst we, day by day, pray that we may do God's will on earth as it is done in Heaven, there is the mysterious harping and the unceasing angelic song, there are white-robed celebrants, there is incense offered by an angel from a golden censer, there is a golden altar before the

Wesley.

also to good actions and right opinions:—" 4. [It consists] not in any *outward thing*; such as forms or ceremonies, even of the most excellent kind. Supposing these to be ever so decent and significant, ever so expressive of inward things: supposing them ever so helpful, not only to the vulgar, whose thought reaches little further than their sight; but even to men of understanding, men of stronger capacities, as *doubtless they may sometimes be*: yea, supposing them, as in the case of the Jews, to be appointed by God Himself; yet even during the period of time wherein that appointment remains in force, true religion does not principally consist therein; nay, strictly speaking, not at all. How much more must this hold concerning such rites and forms as are only of human appointment? The religion of Christ rises infinitely higher, and lies immensely deeper, than all these. *These are good in their place;* just so far as they are in fact subservient to true religion. And *it were superstitious to object against them*, while they are applied only as occasional helps to human weakness. But let no man carry them further. Let no man dream that they have any intrinsic worth; or that religion cannot subsist without them. This were to make them an *abomination* to the Lord." *Ss.* i. 60.

I have given the paragraph entire. Now for the judgment. *Whose language is this?* With

High Churchmen.

Throne of the Almighty; there are prostrations made by angels and by elders; there is, in everything, solemn and gaudeous ceremonial; there is, in everything, the absence of that bareness and coldness which some tell us are alone truly spiritual; there is, in everything, the presence of that kind of worship which the Church Catholic, however imperfectly, strives to realize here on earth, as twice given by the Revelation of God. It is of no consequence whether the words of S. John be regarded as descriptive of the present, prophetic of the future, or even as symbolical only, in accommodation to human ideas: the fact that God has so chosen these terms whereby to express service of the highest, most spiritual, and most acceptable kind, is sufficient for our correct guidance in matters of Christian worship. In any case the truth stands the same—that a Ceremonial Worship, outwardly glorious, is the only worship revealed in the Bible—a fact which can never be safely ignored by "*Bible* Christians."

Nor is this Divine ordination of Ceremonial Worship without good reason, even as it is humanly evident. Man has a body as well as a soul; it is part of his complex nature—as much part of himself as the spirit which God breathed into it: hence God requires the united homage of the whole man; to give God the worship of the spirit, and to withhold that of the body, is to offer Him a maimed offering.

Wesley.

all their hearts High Churchmen subscribe it, to its very last word. Their opponents require to have it divided in halves: the *misuse* of Ritual they are forward to proclaim; the *use* of Ritual they can by no means allow.

No one would expect that Wesley—living at a time, barren beyond comparison, when "Ritualism" in conjunction with earnest work and multiplied services, was never once heard of—has left many notices of what is now so called: nevertheless, in his own course and character as a Church *Revivalist*, there is abundant to show that John Wesley would have been anything but a foe to "Ritualism," if he had found it associated, as it now undeniably is, with a deeper spiritual life, this being manifested by the same signs as vouched for it in his own day. Of this we see something in his coming, *con amore*, to the defence of the Primitive Church—her forms, faith, and worship—against Dr. Middleton (a Low Churchman), who had professed to write "because of the late increase of Popery in this kingdom," charging the early Church with various corrupt abuses, in a manner, "well-imagined," says Wesley, "to prejudice a Protestant reader in your favour." And what were these abuses? "You instance, first—in mixing the wine with water in the Holy Sacrament; you instance next—in their sending the Bread to the sick; then, their styling It 'the Sacrifice

High Churchmen.

The body equally with the spirit partakes of the fall; it ministers to sin; it is punished by suffering, sickness, and death; with the soul it has been redeemed; with the soul it will, in the resurrection, be renewed, and with it consciously partake of that blessedness which is held in store. Hence it *must* take part in that exercise which is for man appointed—it must "worship the Lord with holy worship:" the head must incline in homage to the Name of Him Who is Lord of all, the lips must articulate, the knees must bend, the whole body must prostrate fall under sense of sin in the Divine Presence. Without a service in which due share is allotted to the body—without bowing, kneeling, and prostrating—worship is not complete; it is essentially defective, lacking one of its elements; the higher part of man brings its tribute of thanks, the lower is "unfruitful." And God has so constituted man—has so intimately blended body and soul together—that man *cannot* pay the duty of the one while in wilful neglect of what is due from the other: the man who comes before God and opens not his lips offers Him no praise; the man who bends not the knee offers Him no prayer: it is simply impossible for one christianly instructed, and unhindered by infirmity, to worship God sitting at his ease.

And in its less and proper degree this is true of *things* associated in Worship. God

Wesley.

of the Body of Christ;'" their practice of "Infant Communion," "praying for the dead," and their use of the "consecrated oil"—" no abuses at all," says Wesley, who stoutly defends these practices. xviii. 153, 154. (1749.)

Other things, as practised by the first Christians, he sets his name to, and records for our instruction: their practice of Trine Baptism — dipping three times, in the Name of the Father and of the Son and of the Holy Ghost; their putting on the newly baptized a white robe in token of purity; the renunciation of Satan with faces turned to the West, and confession of Christ with faces turned to the East: many of these, with some other points of Primitive Ritual connected with the Holy Eucharist, namely, Turning to the East on the recital of the Creed; the preparatory Dedication of the Elements to be used (Prothesis); their solemn Oblation; that well-known feature in every early Liturgy, the Invocation upon them of the Holy Ghost; he specifies elsewhere also (Dublin MS.) and pointedly adds, these, " I think it my duty, so far as I can, to observe." To the practice of the early Church he continually refers, and for a very emphatic reason—" May we be followers of them in all things, as they were of Christ." This was the object for which alone Mr. Wesley lived—to bring back—to revive—the Church's forgotten Doctrines and neglected Practices.

High Churchmen.

has clearly shown in the Revelation He has made, that it is His pleasure to accept as common Lord of all, not only the worship of the human spirit and body, but that of all creation. Every thing which He has made may render Him its several tribute: the sweet odours of the earth, its varied riches, its glorious harmonies, its lights and colours, all, in the hand of man, in the temple of God, may unite in one consentient hymn of praise: thus verifying the lines so often sung—

"The whole creation join in one
To praise the sacred Name."

In the spirit of David, whose Psalms are so peculiarly fitted for this Holy Worship, the Church makes *all* things minister in the sanctuary to the honour and glory of God.

Divine Wisdom is justified also in the ordination of a Ritual

Wesley.

And early Methodists said this, and were not ashamed of the acknowledgment: in no more appropriate words could they sum up — as they did in his epitaph—the aim and end of all his labours, "To enlighten these nations, and to *revive, enforce, and defend* the pure Apostolical *Doctrines and Practices of the Primitive Church.*" *

Opponents, like this Dr. Middleton of *The Church Association* stamp, say that Ritualism is the child's love for gewgaws; Wesley, by a truer appreciation, shows that such has ever been the Church's manner of teaching those, "whose thought," as he observes. "reaches little further than their sight." Opposition to such "helps to human weakness," they account a virtue; he proclaims it a "superstition." From the presence of forms and attitudes, they draw the infer-

---

* Love of the Primitive Church involves a love of Ritual, and fosters also a native growth—and Ritual among the early Methodists became indigenous, and had a place on every fitting occasion. Many instances might be given, some of them very touching ones:—Fletcher lay sick at Madeley, and his friends went in a body "to the Church and *sang a hymn of supplication to the Lord.*" Asbury met Dr. Coke for the first time, on American soil, "and kissed him, pronouncing at the same time a primitive salutation." Dr. Adam Clarke, on entering an inhabited dwelling, "did so with a 'Peace be to this house.'" Their yearly Covenant was an occasion of much solemn and impressive ritual; and the world therein found occasion, as now it does; to charge with "solemn trifling and theatrical manœuvres" all who dared to offend against its code of cold proprieties. Preceded by a fast, and consummated by the Eucharist, this Covenant of Marriage to the Lord was made in the most formal and solemn manner. It was read aloud from the pulpit, "all the people kneeling," and saying at its close, "Amen, so be it." The preacher, then, at his discretion, might add, "This covenant I advise you to make, not only in heart, but in *word;* not only in word, but in *writing;* and that you would with all possible reverence *spread the writing before the Lord,* as if you would present it to Him as your act and deed. And when you have done this *set your hand to it: keep it as a memorial* of the solemn transactions that have passed between God and you, that you may *have recourse to it* in doubts and temptations." Then was sung the Covenant Hymn, all the people still kneeling; at the end of the 6th verse the people rose to their feet, and lifted up their hands in token of assent; the hymn was then sung to its close. And as showing that instances of excess, foolish indeed, but pardonable, are not peculiar to the present Church Revival, but are rather what all revivals are liable to, cases have occurred in the palmy days of Methodism, when in the most solemn manner the covenant entered into has been "signed with the blood of the creature"!

High Churchmen.

Worship by its power to teach. Man's nature is such that it is more impressed by what it sees with the eye than what it hears with the ear. No Sermon on Reverence discourses so well as a thousand heads bowed before the Holy Name of Jesus. No words declare the Presence of the Almighty so convincingly as the prostrate forms of His worshippers. No eloquence can impress the truth, "This is the House of God and the very Gate of Heaven," with power equal to that which makes it most resemble Heaven—the honoured Altar, the smoking Incense, the white-robed Choir, the swelling Music, the resounding Praise. All men bow to its influence, while the young and the unlettered "whose thought reaches little further than their sight" are taught almost entirely by it.

To the world, Ritual is an *appointed witness* of the Truth it flies from. Not more surely does the ascending spire point to Heaven, and the seventh-day worship to its holy rest, than a correct Ritual to the faith which it embodys and by its forms makes visible. "Show me thy faith without thy works and I will show thee my faith by my works," is a principle fairly of application wider than is sometimes assigned to it; and so the world feels and confesses:—to quote its words on one point only—the Burial of the sainted dead—"Of course," says a leading daily Journal, "at the bottom of all this desire to

Wesley.

ence of unreality and absence of inward power; Wesley, therefrom, draws the precisely opposite inference, "Surely there is much of the power of godliness where there is so much of the form." xxix. 255.

Children and adults were taught by him to bow at the Name of Jesus, and on the mention of the All-Holy Name; the former in *Hymns* composed for their use, the latter in *Prayers* for every day in the week:— " May I ever have awful thoughts of Thee, never mention Thy Venerable Name, unless on just, solemn, and devout occasions, nor even then without acts of adoration." (x. 42.) Attitudes that were reverent and proper in holy worship were prescribed for observance by all members of his Society:—" Let us constantly kneel at prayer, and stand during singing, and while the text is repeated;" (*Myles Chron. Hist.*, p. 75) and suitable directions were given both for their going out and their coming in.

All were taught the propriety of turning to the Altar and the Cross, and of making all offerings through the Altar for "favour and acceptance." Musical Celebrations and Choral worship, Wesley had a keen relish for, and expressed his high approval of. Hymns, too, were sung in the Office of Holy Communion, and in *Procession* "before the body" at Funerals, the priest taking part: "I did this the rather," says Wesley on one

High Churchmen.

relieve death of the added gloom which the vulgar pomp of modern undertakers have attached to it, there lies the High Church tenaciousness of the doctrine of the Resurrection of the Flesh. We are not so far away as we fancy ourselves, from those old Egyptians who believed that after 3,000 years the soul would return to the poor mummy, and resume again, in glorified shape, its garment of clay." Yes, even *so* do we believe, and *thus* " by our works is our faith made manifest ;" and will, by God's help, so continue. The voice of song shall show that we mourn not as those without hope ; lights, that even the grave is not dark, since death hath been overcome ; Holy Communion, that "we that remain" and "they that sleep" are still one in Christ ; and the reverent care with which we lay our brother down in mother earth, our true belief that with *that* flesh shall we arise and see God.

This is the true issue between Ritual and its opponents ; it is the battle of Faith against Unbelief; the Church of God against the world. The *principle* of Ritual cannot be overthrown. Its *practice* is only a question of degree. Formalism is not the presence of forms but the absence of spirit. And when with deeper faith and warmer love, we pay both outward and inward honour, we do that which God commanded, that by which He lures us onward in our Heavenward way, and that which, as

Wesley.

occasion, "to show my approbation of that solemn custom and to encourage others to follow it." (*Jl.*, Oct., 1763.) The priest's cassock—a vestment which draws down the censure even of Bishops —Wesley wore constantly, even when on travel, and while preaching in the open streets. (xxviii. 292.) And in ministering to the sick, gave a *priest's* blessing, by solemn imposition of hands:— " I then by imposition of hands, as *usual*, gave him a blessing." (xxx. 266.)

But there is other proof, and from another quarter.

In 1738. Wesley paid a visit to the Moravians in Germany, and attended their place of worship at Bertholdsdorf. Marking only their singular custom of sitting to sing, and, by a curious coincidence, using the very same disparaging word of a novel and inelegant vestment in use, which naughty Ritualists have sometimes done of a similar vestment, worn without authority, by English Bishops. thus begins and ends his description of the Service :—

"Two large candles stood lighted upon the Altar; the Last Supper was painted behind it; the pulpit was placed over it, and over that a brass image of Christ on the Cross. The minister had on a sort of *pudding-sleeve* gown, which covered him all round. At nine began a long voluntary on the organ, closed with a hymn, which was sung by all the people *sitting* (in which posture. as is the German custom, they sung all that followed).

| High Churchmen. | Wesley. |

man is made, soul, mind, and body call for and of necessity require. Then the minister walked up to the Altar, bowed, sung these Latin words—*Gloria in excelsis Deo;* bowed again and went away. This was followed by another hymn, sung, as before, to the organ by all the people. Then the minister went to the Altar again, bowed, sung a prayer, read the Epistle, and went away. After a third hymn was sung, he went a third time to the Altar, sung a versicle (to which all the people sung a response), read the third chapter to the Romans, and went away. The people having then sung the Creed in rhyme, he came and read the Gospel, all standing. Another hymn followed," then extemporary prayer in the pulpit and sermon. "Then he read a long intercession and general thanksgiving, which before twelve concluded the service." xxvi. 303.

Here is Ritual, the most full and minute. A brass Crucifix; two candles burning on the Altar; a picture behind it; three several advances to and bowings to the Altar; the minister singing the words, "Glory be to God on High," in the old familiar Latin, bowing again and returning. The whole service, creed and prayer, versicle and response, sung, by the minister and by the people. How would every one but "a Papist at heart" have burned to cry aloud, and deliver his testimony, against such a mass of idolatry, mummery, and superstition! But what says Wesley, the very champion of spiritual religion?—He sees all, he hears all, and all he utters is unqualified praise; of censure he says not a word.

Yet more followed. Wesley describes a joyous procession after the evening service at Hernhuth, in which all the unmarried men, as their custom was, took part, "walking round the town singing praise with instruments of music." On the Tuesday following he witnessed also their manner of burying, not douly and sad, as commonly the case with us, but joyous, in prescribed order and regulated march, " singing as they went," from the chapel where the little body had lain, to "God's ground," where it should be buried: "the children walking first, next the Orphan-Father (so they call him who has the chief care of the Orphan-House), with the minister of Bertholdsdorf; then four children bearing the corpse, and after them, one of the Brethren and the father of the child. Then followed the men, and last of all the women and girls. They all sung as they went: being come into the square where the male children are buried, the men stood on two sides of it, the boys on the third, and the women and girls on the fourth. There they sung again: after which the minister used a short prayer, and concluded with that blessing, 'Unto God's gracious mercy and protection I commit you.' " "Seeing the father, (a plain man)," Wesley asked, " How

Wesley.

do you find yourself?' He said, 'Praised be the Lord, never better. He has taken the soul of my child to Himself. And I have seen according to my desire his body committed to holy ground.'" Thus was every vestige of gloom cleared away.

Wesley states that The Brethren had thus testified their adherence to the public worship of God at Bertholdsdorf (that just desscribed) in a document addressed to the Emperor:—

"'The public worship of God at Bertholdsdorf, which we have hitherto frequented, we are the less able now to forsake, because we have there an assembly of true believers, a doctrine free from error, and a pastor who, having laboured much in the Word, is worthy of double honour. Therefore we have no cause to form any congregation separate from this.'" Wesley spent there another Sunday; and as the Moravians found no fault with the "Ritualistic Service," neither did he: but after having seen something of the inward life as well as the outward form, he says, "I was constrained to take my my leave: I would gladly have spent my life here: O when shall *this* Christianity cover the earth as the waters cover the sea." Id. 311, 318.

So would Wesley have chosen his company, with their adopted Worship and Ritual—a ritual which commonly included Incense also, and Unleavened Bread, and the Eucharistic Vestments—undeniable evidence that Wesley could have accepted the very highest Ritual at present in use in English Churches.

Indeed, some of the early Methodists educated under Mr. Wesley's especial direction and afterwards his valued fellow-labourers, went further, and made these two latter points, the use of Unleavened Bread and Eucharistic Vestments, essential to a service in due order. Dr. Adam Clarke for example: On the first, he says, "If any respect should be paid to the primitive institution, in the celebration of this Divine Ordinance, [the Holy Eucharist] then unleavened, unyeasted bread should be used ... the use of common bread in the Sacrament of the Lord's Supper is highly improper." (*St.* iii. 42, 43.) Equally strong is Dr. Clarke on the Vestments, in his learned Commentary on the Bible, a work in the highest repute among contemporary Methodists. On Exodus xxviii. 2., "And thou shalt make holy garments for Aaron thy brother, for glory and for beauty," his comment is as follows:—"Four articles of dress were prescribed for the priests in ordinary, and four more for the high priest. Those for the priests in general were a coat, drawers, a girdle, and a bonnet. Besides these, the high priest had a robe, an ephra, a breastplate, and a plate or diadem of gold on his forehead. The garments, says the sacred historian, were for honour and for beauty. They were emblematical of the office in which they ministered, 1st. It was honourable. They were ministers of the Most High, and employed by Him in transacting the most important concerns between God and His people—concerns in which all the attributes of the Divine Being were interested, as well as those which referred to the present and eternal happiness of His creatures. 2nd. They were for beauty.

Wesley.

They were emblematical of that holiness and purity which ever characterize the Divine nature, and the worship which is worthy of Him, and which are essentially necessary to all those who wish to serve Him in the beauty of holiness here below, and without which none can ever see His face in the realms of glory. Should not the garments of all those who minister in holy things *still* be emblematical of the things in which they minister? Should they not be for glory and beauty, expressive of the dignity of the Gospel ministry, and that beauty of holiness without which none can see the Lord? As the high priest's Vestments under the law were emblematical of what was to come, should not the Vestments of the ministers of the Gospel bear some resemblance of what is come? Is then the dismal black now worn by almost all kinds of priests and ministers for glory and beauty? Is it emblematical of anything that is good, glorious, or excellent? How unbecoming of the glad tidings announced by Christian ministers is a colour emblematical of nothing but mourning and woe, sin, desolation, and death! How inconsistent the habit and office of these men! Should it be said, 'These are only shadows, and are useless, because the substance is come'? I ask, why then is black almost universally worn? Why is a particular colour preferred, if there be no signification in any? Is there not a danger that, in our zeal against shadows, we shall destroy or essentially change the substance itself? Would not the same sort of argumentation exclude water in Baptism, and bread and wine in the Sacrament of the Lord's Supper? The white surplice in the service of the Church is almost the only thing that remains of these ancient and becoming vestments which God commanded to be made for glory and beauty. Clothing, emblematical of office, is of more consequence than is generally imagined. Were the great officers of the Crown, and the great officers of Justice, to clothe themselves like the common people when they appear in their public capacity, both their persons and their decisions would be soon held in little estimation." This testimony, from so unexceptionable a witness as "the great Methodist Commentator," cannot be without influence on those called by the same name as he, unless in them reason is weaker than prejudice.

Of course, we need not to be told of works published by Mr. Wesley's assistants after his death, that they did not receive his sanction. Nor is any such sanction needed. They may however serve to illustrate by their kindred light what is abundantly proved without them—That John Wesley as a High Churchman did not shrink from a High Ritual.*

* The author of *The Relations of John Wesley and of Wesleyan Methodism to the Church of England investigated and determined* has admitted, that Wesley "held from 1735-1740 views as ritualistically exalted as those of any Romanising Ritualist of the present day." With this admission the controversy is ended: Wesley himself has declared, that such as his views were in 1740, such they continued for the rest of his life:—"I have *uniformly* gone on for fifty years (1739-1789), *never varying* from the doctrine of the Church at all." But, with sufficient inconsistency, Dr. Rigg

recedes from this position, and fixes the time of Mr. Wesley's visit to Germany, 1738, for a complete change in his views—" Wesley up to 1738 had been a High Church Sacramentalist, all his life afterwards he taught the Evangelical doctrine of salvation by faith." Now, whichever date be taken, this witness cannot be true, for the conclusive reason that the known dates of most of the foregoing quotations exceed far beyond the year within which this writer would confine them ; *e.g.*, Wesley's defence of the Primitive Church against Dr. Middleton was written in 1749. However, this visit to the Moravians in Germany is confidently referred to, as the time and occasion of Wesley's sacrifice of Sacraments and Ritual to the doctrine of simple faith. Nothing could be more unfortunate: this was exactly the period and the company in which Wesley was brought face to face with a higher Ritual than he had ever before seen. Wesley was charmed, and expressed his admiration of all he saw and heard in no measured terms. What eventually followed is told in a word (and has been related in a previous chapter, XI.)—on account of the Protestant doctrine of "faith alone" taught by Luther and the Moravians alike, Wesley renounced, *not his own first faith*, but, all connection with both Lutherans and Moravians, for the express purpose of maintaining it.

CHAPTER XVI.

OF HONOUR WHERE HONOUR IS DUE.

High Churchmen.

Honour to God of necessity *includes* due honour to all which relates to Him. This is no less a charge of Holy Scripture than it is a sentiment of regenerate human nature. "Ye shall reverence *My* sanctuary:" ye shall "hallow *My* Sabbaths: at the Name of Jesus every knee shall bow:" "such honour have all *His* Saints:" these, pertaining to Him as Lord of all, and deriving from Him all which makes them holy, demand a relative honour from us. The purified instincts of human nature teach no less. We honour a Sovereign, a Benefactor, a Parent, by showing respect unto his words, his ordinances, his messengers, his family, —all which proceeds from him: this detracts not from, but is part of the honour which is his due. To withhold such honour, *e.g.*, from Christ's Sacraments, or from Christ's Church, under pretence of honouring *Him* the more, is in the highest degree unphilosophical and dishonouring.

Wesley, 1746-1781.

And as Wesley did not shrink from the adoption of a high Ritual, so neither did he shrink from the use of Catholic phraseology, nor from the expression of reverential regard for whatever to Catholics is dear. That love and devotion which is due to the Catholic Church (but which Protestants call *Churchiolatry*),[*] Wesley thus justifies and explains:—

"In Him the Corner Stone
 The living stones conjoin,
Christ and *His Church* are ONE,
 One Body and One Vine."

The immunity of the Church from error he expresses thus:— "The Catholic Church ... is secured against error, in things essential, by the perpetual presence of Christ, and ever directed by the Spirit of Truth in the truth that is after godliness." (xxxi. 73.) He "was ordained," he tells us, "as a member of a college of divines founded to overturn all heresies and defend

---

[*] Such language proceeds on an entirely false assumption as to what the Church is. Change the term, substitute for the word *Church* its Scripture synonym "The Kingdom of God," or "The Body of Christ," and the objection vanishes. For *them* to give such honour to corporations of their own creation, and dependent upon their own will for continuance from day to day, would indeed be "Churchiolatry." But we have yet to learn how honour to the Body can be a dishonour to the Head.

High Churchmen.	Wesley.
At best, it is a culpable error; at worst, it is the sin of an irreverent, rebellious heart. All, therefore, which pertain to Christ—His Body, the Church, His Members the Saints, His Ordinances the Sacraments, down even to "the hem of His garment"—High Churchmen religiously venerate and esteem.	the Catholic Faith." (xvi. 151.) Accordingly, speaking for himself and his people, he says, "The fundamental doctrine of the people called Methodists is,—whosoever will be saved before all things it is necessary that he hold the true faith." xxxi. 51. When he drops the Catholic terminology, as he does here, in writing to this Protestant, it is, he explains, that he may not lose

his labour in speaking to the ignorant and prejudiced—"it was for the readers of *your* class that I changed the hard word Catholic into an easier." All the terms of highest import he continually uses in speaking of the Mysteries of God:—" The Eucharist " " is Offered " " a Sacrifice " " by the Priest " " on the Altar." He yet teaches that " Angels round our Altars bow " while the holy and " tremendous Mysteries " are being celebrated: that they also by an unseen ministry " in a thousand ways " succour us; " they may remove many doubts and difficulties, throw light on what was before dark and obscure, and confirm us in the truth that is after godliness. They may gently move our will to embrace what is good and flee from that which is evil. They may many times quicken our dull affections, increase our holy hope or filial fear, and assist us more ardently to love Him Who has first loved us; yea, they may be sent of God to answer that whole prayer put into our mouths by pious Bishop Ken:—

> " ' O may Thy Angels, while I sleep,
> Around my bed their vigils keep;
> Their love angelical instill;
> Stop every avenue of ill;
> May they celestial joys rehearse,
> And thought to thought with me converse.' " *Ss.* ii. 162.

What a winning setting-forth is this, of the Church's teaching, on the Festival of *SS. Michael and All Angels* in the Collect appointed for the day.

Nay, Wesley is again in company with " pious Bishop Ken " * in

---

* " Guardian, when chill my love shall grow,
Up to fresh flame the embers blow;
Chide warmly my neglect,
And your own love traject;
Or rather sing of the Lamb slain,
And love, though dying, shall revive again."
—*Poem for Michaelmas Day.*

Wesley.

believing that there may be even Invocation of the Blessed without the grave charge of idolatry being thereby justified:—

> " *Aid me*, ye hov'ring Spirits near,
> Angels and ministers of grace,
> Who ever, while you guard us here
> Behold your heavenly Father's face:
> Gently my raptured soul convey
> To regions of eternal day."

Hymn for Midnight, from *Hymns and Sacred Poems* by J. and C. Wesley: and what is something more—pronounced by its Methodist Reviewer (when a stanza following had received from John Wesley the substitution of "faith" for "death") to be "a fine composition of evangelical character."

With Wesley, the Spirits of the faithful departed, as well as Angels, were objects of reverent regard:—" Angels are said to be 'ministering spirits;' but may not reasonable human creatures be made so too; and as they are like unto angels, may they not be as proper at least for the service of men? They have the same nature and affections. They feel our infirmities, and consider us more than abstract spirits do. Souls departed have life, sense, and motion, capacity of being employed, and no doubt have inclination to it, and whither may they be more properly sent than to those of their own nature to whom they are allied and from whom they so lately came?" And though we may give to none the worship due to God alone, " yet we may esteem them very highly in love for their work's sake." *Mag.* xiv. 553. *Ss.* ii. 165.

In his profession of faith Wesley includes the Perpetual Virginity of " the Blessed Virgin Mary, who, as well after as before she brought Him forth, continued a pure and unspotted Virgin." xix. 6. (1749.)

Though observing all days by the Church's appointed service of prayer and praise, he reserves a special observance and love for Saints' Days: " Sunday, Nov. 1. Being All Saints' Day (a festival I dearly love) I could not but observe the admirable propriety with which the Collect, Epistle, and Gospel for the day, are suited to each other:" thus with Wesley, as with other High Churchmen, the Saint's Day takes precedence of the Sunday when the latter is an *ordinary* one. " Tuesday 23. I rode to Shoreham and preached at five in Mr. P——'s house; but the next day I preached *in the church*, being S. Matthias' Day." (xxxii. 161.) He states that by preference he always preaches in a church, but if the church cannot be had, or be not available, he chooses to take his stand under the shadow of the market Cross, and there to preach Christ—" I, if I be lifted up from the earth, will draw all men unto Me:" the almost innumerable references that might be given, of this his practice, are evidence that

Wesley

Crosses in public places were much more numerous in England a century ago than is the case now. (*e.g.* xxix. 112, 122, 132.) Monastic Buildings too had suffered less decay: *Journal*, Oct. 29, 1781—" Walsingham ... I walked over what is left of the famous Abbey. We then went to the Friary; the Cloisters and Chapel whereof are almost entire. Had there been a grain of virtue or public spirit in Henry the VIIIth, these noble buildings need not have run to ruin."—A paragraph which shows how little of the Iconoclast there was in Wesley; and in thorough keeping with his earnest prayer, on beholding the ravages of the " zealous Reformers," as he scornfully calls them, in the wanton demolition of Arbroth Abbey: —" God deliver us from reforming mobs !"

CHAPTER XVII.
OF OBEDIENCE TO CHURCH AUTHORITY.

1. TO RUBRICS.

High Churchmen.

The Church's Directions in the Book of Common Prayer are there only to be obeyed: and every ordained Minister of the Church of England has bound himself by solemn oath to obey them faithfully. The general neglect, and even contempt of them, after this solemn vow of obedience, is surely one of the most portentous facts of this age. Pleas there may be many, but justification of an oath taken to be knowingly falsified there can be none. Custom cannot set the Rubrics aside. and centuries of neglect cannot repeal them. They bind all equally, Bishops as well as Priests, and in favour of none has the Church anywhere lodged a dispensing power. The attempt to procure their reversal, with the avowed object of putting in the right those who have not kept them, and of putting in the wrong those who have, is a proceeding as iniquitous as it is detestable.

Satisfied with a literal fulfilment, they do not repress those who in the largeness of their zeal, exceed their legal obligations. To *tie down* to Rubrics, which are satisfied by being fulfilled, is to

Wesley, 1737, 1744, 1790.

In an age, when such a thing was barely thought of by others, Wesley was the very pattern of exact compliance with the requisitions of the Church: firmly enforcing her discipline (sometimes at the peril of his life), and observing her Rubrics with punctilious accuracy. Yet was it objected, "'That we do not observe the laws of the Church and thereby undermine it.' What laws? The Rubrics or Canons? In every parish where I have been curate yet, I have observed the Rubrics with a scrupulous exactness, not for wrath but for conscience sake. And this, so far as belongs to an unbeneficed minister, or to a private member of the Church, I do now [1744]. I will just mention a few of them, and leave you to consider, which of us has observed, or does observe, them most:—

"1. 'Days of fasting or abstinence to be observed:

"The forty days of Lent.
"The Ember days at the four seasons,
"The three Rogation days,
"All Fridays in the year, except Christmas Day.'

"2. 'So many as intend to be

High Churchmen.

defeat the very end for which they were given. In an age of Puritanism and departure from Catholic custom, the Church of England laid down, as of obligation, the highest rule in each case which could be conveniently enforced. Hence, when the Rubrics stop short of full and express directions, High Churchmen are justified by her own words and evident intention in deferring to what hath been customary "in times past," unless (let it be honestly said) this, in any given instance, has been specially excepted. And such is, indisputably, the principle on which all societies whatsoever are governed—that is the law and rule of obligation which hath been formerly received, and never by any subsequent enactment set aside.

For Priests, such as Wesley, who are scrupulously exact in obeying the Rubrics, to be accused of contravening them because they do not make them the full measure of their duty; while others, who ignore them altogether on six days of the week and violate them on the seventh, are allowed to go without rebuke, is an offence to be visited with severest reprobation, and which none but the enemies of the Church can condone.

Wesley.

partakers of the Holy Communion, shall signify their names to the curate, at least some time the day before:

"'And if any of these be an open and notorious evil liver—the curate shall advertise him, that in any wise he presume not to come to the Lord's Table, until he hath openly declared himself to have truly repented.'

"3. 'Then (after the Nicene Creed) the curate shall declare unto the people, what Holy-days, or Fasting-days, are in the week following to be observed.'

"4. 'The minister shall first receive the Communion in both kinds himself, and *then proceed* to deliver the same to the bishops, priests, and deacons, in like manner, if any be present, and *after that* to the people.'

"5. 'In Cathedral and Collegiate Churches and Colleges, where there are many priests and deacons, they shall *all* receive the Communion with the priest, *every Sunday at the least.*'

"6. 'The Children to be baptized must be ready at the font, immediately after the last lesson.'

"7. 'The curates of every parish shall warn the people, that without great necessity they procure not their children to be baptized *at home* in their houses.'

"8. 'The curate of every parish shall diligently upon *Sundays and Holy-days*, after the second lesson at evening prayer, *openly in the church*, instruct and examine so many children as he shall think convenient, in some part of the Catechism.'

"9. 'And whensoever the Bishop shall give notice, &c.

"Now the question is, not whether these Rubrics ought to be

Wesley.

observed (you take this for granted in making the objection), but whether in fact they have been observed by you, or me, most? Many can witness, I have observed them punctually, yea, sometimes at the hazard of my life: and as many, I fear, that you, have not observed them at all, and that several of them you never pretended to observe. And is it *you* that are accusing *me*, for not observing the Rubrics of the Church? What grimace is this? 'O tell it not in Gath! Publish it not in the streets of Ascalon!'

"With regard to the Canons, I would in the first place desire you to consider, two or three plain questions:

"1st. Have you ever read them?

"2nd. How can these be called 'The Canons of the Church of England'—seeing they were never legally established by the Church —never regularly confirmed in any full Convocation?

"3rd. By what right am I required to observe such canons as were never legally established?

"And then I will join issue with you on one question more— *Whether you or I have observed them most?* To instance only in a few:

"Can. 29. 'No person shall be admitted godfather or godmother to any child, before the said person hath received the Holy Communion.'

"Can. 59 ... Can. 64 ... Can. 68 ... Can. 75. &c.

"Now let the clergyman who has observed only these five canons for one year last past ... cast the first stone at us for not observing the Canons of the Church of England." xiv. 155-158.

The characteristic impudence of those who are first in breaking the law in being the first to charge the offence upon their non-offending brethren, is only to be paralleled with their equally characteristic ignorance in setting down as violations of the law acts of obedience to it. Wesley, on one occasion, was taken into custody and tried by a grand jury, being charged with having broken the laws of the Church and Realm. Of the ten Articles of Indictment, four were such as contravened no law; five were what the law required (two of them cases of repelling from Holy Communion, two of them refusals to accept as Sponsors any other than Communicants, one the refusal to Baptize otherwise than by immersion, except it should be certified that the child was weak and unable to bear it), the remaining tenth, the refusal to bury one who had died contemning the faith and communion of the Church!*

---

* Methodists say, "such was Wesley in early life." Only fifteen months then before his death he affirmed his unaltered sentiments on this head—"I hold all the doctrines of the Church of Eng and, I love her Liturgy. *I approve her plan of discipline*, and only *wish it could be put in execution.*" (*Mag.* 1790, p. 287.) Thus both at the beginning and at the close of his life, his practice and his prayer were one—"Restore to Thy Catholic Church her ancient discipline." x. 79.

Wesley.

Surely, Wesley well earned, by his unflinching obedience to the Church's rule and discipline, the right to say to those who showed a disposition to be law-menders rather than law-keepers—" Do not *mend* our rules, *keep* them."

2. OBEDIENCE TO BISHOPS.

High Churchmen.

The Right and Rule of Bishops is Divine: on this sure principle High Churchmen ground their obedience. They obey them in Christ and for conscience sake; they obey them as Angels of God without questioning and without reserve. They attach no conditions of their own and would willingly be left ignorant of any. For thus only is obedience perfect and worthy of the name.

But this duty of obedience does not end with priests: bishops must themselves be subject: they, too, must acknowledge a law which is higher than themselves—the law of that branch of the Church whereof they are ministers in particular, this being everywhere, and always, in due subordination to the Church Catholic; to whose requirements all branches, as such, are necessarily bound. Without this, obedience is, and must be, impossible: for he who sets aside the laws of the Church to govern arbitrarily by his own will—whether he be bishop or priest—not only sets the example of disobedience, but makes disobedience on the part of those whom he would coerce an imperative

Wesley, 1735-1777.

Wesley early showed that none had more reverence than he for the Rule of Kings and Bishops. "All power is from above," was ever his principle. The Divine Right of the former he maintained against American Republicans: the Divine Right of the latter he proclaimed against English Dissenters, and called upon the Bishops to sustain it themselves:—

"Bold let them stand before their foes,
And dare assert their Right Divine."

But he was early taught the restraining application—that Rulers to be obeyed must themselves be subject, and exercise their right of rule in accordance with law, not in opposition thereto. Church Authorities, in Oxford, would have starved Methodism in its very birth, by putting their *veto* on Weekly Communion. The struggle terminated in a miserable promise being extorted from two, that "for the future they would only communicate three times a year," and in Wesley and his fellows being still more determined "to communicate at every opportunity." State Authorities, in

High Churchmen.

duty. Even a Divine command—"Obey them which have the rule over you and submit yourselves"—does not bind in obedience to the priest in matters against the Church's direction; and bishops, though they were Angels from Heaven, are not to be obeyed in things contrary to what the Church hath received. True, the determination of what the Church hath received does not belong to the priest, but as little does it belong to the bishop, and least of all to him who recognizes no authority in the Church higher than his own will. The will, even of a king, does not bind the meanest of his subjects; how much less does the will of a bishop bind a priest who has received the same commission to do, and to teach, as he? This is continually forgotten, and from quarters which furnish the reiterated cautions against Popery, there comes the persistent championship of the hyper-papal theory. "*Sic volo, sic jubeo, stet pro ratione voluntas*—As I will, so, order, the will stands for the reason;" which would convert as many prelates as assumed it into as many popes. And hence has arisen the odious necessity of having all professions qualified in express terms: The authority of the higher commands the obedience of the lower only so far as it is in accordance with the Church's own law. By her law both are bound, and within her law lies the right of rule in the bishop and the duty of submission in the priest.

Wesley.

Georgia, attempted to proscribe by pains and penalties obedience to the Church's rule and discipline: Wesley told them—priest-like—that he did not acknowledge their power of interference, and that according to the Church's rule, and not otherwise, would he administer the Mysteries of God.

It could not be expected that a man with such a sense of the supremacy of law over the mere will of the individual, would not meet with other occasions which demanded the same stand to be made against arbitrary and illegal exactions; and which, by their frequent repetition, would also justify and seem to require professions of obedience to rulers to be so qualified in express terms. Both came to pass. Wesley, popularly and persistently charged with disaffection towards both the Bishops and the King, by those who should have known better, was not afraid to declare that neither King nor Bishop was necessarily to be obeyed:—" I hastened away in order to be at Peele-town before the Service began. Mr. Corbett said, 'He would gladly have asked me to preach, but that the Bishop had forbidden him; who had also forbidden all his clergy to admit any Methodist preacher to the Lord's Supper.' But is any clergyman obliged, asks Wesley, either in law or conscience, to obey such a prohibition? By no means. The *will* even of a King does not bind any English subject, unless it be seconded by an

I

High Churchmen.

The priest owes a duty still higher than that of obedience to his bishop, and that is obedience to the Church, whereof both are ministers. Even were the Ignatian formula correctly rendered—"*Do nothing without the Bishop*"—which it is not,* it would then be a precept subject to this obviously necessary qualification; and require also to be read in the light of other times than our own: So long as the Church is suffered to have no voice in the appointment of her chief pastors, the Church's children cannot leave her interests wholly in their hands, nor for themselves promise unconditional obedience.

Wherefore, this is the profession which High Churchmen in conscience make and avow:— The *first thing they desire* is to obey their Ecclesiastical Superiors wholly and without reserve; the *last thing they will do* is to obey the arbitrary illegal exactions of *any*; least of all when these are in weak and unworthy compliance with popular clamour, or, at the dictation of the world.

Wesley.

express law. How much less the will of a Bishop? 'But did you not take an oath to obey him?' No: nor any clergyman in the Three Kingdoms." (*Jl.* xviii. 45.) "We then promised to submit (mark the words) to the *godly admonitions* and injunctions of our ordinary. But we did not, could not, promise to obey such injunctions as we know are contrary to the Word of God." xiv. 159.

Goaded thus by arbitrary and illegal exactions†—which were made to the grievous injury of the Church, as Bishops now are ready to confess—Wesley determines that for the future obedience, for him and his people, shall be determined and stand thus:—"We profess: 1. That we will obey all the laws of the Church (such we allow the Rubrics to be) so far as we can with a safe conscience. 2. That we will obey with the same restriction, the Bishops as executors of those laws. But their *bare will*, distinct from those laws, we do not profess to obey at all." xxviii. 350.

---

* οὐδὲν ἄνευ ἐπισκόπου is by an abuse of quotation frequently defrauded of its latter clause καὶ τῶν πρεσβυτέρων—*and the presbyters*: i.e., The obedience here enjoined is not to the Bishops in particular by the priests, but to the Clergy in general by the people.

† Wesley's spirit was fired too by observing that the shield of condonation is ever cast over those who sin in defect, while any instance of excess meets with a sharp and speedy punishment. In 1768, "Six Students belonging to Edmund Hall were expelled the University, for holding Methodistical tenets, and taking upon them to pray, read, and expound the Scriptures, and sing hymns in a private house. The sentence was pronounced in the *chapel* (!)." Dr. Dixon, the principal of the College —to his honour be it said—defended the young Methodists and properly "observed that as these six gentlemen were expelled for having too much religion, it would be very proper to enquire into the conduct of some who had too little."—*Myles' Chronological History*, p. 122.

CHAPTER XVIII.
INSTITUTION AND DESIGN OF METHODISM.

Wesley and High Churchmen.

It is time to consider facts, as apart from professions: Wesley's institution and sole leadership of a huge Society is with many accepted as proof positive of a breach of Church Communion, endangering Church doctrine and discipline, notwithstanding his constant disclaimers. But why should it?* A religious Society within the Church, as Wesley says, "is *no new thing.*" In this Church of England have been recognized, again and again, Societies more or less independent of Episcopal control, because confined to no diocese, and yet under the necessity of being directed by one only, himself ubiquitous. Such were those of S. Benedict and S. Francis, orders of revivalists, stirrers up of religion in the souls of men—preachers and proclaimers of the Gospel to the poor. Such are those of which the germs have been planted by Mr. Leycester Lyne (otherwise Father Ignatius) and several others in our own day; not, in the least, to supersede or to oppose the parochial ministers, but to be *extra*-ordinary messengers of God, bringing His Gospel to the poor, and bringing the poor to the higher ministrations of the Church in whatever parish they may happen to dwell. That there is need, nay, urgent necessity for this is plain to every one who cares to think. In all our cities and towns, notwithstanding multiplied evangelistic agencies, there are unmanageable multitudes, living in brute ignorance and vice—heathens, nay, worse than heathens, at one time many of them christened men—now practising by day and by night every kind of sin. To these, churches are nothing. It is the living voice of the world-forsaking, self-denying man of God through which alone they must be arrested. (xv. 162, 163.) The Church with her *ordinary* agencies *may* overtake them, but in the meantime how many *must* live unreclaimed, and die as they have lived? It was to these, especially, that Wesley addressed himself. (*Id.* 163.) It is perfectly certain, both from his repeated assertions and from his well-known love and zeal, that such was Wesley's design in founding and directing his Society. All other Societies, he points out, (*Id.* 312) have an

---

* " That a religious society may be form\~d in a Church, for the purpose of prayer and mutual edification, distinct from that fellowship which is implied in ordinary Church Communion, without partaking of the nature of schism, is a matter so obvious to reason and common sense, that we suppose it will not be called in question by any reasonable man."—*Centenary of Methodism*, Dublin, p 231.

Wesley and High Churchmen.

origin essentially different from *this:* " they began by condemning others and by separating themselves therefrom: we began by condemning ourselves and by continuing in the Church wherein we were called." " We, by such a separation should not only throw away the peculiar glorying which God hath given us ... but should act in direct contradiction to that very end for which we believe God hath raised us up. The chief design of His providence in sending us out, is undoubtedly to quicken our brethren: and the first message of all our preachers is to the lost sheep of the Church of England." (xxiii. 119.) " We look upon the clergy, not only as a part of these our brethren, but as that part whom God, by His adorable providence, has called to be watchmen over the rest; for whom therefore they are to give a strict account." " We look upon ourselves, not as the authors, or ringleaders of a sect or party; *it is the farthest thing from our thoughts:* but as messengers of God, to those who are Christians in name, but heathens in heart and in life; to call them back to that from which they have fallen, to real, genuine Christianity." (xxiii. 121, 122.) Wesley solemnly re-affirms this —almost in the same words—and reminds his preachers also of it, nine months only before his death:—" Ye were, fifty years ago, those of you that were then Methodist preachers, *extra*-ordinary messengers of God, not going in your own will, but *thrust* out, not to supersede, but ' to provoke to jealousy,' the ordinary messengers. In God's Name, stop there .. Be Church-of-England-men still. Do not cast away the peculiar glory which God hath put upon you, and *frustrate the design of Providence—the very end for which God raised you up.*" *Mag.* 1790, p. 234.

So far, then, from the Methodist Society being a breach of Church Communion, it was, considered not *as it is,* but as Wesley designed it should be.* and as to the last he maintained it, the very means through which alone, in the case of thousands, communion with the Church became a realization and a truth. " You may," says he, " easily be convinced of this, if you will only weigh the particulars following: 1. A great part of these went to no church at all before. 2. Those who did sometimes go to church before, go three times as often now. 3. Those who never went to church at all before, do go now *at all opportunities.* 4. The main question is, Are they turned from doing the works of the devil, to do the works of God? Do they now live soberly, righteously, and godly in this present world? If they do—if they live according to the *directions* of the Church, believe her *doctrines*, and join in her *ordinances*—with what face can you say that these men *separate* from the Church of England?"

---

* " The design of Methodism (is) not to separate from the Church, but to unite together all the children of God that were scattered abroad." April 14, 1789.

Wesley and High Churchmen.

(xv. 174.)' "The real truth is just the reverse of this: we *introduce* Christian fellowship, where it was utterly destroyed." "These were not Christians before they were thus joined. Most of them were barefaced heathens:" *(Id.* 199, 200)—but now under this Rule:—" In the year 1743," writes Wesley, "I published the Rules of the Society, one of which was that all the members thereof should constantly attend Church and Sacrament." And to this he added, " Those who are resolved to keep these Rules may continue with us, and those only."* (xxxi. 261.) And of others, who did previously assemble with their brethren of the Church of England, Wesley asks, " And do they now forsake *that* assembling themselves together? You cannot, you dare not say it. You know, they are more diligent therein than ever; it being one of the fixed rules of our societies ' That every member attend the ordinances of God,' *i.e.*, do *not divide from the Church.* And if any member of the Church does thus divide from or leave it, he hath no more place among us." xiv. 161.

* Only in the case of those *private* members of the Society who were in conscience dissenters from the Established Church was this rule relaxed.

CHAPTER XIX.
ALLEGED VIOLATIONS OF CHURCH ORDER.

Wesley and High Churchmen.

Methodism grew out of the Church's necessity: it was her lost souls that it sought to save: and it ill becomes Churchmen to cavil at the means which alone met it.

Four Violations of Church Order have been charged against Wesley:—
1. Preaching in the open air.
2. Use of extemporary prayer.
3. Employment of lay-preachers.
4. Assignment of their place of labour within the Society. *Jl.* xxi. 145.

He was himself, at first, he tells us, "so tenacious of every point relating to decency and order, that I should have thought the saving of souls almost a sin, if it had not been done *in a church*." (xxvii. 64.) Happily, Wesley got over this scruple. Because the Church's message was not heard inside, was a sufficient reason why it should be proclaimed outside. Here, then, a single Collect would suffice, or a short extempore prayer might be used. (xv. 313.) And this, again, might be fittingly done by pious "lay brothers:" for only so, could the means become co-extensive with the need.

Wesley was not unaware of their lack of due mission; and importuned in vain the Bishops to supply it:* the very urgency of the need prevented this: for Bishops, no less than priests and people, were content with things as they were, and determined, while tolerating every degree of sloth and defect, to tolerate no "innovation" or "excess." This being the attitude of the Bishops, Wesley had one only question to determine, whether he would silence his preachers, disband his societies, and confine his own ministrations within a single parish—in fact, acknowledge his whole work a mistake, and with his own hands undo it—or, incur the charge of *insubordination* to Church Authority. To this there could be but one answer. Notwithstanding such a charge, continually repeated, and attended too with every other species of discouragement, Wesley ever sought to bind all in love and fellowship to the Church; and to the last showed a jealous concern lest any preacher of his should overstep his

---

* His subsequent action (however much for a time he hesitated) was, as he shows, entirely justified by a Rule in the Great Western Church, "even in some of their strictest orders"—to compare like things with like—which dealt with the same case and resolved it in the same way:—"If any lay brother believes himself called of God, to *preach* as a missionary, the Superior of the Order, being informed thereof, shall immediately send him away." xv. 150.

Wesley and High Churchmen.

appointed and proper sphere of labour. For the guidance of the Society he asks (in a Code of Directions as revised and republished by him eighteen months only before his death)—" How should an Assistant [Superintendent Preacher] be qualified for this charge? By ... loving the Church of England, and resolving not to separate from it." (xv. 308.) Every Helper [Itinerant or Local Preacher] shall be asked, "Do you constantly attend the Church and Sacrament?" (*Id.* 325.) How this rule included the private members, and was, on occasion, enforced, has been seen (page 23). And nothing in the Society was to be accepted as setting it aside: "In visiting the Classes, ask every one, 'Do you go to Church as often as ever you did?' Set the example yourself: and *immediately alter every plan that interferes therewith.*" (*Id.* 311.) And, consequently, no service was allowed to be held in Church hours: "All over England we fixed both our morning and evening service at such hours as not to interfere with the Church." "Our own service is ... not such as supersedes the Church service. We never designed it should: we have a hundred times professed the contrary. It presupposes public prayer, like the sermons at the University. Therefore I have over and over advised, 'Use no *long* prayer, either before or after sermon.' Therefore I myself frequently use only a Collect, and never enlarge in prayer unless on some extraordinary occasion. If it were designed to be instead of Church service it would be essentially defective." (*Id.* 313.) Being "vehemently importuned," at Deptford, to dispense with this rule in that particular case, he says, "It is easy to see that this would be a formal separation from the Church ... obliging our brethren to separate either from the Church or us. And this I judge to be not only inexpedient, but totally *unlawful* for me to do." (*Jl.*, Sept. 24, 1786.) The year after he writes of the Deptford people, who still "were mad for separating from the Church"—"I told them if you are resolved, you may have your service in Church hours. But remember! From that time you will see my face no more." To the last, Wesley stedfastly withstood any intrusion of the Methodist preachers on the priestly office, and was never so emphatic as when clearing them from even the implied charge:—"They no more take upon them to be priests than to be kings. They take not upon them to administer the Sacraments, an honour *peculiar to the priests of God.*" (xv. 154.) Asserting, within a few months of his death —"If any preacher had taken such a step, we should have looked upon it as a recantation of our Connexion," and a "renunciation" of "the first principle of Methodism, which was wholely and solely to preach the Gospel." Thus his whole life, both in the Society and out of it, was a fitting comment on his own true text, *The true Methodist is no other than a true Churchman.* xi. 186.

CHAPTER XX.

OPPOSITION TO METHODISM.

1. FALSE ACCUSATIONS.

Wesley and High Churchmen.

The Restoration of the Catholic Religion "*whole* and *undefiled*" was ever Wesley's motto. As against this he knew no authority, whether of King or Parliament, Bishop or Protestant mob. "That which is first is true;" and Truth had his supreme allegiance. He courted no worldly favour, neither did he fear its frown. Timorous counsels he heeded not, and "prudence" he despised. "God deliver me," says Wesley, "and all that seek Him in sincerity from what the world calls 'Christian Prudence.'" "*Prudence* had made the little company at Oxford leave off singing Psalms," and Wesley had sense enough to see, and was prompt in urging, that concessions serve only to whet the appetite they are intended to appease. (xxvii. 28.) That such a man, with such an object, should be opposed, was the most natural of all natural things: but it never occurred to the early Methodists that Truth was determined by rowdy majorities, and their leader was not a man to flinch, having put his hand to the plough. So on the struggle went between the priest and the world-power. It is interesting to read, in Mr. Wesley's words, a narrative of events in his day which find their exact parallel in our own: —the same charges, opponents of the same character, working by the same unscrupulous means, the same unbridled mob-violence, the same proscription of law in favour of the popular will. Gossips, newsmongers, ballad-vendors, and buffoons all ranged on the same side, and Wesley appealing to "men of reason and religion," and asking only to be let alone.

The capital charge, of course, was, "That he was a *Papist*," "a Jesuit in disguise;" as such he was assailed, both on his going out and on his coming in, with those hoots and cries (now again familiar), "Go to Rome;" "Go to Rome, and kiss the pope's slipper." It was loudly and confidently affirmed "that the Methodists are carrying on the work of Popery;" "that it was all Jesuitism at the bottom;" "that they are close friends of the Church of Rome, agreeing with her in almost everything but the doctrine of merit." (xvii. 38.) "Cautions to all Protestants" were given, warning the populace against these "Papistical imitators," as Wesley and his people were called. Placards were "stuck up in public

Wesley and High Churchmen.

places" and paraded through the streets, exhibiting a "comparison between the Papists and the Methodists." Men of ponderous learning—Bishops—"by quotations from our own writings compared with quotations from popish authors," find, says Wesley, "a parallel as exact as one egg is like another."* His practice of "recommending 'popish' books," and republishing, for his societies, their spiritual biographies and manuals of devotion, was indeed too good a thing not to be made the most of by his Protestant adversaries. But Protestants are also good story-tellers—To the current rumour, "That I was a Papist, if not a Jesuit," some added "that I was born and bred at Rome, which many cordially believed." One had "heard Mr. Wesley told to his face that he kept two popish priests in his house." Another had "heard at an eminent dissenting teacher's, 'That it was beyond dispute Mr. Wesley had received large remittances from Spain, in order to make a party among the poor: and that as soon as the Spaniards landed he was to join them with 20,000 men.' " xxvii. 298.

So often were these charges repeated, and with so much assurance, that many simple Methodists themselves were disquieted. Of one such Mr. Wesley writes, " Mrs. S., who was still torn in pieces with sorrow, and doubts, and fears. Her chief fear, she said, was 'That we are all Papists.' ... She said 'Why, it is not long since I met with a gentleman who told me, he was a Roman Catholic. And when I asked him if Mr. Wesley was a Papist, he would not say Yes or No, but only, ' Mr. Wesley is a very good man, and you do well to hear him.' " Worse than this man of silence, there follows next the abominable gossip :—" Besides, it is but two or three nights since, as I was just setting out to come to the Room, Miss G. met me and said, ' My dear friend, you shan't go; indeed you shan't: you don't know what you do. I assure you Mr. Wesley is a Papist: and so am I: he converted me. You know how I used to pray to saints and to the Virgin Mary. It was Mr. Wesley taught me when I was in the Bands. And I saw him rock the cradle on Christmas-eve. You know I scorn to tell a lie.' "—" Poor Mrs. S. was utterly confounded," says Wesley. (xxviii. 110.) And poor John Wesley! by all accounts he *must* have been a Papist. In such a charge all mere Protestants joined. One solemnly "averred 'That Mr. Wesley was unquestionably a Jesuit." (xxix. 158.) Another averred "That Mr. Wesley preached nothing but Popery, denying Justification by Faith, and making nothing of Christ." (*Id.* 195.) Calvinistic Methodists " affirmed that they had heard both my brother and me many times

---

* How any respectable Methodists, calling themselves by his name, can for very shame now join in these very cries, and make the same charges against those who are herein even as he, may well be left for them to explain.

Wesley and High Churchmen.

preach Popery." (xvi. 84.) And " J. M. gave me a full account of J. B.'s renouncing all connection with me ;" adding, in the midst of the congregation " he spread out his arms and cried ' Popery, Popery, Popery!' " (xxix. 196.) " Mr. A—ns, a dissenting minister, also publicly affirmed ' we were all Papists, and our doctrine was mere Popery.' And Mr. B., another dissenting minister, went a step further still, for after he had confessed many texts in the Bible are for them, he added, 'but you ought not to mind these texts: for the Papists have put them in!'" (xxviii. 143.) One zealous prelate raved against the Methodists in the most approved fashion—" The whole conduct of the Methodists is but a counterpart of the most wild fanaticisms of Popery:" and another, more sober (the Bp. of Exeter), as if gravely summing up the entire case with judicial impartiality, thus delivers himself:—" We may see in Mr. Wesley's writings that he was once a *strict Churchman*, but gradually put on a more *Catholic spirit*, tending at length to *Roman Catholic*. He rejects any design to convert others from any communion, and consequently not from Popery." Wesley admits the former half of the allegation, and bestows a simple denial on the latter. xvi. 344.

"I have often enquired," says Wesley, "who were the authors of such report (that I was a Papist), and have generally found, they were either bigotted dissenters, or ministers of our own Church ... And I can no otherwise think than that they either spoke thus from gross ignorance ... or they wilfully spoke what they knew to be false—probably thinking thereby to do God service!" xvi. 317.

Magistrates vied with Bishops in giving the calumny countenance: the former required Wesley to sign a declaration against Popery; the latter denounced him at their visitations, and the clergy and ministers of every name and degree were not a whit behind their superiors in declaiming against this disturber of the Church's *peace*. " Every Sunday," says C. Wesley, " damnation is denounced against all who hear us; for we are ' Papists,' ' Jesuits,' ' seducers,' and bringers-in of the Pretender."

In the midst of all this fervid denunciation of Papists and Popery, how apposite is that reflection of Wesley:—" I could not but reflect on the many advices to beware of the increase of Popery: but not one that I remember to beware of the increase of Infidelity. This was quite surprising when I considered—1. That in every place where I have yet been, the number of the converts to Popery bore no proportion to the number of the converts to Infidelity. 2. That as bad a religion as Popery is, no religion is still worse; a baptized infidel being always found upon trial twofold worse than *even a bigotted* Papist." (xxvi. 163.) A reflection which has oftentimes lately occasioned a similar exclamation of surprise: How is it that

Wesley and High Churchmen.

the full latitude of the existing law is claimed in favour of infidels (as Wesley would account them), while the same law must be over-ridden by new enactments against the Ritualists! The morbid tenderness shown for whatever is derogatory to the honour of our Blessed Lord, and the bitter and relentless hate for whatever is an unaccustomed act of service done to Him, is one of the most appalling facts of this age.

The true relation of Methodism to Popery was however shown by the *discredit* which Papists strove to cast upon it. "I remember well," says Wesley, "when a well-dressed man had gathered a large company, and was vehemently asserting that 'those rogues the Methodists were all Papists;' till, a gentleman coming by, fixed his eye on him and cried, 'Stop that man: I know him personally: he is a Romish priest.'" (xvi. 351.) Again: I was expounding, says Wesley, "when one cried out, 'Thou art a hypocrite, a devil, an enemy to the Church. This is false doctrine. It is not the doctrine of the Church.'" "The day after I received the following note, 'Sir, This is to let you understand that the man which made the noise last night is named John Beon. He is a Romish priest.'" (xxvii. 205.) Nor do the people called Ritualists fare better at the hands of those whom they are supposed to strengthen than did the people called Methodists. The only conclusion consistent with reason is—that what is opposed by Papists has *not* "a tendency to Popery."

Not only as "a Papist," but also as "an *Innovator*" did Wesley excite against himself the determined hostility of all easy-going people who wished for nothing so much as to be left to the even tenor of their way. In a singular manner were combined against him all who before were at enmity. He was "strongly opposed both by the Calvinists and Socinians;" and "the Presbyterian minister wrote to the Popish priest," to secure their flocks against the dreaded contamination. Being neither Protestant nor Papist, Wesley puzzled the intelligent public: "We like nothing you do—your sermons are satires—we wont hear ourselves abused." "Besides, say they, *they* are *Protestants*: but as for *you*, they cannot tell what religion you are of. They never heard of such a religion before. They do not know what to make of it." (xxvi. 135.) Accused of holding principles contrary to "our Protestant Church," Wesley sufficiently replies, "I do not espouse any other principles but what are consonant to the Book of Common Prayer." Foiled here, his adversaries return to the attack in a truly characteristic manner—"*You would if you durst* as is evident from some *innovations* you have already introduced." It being alleged "that the doctrines of these men are false, erroneous ... new, and unheard of till late," Wesley replies, "that every branch of this doctrine is the plain doctrine of Scripture interpreted by our own Church. Therefore it cannot be either false or erro-

Wesley and High Churchmen.

neous;" neither are they new, but "old as God's revelation to man:" and trenchantly adds, "If therefore they were *unheard* of till late, the greater guilt is on those, who as ambassadors of Christ ought to publish them day by day." (xv. 136, 137.) Let all such modern accusers of their brethren take to themselves this answer, and as Wesley says, "digest it how they can."

Again, he is accused of holding "*false and dangerous*" doctrines on the Holy Eucharist by those whom he reminds, and truly, that they do not accept the plain teaching of the Church on the subject—hence the accusation. While such is their estimate of a priest's duty to the Church, that acts of obedience to her requirements are adduced as damning evidence against him. (xxvi. 205.) So, within a century, doth history reproduce itself!

Another charge, and again one with which we are made familiar, "Old wise men, particularly the Bishop of London," asked, somewhat contemptuously, "A *few young raw* heads—What can they pretend to do?—They are only a few." Wesley reminds his Lordship, and all others whom it concerns, that it is precisely the few who are irresistible if their cause be right: and acutely remarks, "I cannot but observe here what great pains have been taken to *keep* them few:" Those are accounted the most meritorious who were the most forward to say all manner of evil against us falsely. Upon such, and such only, have Episcopal smiles and more substantial favours been bestowed. Those who have been convinced from time to time that they ought to join hearts and hands in the work have been withheld by alluring promises: while, on the other hand, the threat and certain prospect of displeasure has waited upon any that should join us. "So that how fully soever they were convinced, they could not act according to their conviction unless they could give up at once all thought of preferment either in Church or State. And many have on this very account been disowned by their dearest friends and nearest relations." "Very good Protestants!" these, remarks Wesley, with quiet sarcasm: Excellent Bishop of L—don, we rejoin, who has earnestly recommended this mode of putting down to all patrons of livings! xv. 142. *Jl.* viii. 43.

Again a charge, once more a familiar one, of *Conspiracy and disloyalty*. "We were represented," says Wesley, "both from the pulpit and the press as introducing Popery, raising sedition, preaching both against Church and State: and all manner of evil was publicly said both of us and those who were accustomed to meet with us." (xxviii. 263.) Such cowardly charges, unproved on the one hand, and impossible to refute on the other, serve their temporary purpose: though they cannot stop the good work, and are perhaps even necessary to its ultimate establishment, yet they do for a time shake the adhesion of the fearful and faint-hearted. Wesley bears testimony to

Wesley and High Churchmen.

this: "I found there had been a shaking among them, occasioned by the confident assertions of some, that they had seen Mr. Wesley a week or two ago, with the Pretender in France; and others, that he was in prison in London. Yet the main body still stood firm together." *Id.* 216.

The next charge is an immense favourite. There was in Wesley's days, as in our own, the inevitable cry against every priest who does a priest's part—that of *Spiritual Tyranny* and usurpation of authority over the conscience:—"Mr. C. gave a long and earnest charge 'To beware of spiritual tyranny, and to oppose the new, illegal authority which was usurped over their consciences.'" xxvi. 204.

Nor was the *Murphyite* faction unrepresented in Wesley's day. Pure waters or foul are all one to him who is himself unclean. It was given out that Wesley was the father of a base-born child, and for this was degraded at College; also, "that the Methodists at their private meetings put out the lights, with abundance more of the same kind." "Disclosures" of the most abominable character were made, professedly by those who had been in the snare and had escaped. and a Chiswell Street Bookseller was found, who was willing to increase his trade by publishing these vile slanders. (Nightingale's *Portraiture*, p. 194.) The publications vended by these depraved traducers "bring together the father-confessor, in the shape of a Methodist preacher. and a single woman—'We must touch lightly.' say they, 'on this abominable subject.' Then they begin to suggest 'what must pass in the maiden's mind,' until 'all modesty and all shame be utterly destroyed.'" *Mag.* xxix. 137.

---

2. "PUTTING DOWN" METHODISM.

Wesley and High Churchmen.

As all truly *Bible Christians* know (S. John xv. 18-20), there is no surer indication of the character of a Religious Revival than its treatment by the world. A spurious revival — an outburst of fanaticism—at best. a temporary effervescence of a mere Sunday religion, has the world's toleration: it may be ridiculed, it may be condemned, but at all events it is met by no vigorous opposition. A true revival. on the other hand, is bitterly and relentlessly opposed. Men of all parties and by all means try to crush it. And "reason good" says Wesley: it disturbs men; it makes demands; it comes with claims to Divine authority; it discovers an *imperium in imperio* —the Kingdom of Christ within the kingdoms of this world,

Wesley and High Churchmen.

warring against its false maxims and covetous ways, giving no quarter, making no concessions, and subjugating for Christ all to itself.

And to none was this better known than to John Wesley. Consequently one of the first lessons he gave his people was not to quail under persecution, "as though some strange thing had happened to them;" but to expect it, and to meet it with a true heart and a good courage. "Do not imagine," wrote he to them, "you can avoid giving offence. Your very name renders this impossible. Perhaps not one in a hundred of those who use the term 'Methodist' have any ideas of what it means. To ninety-nine of them it is still heathen Greek: only they think it means something very bad, either a papist, an heretic, an under-miner of the Church, or some unheard-of monster. It is vain, therefore, for any that is called a Methodist ever to think of not giving offence." (xvi. 9.) How true! Whether spoken of "Methodist" or "Ritualist;" and singular that these names should so exactly match each other—meaning as each does, neither more nor less, than *a precisian* (*Id.* p. 10)—one exact in walking in the Church's way. This also, and this only, meets Mr. Wesley's definition of the term "Methodist:" "A true Methodist being no other than a true Churchman." "And as much offence as you will give by your *name*, you will," continues Wesley, "give still more by your *principles:*" "to bigots" on the right hand and on the left—those for, and those *against*, "modes of worship and ordinances;" "to men of forms," high and dry; "to moral men so-called;" "to men of reason, by talking of inspiration and receiving the Holy Ghost;" "to open sinners" of every kind, by your life and by your open rebukes. ... "Either, therefore, you must consent to give up your principles, or your fond hope of pleasing men." *Id.* 10.*

But then, as now, there were these additional circumstances of exasperation: "It is a provoking circumstance," Wesley points out, "that you do not leave your brethren quiet. You still rank yourselves among them. 'If you would but get out of their sight!' But you are a continual thorn in their side as long as you remain with them." "Add to this," that you are continually swelling your numbers out of their ranks: "but the fear of losing (so they account it) more of their members, gives an edge to their zeal, and keeps all their anger and resentment in its strength." "And (which cannot but anger them the more) you have neither power nor riches, yet they, with all their power, and money, and wisdom, can gain no ground against you." (*Id.* 11.) Could the parallel come closer? Yes, closer still! The Methodists were a power in themselves;

---

* These two are for ever incompatible. Methodism now basks in the world's smile only so far as it has lost its own original savour.

Wesley and High Churchmen.

they were rich in spiritual goods; and however exasperated their opponents might be, they did not mean to budge; "they knew their calling," it was—not to *leave* but to *leaven* the Church. (xv. 247.) But if so, continues Wesley, "you cannot but expect that the offence arising from such a variety of provocations will gradually ripen into hatred, malice, and all other unkind tempers." (xvi. 11.) Forewarned is forearmed.

A stedfast adherence to Catholic Truth and Primitive Order secured Wesley an easy victory over his many assailants. One by one they were convicted of not holding the principles of their own Church, and of assailing him simply because he did. But those worsted in argument, had famous weapons in store. The Press was open to anonymous slanderers: "slashing articles" were got up, dignified and rendered authoritative by the editorial " we." Samson was brought to grind in the mill, and venal writers made sport for debased readers. Wesley appropriately reminds his brave assailants that "any scribbler with a middling share of low wit, not encumbered with good nature or modesty, may raise a laugh on those whom he cannot confute, and run those down whom he dares not look in the face." xvi. 275.

It has often been a subject of congratulation amongst our opponents that *Punch* and *Judy* are with them: it must be very assuring to them to learn that the same commendable element was in full force against Wesley and his fellows. "Men of wit in Christ Church," writes Wesley in his *Journal*, "entered the list against us, and between mirth and anger made many pretty reflections upon *The Sacramentarians* as they were pleased to call us. Soon after their allies at Merton changed our title and did us the honour of styling us *The Holy Club*." (xxvi. 97.) Again: "The following advertisement was published:—'For the benefit of Mr. Este. By the Edinburgh company of Comedians. On Friday, Nov. 4, will be acted a comedy called, "The Conscious Lovers;" to which will be added a farce called "Trick upon Trick, or Methodism displayed."'" (xxviii. 191.) These grave arraignments of Methodism were treated as lightly as they deserved, " We do not concern ourselves," said the impurtable Father of Methodism, "to be under any obligation to regard them, much less to take them for *arguments*." xxvi. 101.

Meanwhile, the new Oxford movement was spreading everywhere, and everywhere giving signs of a vigorous vitality. Men saw with increasing concern that it triumphed in argument, outlived abuse, and would not die by witticisms. Still, ultimate success was declared to be impossible: for was it not treason against the Englishman's religion—it laid claim to Divine authority—it bore not the stamp of our sovereign lord the King? Daily Services. Weekly, at times

Wesley and High Churchmen.

daily. Celebrations, earnest preachings, revival of long-forgotten doctrines and discarded discipline, hearing confessions and directing penitents, with such "pomp and grandeur" in their public offices and processions, " solemn trifling and theatrical manœuvres" as they were charged with, could not long be tolerated by the British public; men, as standing in the presence of some superior power, shrieked aloud for protection. And so at last the *fiat* went forth—*Methodism must be put down:* and forthwith, clergymen, popish priests, protestant ministers, mayors, sheriffs, aldermen, magistrates, lawyers, captains, doctors, M.P.s, and peers of the realm hasted to fulfil the decree. The Noble Lord said to the Bishop, and the Bishop returned answer to the Noble Lord—" It will not do, it must be *put down.*"* " As a bitter spirit of intolerance was thus manifesting itself," writes Mr. Myles in 1812, they could not but look on their societies "with apprehension. The press was teeming with the grossest slander and falsehood against them, their religious practices traduced and vilified, and they themselves represented as ' vermin, fit only to be destroyed.'" † " Certain popular publications," says the same writer, in every issue gave currency to these representations, until "the Legislature was loudly and repeatedly called upon to adopt measures of coercion against them, under the pretence that Methodism was inimical to public security and morals." *Chron. Hist.*, p. 384.

But these early Methodists, notwithstanding all these engines of oppression, were really happy in one thing—the rich idea had not then occurred to dignify such persecution with the name, and give it the force, of law—by *post facto* legislation: thus brute force directed against their persons, making them a host of friends, would in time expend itself, and leave their *status* in the Church unaltered.

However, the process of *putting down* commenced, and "the good protestant mob," as Wesley sarcastically designates it, took aptly to their work. A few samples may be suggestive. " Public notice," says Wesley, was given at Walsal, by a paper

---

* Lord Sh—bury and the Bishop of L—don in the House of Lords.

† Of their religious practices which were "traduced and vilified," for which also they were "represented as 'vermin fit only to be destroyed,'" the one specially singled out as justifying the harshest language and treatment that could be applied, was that of Confession. (See chap. vi.)

A "memorable presentment" had been made against Charles Wesley:—" We find and present Charles Wesley to be a person of ill-fame, a vagabond, and a common disturber of his Majesty's peace, and we pray he may be *transported*"! *Jl.* viii. 6.

Dr. McN——, in our own day, in language which applies to all High Churchmen who fulfil the Church's direction, has declared that *transportation* does not go far enough. —"I would make it a *capital offence* to administer Confession in this country. Transportation would not satisfy me, for that would merely transfer the evil from one part of the world to the other. Capital punishment alone would satisfy me. Death alone would prevent the evil. That is my solemn conviction." !!!—(*Sermon* as reported in the *Liverpool Mercury.*)

Wesley and High Churchmen.

posted up in the market place, "'That all who designed to assist in breaking the windows and plundering the houses of the Methodists should be ready at ten o'clock the next morning on the Church-hill.' Thence they marched down, some armed with swords, some with clubs, and some with axes." (xv. 133.) They "broke open the doors," dashed out the windows, and "cleared them away, lead, bars and all;" stripped off the roofing lead, threw down the tiles, pulled down one room, the joist of which they carried away, and destroyed or stole whatever they could lay their hands on." "Counters, boxes, drawers, were rifled and broken up, and all that axe or hammer could break." "Bible and Common Prayer-Book," where they fell into their hands, they "tore all to pieces:" "cut up bed and bedstead, and piled on the fire, chairs, bundles of linen, and other household goods." (xv. 131-134.) Their preaching-houses were everywhere points of attack. The mob, headed by a canting ballad-singer "with ballads in one hand and a Bible in the other" (*Jl.* vii. 143) burst open the doors, "brought out all the seats and benches, tore up the floor, the door, the frames of the windows, and whatever of woodwork remained, part of which they carried off for their own use, and the rest they burnt in the open street." They went to their meetings, and "blew horns," "beat drums," "fired pistols," forced into their midst "dogs and bulls," "threw amongst them crackers" and "squibs," "played the fire-engines upon them," pelted them with "potatoes," "stones," "rotten eggs," "clods," and "dirt." Acts of violence against their persons were of every kind and degree, "the mob fell upon them, both on men and women, with clubs, hangers, and swords." Girls of pure character were infamously accused, women with child endangered in life, and men stripped bare, dragged over the stones, dipped in skin-pits, pools, and mud-holes, and beaten till half dead: "the outrages that were committed," says Wesley, "it is scarce possible to describe." "Thus were a loyal and unoffending people treated ... and then were publicly branded in the *Whitehall and London Evening Post*, for rioters and incendiaries!" *Cent. of Methodism*, p. 113.

And who were the chief inciters to these outrages? Will it be believed?—The ministers of the law themselves, whether clerical or lay! Speaking in reference thereto, Wesley says, "I do not speak without ground. I have heard such sermons (in Staffordshire particularly) that I should not have wondered if as soon as we came out of the church the people had stoned me with stones: and it was the natural consequence of what that poor minister had lately heard at the Bishop's visitation: as it was one great cause of the miserable riots and outrages which soon followed." (xv. 161.) One worthy Mayor, when applied to for protection, "said aloud in the midst of the mob, 'it is your own fault for entertaining these preachers: if you will turn them out of your house, I will engage there shall be

Wesley and High Churchmen.

no harm done; but if you will not turn them out you must take what you can get.' 'Huzza!' cried the mob, and stones flew faster than before." (*Jl.* vii. 144.) On another occasion, after an infamous outrage, "one offender was carried before Mr. G., who came back and told his companions, the Justice said, 'That they might go home about their business.'" "Wretched magistrates," says Wesley, "who by refusing to suppress, encouraged the rioters, had long occasioned continual tumults here." (xv. 132, xxx. 268.) In another place, "the Mayor being sent for, came with a party of soldiers, and said to the mob, 'Lads, once, twice, thrice, I bid you go home. Now I have done.' He then went back, taking the soldiers with him. On which the mob, pursuant to their instructions, went on and broke all the glass and most of the window frames in pieces." (*Jl.* viii. 49.) Another time, according to an eyewitness—" Mr. Mayor then appearing, he (deponent) demanded his assistance to suppress a riotous mob ... the Mayor then went, and looked on many of the people covered with dust and blood, and some of them still remaining (for protection) in the house, fearing for their lives. J. C. and J. R., Esquires, Sheriffs, and H. M., Esq., Alderman, turned them out to the mob and nailed up the doors." (*Jl.* vii. 143.) Once more. On one of the aggrieved Methodists applying to D. C., Esq., then Mayor, desiring him, "that he would put a stop to these riots, asking at the same time whether he gave the said Butler (the ballad singer and Bible bearer), leave to go about in this manner? Mr. Mayor said, 'He neither gave him leave, neither did he hinder him.'" (*Id.* 141.) Another refused them a warrant, and turned them away with the rebuff, "I will neither meddle nor make:" So applicants to the Justice "came off without any justice at all." xviii. 26.

Nay, with characteristic audacity, these "very good protestants" procured that the charge resting upon them should be transferred to the sore shoulders of those whom they had been lading with stripes, and the worthy magistrates, nothing loath to stand on the popular side, issued the following proclamation:—.

"To all high constables, petty constables, and other of his Majesty's peace officers, &c. "Whereas we, his Majesty's Justices of the peace, ... have received information, that several disorderly persons styling themselves Methodist preachers, go about, raising routs and riots, to the great damage of his Majesty's liege people, and against the peace of our sovereign lord the King: These are in his Majesty's name to command you and every one of you, within your respective districts, to make diligent search after the said Methodist preachers, and to bring him or them before some of us, his said Majesty's Justices of the peace, to be examined concerning their unlawful doings. Given under our hands and seals," &c. xxvii. 183.

So regular did these perversions of justice become, that opponents turned this also to account, and it was industriously bruited abroad, "'There is no law for the Methodists:' hence," says Wesley, "continual riots followed." xxxi. 284.
Even that most contemptible of all species of oppression—stopping the poor relief—was then (as it also has been in this day) had recourse to: " Elizabeth Lingham, a widow with five children ... had her parish allowance reduced from 2s. 6d. to 1s. 6. a-week." (xviii. 22.)—pinching the bellies of the widow and her poor orphans are fair and noble ways of enforcing contentment with a corrupt custom which provides the means of grace for only one day in the week! "'Liberty of conscience' and 'right of private judgment' are good and specious words," says Wesley, " but how reconcileable they are to such conduct as this let all the world judge."

" The Sacramentarians," as they were called from their love of the Blessed Sacrament, were plied alternately with promises and threats; while the rioters were bribed with money, primed with drink, and incited by the promise of plunder: one was told by " their captain," "'That if she would have nothing to do with these people not a pennyworth of her goods should be hurt.' She made no reply ; and the work of breaking and plundering commenced." To another, who was witnessing the spoiling of his goods, " some gentlemen promised that the mob should desist if he would sign a paper implying, ' That he would never hear those parsons more.'" He sturdily refused ; and the spoliation went on. (xv. 134, 135.) Some bought themselves off with sums of money, and for the time escaped. Others threatened: " H. O. came to J. G—'s house, saying, that if he did not leave following this way, he had a hundred men at his command, who should come and pull his house down." " About the same time the Rev. Mr. E. came, and meeting some others at Thomas Forshew's they drew up a writing, and the town's crier gave public notice ' That all the people of the Society must come to Mr. Forshew's and sign it; or else their houses would be pulled down immediately ' ... Several signed through fear. They made every one who did, lay down a penny—' *to make the mob drink*.' " (*Id*. 131, 133.) " Strengthened with drink and with numbers, and with one Captain G. at their head, they returned to the attack, bawling out ' Now, Hey, for the *Romans*,' 'down with the heretic dog,' and ' the good Protestant mob,'" says Wesley, " marched in grand procession and burnt me in effigy."

Protestantism is powerfully enforced by drink : and when there is found a churchwarden who is willing to provide the latter out of pure love for the former, it may be said of him that he shows a proper faith in his principles, and a commendable care that they should carry their greatest weight. Wesley bears witness to work done by this agency : —" Many of the mob came in and said. ' Come now, d———n you

Wesley and High Churchmen.

Dorset, we have done our work; pay us our wages:' and I saw the drink come in, in large jugs, and every one drank what he would." (xviii. 20.) Well may we, with Charles Wesley, be excused in assigning our place anywhere than " beneath the standard " of *our common Protestantism!* In one of his spirited poems he makes the mob say:—

> " Old Wesley, too, to Papists kind,
> Who wrote against them for a blind,
> Himself a Papist still at heart,
> He and his followers shall smart.
> Not one of his fraternity
> We here beneath our standard see."

And in the same poem severely satirizes the magistrates who trailed their office at the tail of the rabble. Nor did the same functionaries always escape at the hands of Wesley the elder: once, " being brought before a Nottingham Alderman with the introduction, 'Sir, I have brought you another Methodist preacher,' he asked," says Wesley, " my name, and then said, ' I wonder you cannot stay at home, you see the mob wont suffer you to preach in this town ' "— Wesley keenly retorted, " I did not know this town was governed by a mob, most towns are governed by magistrates." xxviii. 362.

And—that nothing should be wanting to make the parallel complete between the Oxford movement in that day and the Oxford movement in this—Rival Funds were started, one for Attack, the other for Defence. Wesley appealed to the law on behalf of liberty which was lawfully theirs: the aggressors denied them this liberty, and promised security to all who should break the law in harassing them:—" Let the heretic dogs indict you; I will bring you off without a farthing's cost." (*Jl.* vii. 144.) Magistrates, then as now, inflicted ridiculously small fines for these breaches of the law endangering life and limb, instead of a term of imprisonment without the option of fine. The fines were " at once paid," " by a gentleman present," and the offender was at liberty again for fresh outrages, and incited thereto by the promise thus made and thus fulfilled. Wesley spiritedly asks, " But is there no way to quell riotous mobs even when magistrates will not do their duty? There is one ... move the King's Bench for an information against them ... The only objection is the expence ... But if we all join hand and heart together, cannot we make this easy to? Cannot we raise a common stock? By the blessing of God we can." (*Min.* i. 44.) So on the struggle went: opposers guaranteeing aggressors safety against the consequences of their violence; and Wesley (who lived on £28 a-year and gave away the rest in alms—*Ss.* ii. 328) and his poor members contributing to a common Fund for Defence their pounds, pence, and mites.—The one representing the C. A., the other the E. C. U.* *God defend the right.*

---

* *The Church Association; The English Church Union.*

CHAPTER XXI.

A CALL TO CANDID CONSIDERATION.

Wesley and High Churchmen.

Wesley saw clearly the whole position, and pointed it out:—
The *Infidel* may disseminate his principles, anywhere, anyhow, "but no mob rises against him: and reason good: Satan is not divided against himself." (*Jl.* ix. 49.) The *Romish* priest may say Mass and sing his office, where and when he likes: but against him no voice is raised: he too is tolerated. (*Jl.* vii. 144.) But against a priest of the Church of England, like himself pledged (xvi. 151) "to defend the Catholic Faith," and "so far as I can, to observe" her Ritual and laws, "the good Protestant mob" cries, *Put him down.*

The *World*, tolerant indeed of a Sunday religion, has the bitterest intolerance for fastings and confessions, frequent prayers and Eucharists, and the priest who comes claiming spiritual authority and a Divine mission, so with the greatest consistency it echoed the cry, *Put him down.*

Magistrates, timid and timeserving, instead of firmly enforcing the law they held a commission to administer, could only yield, and re-echo the cry of those that broke it, *Put him down.*

Bishops ignored the new movement so long as they might have assumed the guidance of it—"I cannot imagine," said the Bishop of London in a Pastoral Letter, "what persons mean by talking of 'a great work of God' at this time, &c." (*Ss.* ii. 111)—and then, finding it a great power, and beyond their control, they set themselves to *stamp it out.* There was room, and favour, and promotion, for the sporting parson, the worldly pastor, for the priest who denied or altogether eschewed his office: only for Wesley and his fellows was there no room.

Wesley pointed out further, that the offence could only cease by the sacrifice of his principles or the abandonment of his position. On the first he says, "Steward of the Mysteries of God, he can abate nothing, he can soften nothing." (xv. 138.) And relative to concessions "to content the people," he says with firmness, "We have not so learned Christ as to renounce any part of His service; though men should say all manner of evil against us, with more judgment and as little truth as hitherto. If the neglect of (what we account) our duties be the one condition of securing our reputation—why—*Fare-it-well!*" (xxvi. 101) On the second he says—"Warm men spare no pains at this very day to drive us out

Wesley and High Churchmen.

of the Church. They cry out to the people, wherever one of us comes, 'A mad dog!' 'A mad dog!' If haply we might fly for our lives, as many have done before us. And, sure it is we should have complied with their desire, we should, merely for peace and quietness, have left the Church long before now—but that we could not in conscience do it. And it is on this single motive—*it is for conscience sake*—that we still continue therein; and shall continue, God being our helper; unless they by violence *thrust* us out." xv. 185.

Wesley appealed to the Bishops: he earnestly entreated them for the sake of Truth and Religion *not to stay this work*: it spoke for itself: sinners were converted; churches were filled; communicants multiplied tenfold. (xiv. 154.) "O that you would no longer shut your eyes against the broad light which encompasses you on every side." He appealed to all "men of reason and religion" —well-intentioned but inconsiderate people who threw in the weight of their influence with those who furiously opposed it. "God begins a glorious work in our land. You set yourself against it with all your might; to prevent its beginning where it does not yet appear, and to destroy it wherever it does ... But know, that for this also, God will require an account of you in the day of judgment." (xv. 176.) He pointed out the sure *origin* of such opposition:—" Satan will stir up his trusty servants to fight, lest his kingdom should be destroyed." (*Min*. i. 44.) " 'Tis an idle conceit, that the spirit of persecution is among the Papists only: it is wheresoever the devil, that old murderer, works, and he still worketh in all the children of disobedience" (xv. 124): and appealed directly to their conscience:—" How long will you fight under the banner of the great enemy of God and man? you are now in his service: you are taking part with the devil against God. Even supposing there were no other proof, this would undeniably appear, from the goodly company among whom you are enlisted, and who war one and the same warfare." He called attention to the *character* of the troops of opposition: "A mixed multitude, of church-goers (who seldom, if ever, go near a church), dissenters, and papists." (xxviii. 205.) "Might not the very sight of these troops show any reasonable man, to what general they belonged? As well as the weapons they never fail to use; the most horrid oaths and execrations, and lawless violence, carrying away as a flood whatsoever it is which stands before it: having no eyes, nor ears, no regard to the loudest cries of justice, reason, or humanity."—And continued his appeal to every one who has conscience, or even self-respect—" Can you join heart or hands with these any longer? With such an infamous, scandalous rabble-rout, roaring and raging, as if they were just broke loose, with their captain, Apollyon, from the bottomless pit." xv. 189.

"How long," asks he again, "will you despise the well-known advice of a great and learned man?—'REFRAIN FROM THESE MEN, AND LET THEM ALONE. IF THIS WORK BE OF MAN, IT WILL COME TO NOUGHT. BUT IF IT BE OF GOD, YE CANNOT OVERTHROW IT—lest haply ye be found even to fight against God.'" xv. 188.

For himself he asked no favour; he desired only toleration, and such protection as the law allows. "I fear God and honour the king," said he: "I earnestly desire to be at peace with all men: I have not willingly given any offence, either to the magistrates, the clergy, or any of the inhabitants ...; neither do I desire anything of them, but to be treated (I will not say as a clergyman, a gentleman, or a Christian) but with such justice and humanity as are due to a Jew, a Turk, or a Pagan." xviii. 119.

Such a spirit *must* triumph ultimately; and it triumphed in Wesley. One good Bishop led the way: of him, "some gentlemen enquired, 'My, Lord, what must we do to stop these new preachers?' The Bishop answered, 'If they preach contrary to Scripture, confute them by Scripture; if contrary to reason, confute them by reason. But beware you use no other weapons than these, either in opposing error, or defending the truth.'" (*Id.* 136.) Other putters-down of "the heretics" were told in open court, that "*Rioters* were not to be *Reformers:* and that his Majesty had nowhere put the reins of government into the hands of mobbers, or made them judge or jury." (*Id.* 10.) The triumph was complete, when on some Methodists being "presented at the assizes as vagabonds," "'it was plainly showed," says Wesley, "'There is law *even for Methodists:*' and his Majesty's Judge took a fair occasion to declare the utter illegality of all riots, and the inexcusableness of tolerating (much less causing) them on any pretence whatsoever." *Jl.* viii. 42.*

* It is not true that these persecutions—disgraceful alike to the clergy, the magistracy, and the people—had any part or share in determining the Methodists to separate from the Church. Persecution was at its height fifty years before the separation took place; and while the fiery trial lasted, it was patiently endured, and separation from the Church was not so much as thought of.

CHAPTER XXII.

STEDFAST UNTO THE END.

1. IN THE CHURCH'S DOCTRINE.

Wesley and High Churchmen.

There is but little difficulty in showing that Wesley in his adherence to the Doctrine and Communion of the Church of England continued faithful to the last. His own repeated and solemn declarations incontestibly prove this. But, says Wesley, on sending an edition of his Sermons from the press, "any man of understanding may now judge for himself," by comparing sermons preached as early as 1738 with those preached during the following fifty years: this is the answer which Wesley once gave "to those who frequently asserted 'That we have changed our doctrine of late, and do not preach now what we did some years ago." (*Ss.* i. vii.) Wesley never accounted those his friends who brought this charge against him: it was Churchmen who preferred it in his day; it is the Methodists themselves in this. Perplexed at finding their Founder in company with High Churchmen, they struggle, at the risk of discovering their own departure from their founder's faith and principles, to make it appear that he towards the end of his life departed from his own. And most curious and contradictory are the results. One deponent (*Methodist Recorder*, Sept. 28, 1868) for example, following a host of others, says that it was in his earlier years only that Mr. Wesley taught Baptismal Regeneration. *The London Quarterly*, in an article attributed to the Editor Dr. Rigg, says, "It was, in fact, in the year 1746 that Wesley may be said to have thrown overboard finally the last of his High Church leanings"—exactly ten years before his Treatise on Baptism was written, which sets forth the High Church doctrine particularly objected to by *The Recorder!* Formerly, it was the custom to say that it was in his earlier and benighted years only that John Wesley held High Church views: now, since that is no longer tenable, as the dates of his *Works* conclusively show, it has actually been suggested by the *Quarterly* Reviewer that when he wrote these he was in his second childhood! "In flat opposition," to use his own words, to each and all of these, Wesley says, "Forty years ago I knew and preached every Christian doctrine which I preach now (1738-1778)." Ten years later, and within two of his death, he declares,

"I have uniformly gone on for fifty years (1739-1789) never varying from the doctrine of the Church at all." A conclusive answer to the statement, by whomsoever made, that Wesley toward the end of his life changed in his views and altered his teaching. Plain evidence, also, that according to the best of Mr. Wesley's understanding, the doctrine exhibited in these pages—set forth in his own words—is that "of the Bible, of the Primitive Church, and, in consequence, of the Church of England." (*Ss.* i. 575.) The weight of these two declarations is not lessened by the deliberateness with which they were made: the first, on a mental review of all his teaching; the second, on explaining to the Society at large, shortly before his death, the design of Methodism from the beginning. *Jl.* xviii. 89, xxi. 145.

If declarations like these can be in any wise strengthened by additional and later testimony, it is at hand. With no less emphasis he asserts in 1790 (nine months later), and makes the assertion a voucher for the short remainder of his life—"I *have been uniform* both *in doctrine* and discipline for above these fifty years; and it is a little too late for me to turn into a new path now I am greyheaded." *Methodism of the Future*, p. 111.

But even this is not all. Wesley not only asserts on every occasion his own unvarying adherence to the doctrine of the Church; he tells the Methodists, that a like adherence on their part also, is essential to their existence as a spiritually living body:—"I am not afraid that the people called Methodists should ever cease to exist, ... but I am afraid, lest they should only exist as a dead sect, ... and this undoubtedly will be the case, unless they hold fast both the *doctrine*, spirit, and discipline, with which they *first set out*." *Mag.* 1787, p. 100.

2. IN THE CHURCH'S FELLOWSHIP.

Wesley and High Churchmen.

Equally conclusive is the way in which Wesley deals with the charge of leaving the Church's *Communion*. The very idea was to him intolerable. He did not so much as allow the question even to be raised by his preachers, except in order "to confirm their adherence to it." (*Vol.* xiii. 353.) He comes down sharply on those who knew no better than to talk of "Wesley leaving the Church." "Leave the Church!" exclaimed he, "what can you mean? You have retailed a sentence from somebody else, which you no more understand than he." (xiv. 159.) "I am now, and have been from my youth, a member and minister of the Church of England: and I

Wesley and High Churchmen.

have no desire nor design to separate from it, till my soul separates from my body." *Ss.* ii. 198.

He reviews the grounds on which such an accusation is made to rest; in order to demolish it utterly: " the whole of the matter is:—

" 1. I often use extemporary prayer.

" 2. Wheresoever I can, I preach the Gospel.

" 3. Those who desire to *live* the Gospel I advise how to watch over each other, and to put from them such as walk disorderly.

" Now, whether these things are, on other considerations, right or wrong, this single point I must still insist on: All this does not prove, either that I am no member, or that I am no minister of the Church of England. Nay, nothing can prove I am no *member* of the Church, till I am either *excommunicated*, or *renounce* her communion, and no longer join in her doctrine, and in the Breaking of Bread, and in prayer. Nor can anything prove, I am no *minister* of the Church, till I either am *deposed* from my ministry, or *voluntarily renounce* her, and wholly cease to teach her doctrines, use her offices, and obey her rubrics for conscience sake." (xvi. 159.) And vehemently declares (not two years before his death) " unless I see more reason for it than I ever saw yet, I will not leave the Church of England, as by law established, while the breath of God is in my nostrils." (June 2, 1789. *Vol.* xiii. 238.)

Wesley, while he lived, also held the Methodists to the Church. He is careful to point out that those are not Methodists who do separate: in ceasing to be Churchmen they cease also to be Methodists. Some indeed broke away even in his life-time, but he stoutly refuses to acknowledge these:—" None of these have any manner of connection with the original Methodists:" " these therefore cannot make *our* glorying void—that we *do* not, *will* not, form any separate sect, but from *principle* remain, what we always have been, true members of the Church of England." *Ss.* i. 575.

Accordingly, separation from the Church was expulsion from the Society. " Such is our rule," says Wesley, " That if any man separate from the Church, he is no longer a member of our Society." (xvi. 157.)

No service was allowed to be in church-hours:—" We fixed both our morning and evening service, all over England, at such hours as not to interfere with the Church." And, though " vehemently importuned," he stedfastly withstood all divergence from this rule, saying, " It is easy to see that this would be a formal separation from the Church " … " and this I judge to be not only inexpedient, but totally unlawful for me to do."* *Jl.* xxi. 21, 1786.

---

* Utterly untrue, is the assertion that Wesley grounded union with the Church on the principle of *expediency alone*—an assertion which is founded on Wesley's *Twelve Reasons against Separation*. But these *Reasons*, on the contrary, contain the most distinct

Wesley and High Churchmen.

Those partial exceptions, sanctioned in a few special cases, by which, Methodists say Mr. Wesley himself deliberately prepared and indicated the way for their subsequent separation, Wesley points to as proving the very contrary:—" Observe! This is done, not to prepare for, but to prevent a separation from the Church." *Jl.* xxi. 143.

He never permitted his preachers to administer the Sacraments:— " Did we ever appoint you to administer the Sacraments—to exercise the priestly office? Such a design never entered into our mind: it was the farthest from our thoughts:" and declared in the official organ of the Society, nine months only before his death, that if his preachers should take upon themselves to administer the Sacraments, they would, by that step, recant their connection with Methodism, and commit the sin of Korah, Dathan, and Abiram.

But bound both preachers and members by the Rules of the Society to constantly attend Church and Sacrament:—" In the year 1743, I published," says Wesley, " the Rules of the Society; one of which was that all the members thereof should constantly attend the Church and Sacrament." " [1763.] On Friday evening, I read to them all the Rules of the Society, adding, Those who are resolved to keep these Rules may continue with us, and those only." (xxxi. 261.) " And these points shall be carried, if only fifty remain in the Society." *Jl.* xvii. 45.

In answer to the question, May it not probably or possibly happen " that your hearers after your death ... will form themselves into a distinct sect?" He replies in full:—

" 1. We are persuaded the body of our hearers will even after our death remain in the Church, unless they be thrust out.

" 2. We believe notwithstanding, either that they will be thrust out, or that they will leaven the whole Church.

" 3. We do, and will do, all we can, to prevent those consequences which are supposed likely to happen after our death.

" 4. But we cannot with a good conscience neglect the present opportunity of saving souls while we live, for fear of consequences which may possibly or probably happen after we are dead." xv. 247.

statement that whether lawful, under any circumstances for others or not, Separation from the Church of England is unlawful for us—the Methodists—and would be still unlawful " were it only " on the ground of being inexpedient:—" By such a separation, we should not only throw away the peculiar glorying which God has given us ... but should act in *direct contradiction* to that very end, for which we believe *God hath raised us up.* We cannot apprehend, whether it be lawful in itself or no, that it is lawful for us: *were it only* on this ground, that it is by no means expedient." Here, if words mean anything, Wesley declares his judgment to be that separation would be " in direct opposition " to the *Divine will and purpose*. By the last words, in the above statement, Wesley ensures that his judgment shall reach to, and embrace all, even those who were disposed to rest *their* adherence to the Church on expediency alone: because, as is well pointed out in the *Centenary of Methodism*, this was the one ground on which all his preachers were, or could be, united, in their adhesion to the Church. xxiii. 119, and *Cent. of Meth.* p. 247.

Wesley and High Churchmen.

In accordance with the promise given in this unexceptionable statement, everything *was done* in the Society "to prevent those consequences." In a Code of Directions drawn up by Mr. Wesley and given to his preachers "as the Rules by which they were to walk," and which received Wesley's "latest revision and correction" a year and a half before his death, these instructions occur:—

"How should an assistant (Superintendent) be qualified for this charge?—By loving the Church of England and resolving not to separate from it. Let this be well observed. I fear, when the Methodists leave the Church God will leave them. O use every means to prevent this. (1) Exhort all our people to keep close to the Church and Sacrament. (2) Warn them all against niceness in hearing—a prevailing evil. (3) Warn them also against despising the prayers of the Church. (4) Against calling our Society a Church, or the Church. (5) Against calling our preachers Ministers; our houses, Meeting-houses; call them plain preaching-houses." (xv. 311.) The most material thing respecting these "Minutes" has yet to be told:—No Preacher was received into full connexion but by *accepting the obligation* thenceforth to observe them faithfully. This official act was indicated and performed "by giving him the Minutes, inscribed thus—' As long as you freely consent to, and earnestly endeavour to walk by, these Rules, we shall rejoice to acknowledge you as a fellow-labourer.'"* *Chron. of W. Methodism*, i. 78, 80, 88.

In answer to the further question, "How he should wish his friends to act in case of the Methodists withdrawing from the established Church?"—his immediate reply was, "I would have them adhere to the Church and leave the Methodists." *Knox's Remarks*, p. 314.

And that this decisive reply was the result of strong unvarying convictions, which began with the beginning and continued to the close of his life, his final declaration on the subject shows. While his last reports of Conferences show something further—that his most trusted preachers unanimously concurred therein:—

1756. "My Brother and I closed the Conference by a solemn declaration of our purpose *never to separate* from the Church, and all our brethren cheerfully concurred therein." *Vol.* xiii. 305.

1785. In consequence of an idle rumour, "I openly declared in the evening that I had now no more thought of separating from the Church than I had forty years ago." *Vol.* iv. 320.

1786. "We *weighed* what was said about separating from the

---

* "This document, which is denominated 'Minutes of several conversations between the Revd. John Wesley, M.A., and others,' is held by all the Preachers as the Collection of the most important and official Rules by which they are to be governed."— *Chronicles of Wesleyan Methodism*, Dr. Warren, i. vii. [1827.]

Wesley and High Churchmen.

Church; but we all determined to continue therein, without one dissenting voice." *Id.* 343.

And of the two last Conferences, both English and Irish, held during his life, in which the subject came prominently forward, he reports:—

1789, July 3, Dublin. "I never saw such a number of preachers before so unanimous in all points, particularly as to leaving the Church; which none of them had the least thought of." *Id.* 464.

1789, Aug. 28, Leeds. "About a hundred preachers were present, and never was our Master more eminently present with us. The case of separation from the Church was largely considered, and we were all *unanimous* against it." *Id.* 466.

This was eighteen months only before his death. Three months later, Wesley said, "I declare, once more, that I live and die a member of the Church of England, and that none who regard my judgment or advice will ever separate from it." (*Mag.*, April, 1790.) This was final—the last declaration he ever made on the subject. A few days after, he writes, "I am now an old man, decayed from head to foot, my eyes are dim, my right hand shakes much, my mouth is hot and dry every morning, I have a lingering fever almost every day." And on the 2nd of March, 1791, after expressing strongly his desire that all things after his death should remain as then by Conference concluded, he fittingly passed away, praying with his dying breath for the Church of his Baptism, his ministry, and his affections.*

* It has indeed been lately asserted by an authorized exponent of Wesleyan Methodism (Dr. Rigg), that "whatever has been carried out [by the Methodists] in the way of practical separation from the Church of England was deliberately initiated by Wesley himself;" and, that "the utmost divergence of Methodism from the Church of England at this day, is but the prolongation of a line the beginning of which was traced by Wesley's own hand." This bold assertion must submit to be tested before it can be received as true. It would be sufficient to place along-side it Wesley's own dying manifesto, in which he distinctly repudiates any connection with those whose divisive tendencies he foresaw, and whose subsequent action he flatly refuses to have fathered upon himself:—"I never had any design of separating from the Church; I have no such design now: I do not believe the Methodists in general design it, when I am no more seen. I do, and will do, all that is in my power to prevent such an event. Nevertheless, in spite of all I can do, many will separate from it; although I am apt to think not one half, perhaps not a third of them. These will be so bold and injudicious as to form a separate party, which, consequently, will dwindle away into a dry, dull, separate party. *In flat opposition to these*, I declare, once more, that I live and die a member of the Church of England; and that none who regard my judgment or advice will ever separate from it." But we will meet Wesley's defamers in detail, on their own chosen ground.

The two capital points which rule the controversy and determine the position of the Methodists in relation to the Church, are, as it is well known, 1. The holding of service in Church hours; and, 2. The administration of Sacraments by the lay-preachers. The above statement cannot be substantiated in respect to the former, except by holding that the exception reverses the rule—an axiom which is universally denied. But Wesley's rule did not permit a simple exception. Four years before his death, he was "vehemently importuned" to allow one such exception, but firmly met the importunities with an emphatic refusal:—"It is easy to see that this [holding the service in Church hours] would be a formal separation from the Church;" and, what would be, " not only inexpedient, but *totally unlawful* for me to do." Services held, and Sacraments given, always by ordained ministers, in London and Bristol, were never regarded, while he lived, as any violation of the rule at all: nor indeed were they, any more than the numerous similar instances allowed in the present day; *e.g.*, in proprietary Chapels. And the only case in which the rule was relaxed, and the society suffered, under strict conditions, to have service in "the Room," was when on account of the open immorality of the minister, or for some other equally urgent cause, all the members, instead of going to Church would immediately troop off to meeting, *i.e.*, to the Dissenting Chapel.

But tested as a principle, the statement breaks down entirely. By it a party of Communists would be able to plead that our Blessed Lord by allowing that for the cause of unfaithfulness, a wife may leave her husband and be married to another man, had thereby set aside the obligation of Christian marriage: in fact, that "the utmost divergence" from the Divine law of their present practice "is but the prolongation of a line, the beginning of which was traced by" the Law-giver's "own hand"!

Equally untrue is the statement when considered in respect to the administration of the Sacraments by the lay-preachers. This Wesley declared, in 1756, would be simply "a sin:" and what he "dared not tolerate." On a review of Methodism, two years before his death, or nine months only if it be dated from its publication in the official organ of the Society, he emphatically protested that "such a thing never entered into his mind;" and would, if adopted, be a renunciation of the "first principle of Methodism." And this, his judgment, was never reversed: "in his latest years," as is by Methodists acknowledged, he only "became more peremptory."

With a change of position, Methodists plead the part which Wesley, "prevailed upon by the undue influence of some of the preachers," took in ordaining Messrs. Mather, Rankin, and Moore to act as his assistants, under the very limited commission to do "what and where I appoint." And very bitterly did Wesley regret this step, as one who acted with him on this occasion has borne witness, "and with tears expressed his sorrow both in public and in private." In public, at the Leeds Conference, 1789; and occasionally afterwards in London, until his death. About six weeks before that event, he said mournfully, of the preachers, "They are now too powerful for me." This is the testimony of a priest who took part with Wesley in these ill-considered acts of ordination, and who conducted the Methodist press under him during the last eighteen months of his life, and who had, therefore, the most ample means of knowing his latest sentiments. (*Centenary of Methodism*, p. 271.) But this is so much more than is needed. For neither had Wesley, in this, an idea of providing the nucleus of a future ministry, separate from the Church on the Presbyterian plan, nor did the Methodists turn it to this or any other account. Just as they were, in Mr. Wesley's life time—as he maintained, without ordination, power, or appointment of any kind—the preachers *admitted themselves*, by their own vote, to the exercise of the priestly office in the administration of the Sacraments. How it can be pretended that this is a course which was "deliberately initiated by Wesley himself"—"a divergence of Methodism from the Church of England at the present day," which "is but the prolongation of a line the beginning of which was traced by Wesley's own hand"—does not appear. Certain, even of themselves, have said, "What parallel the ingenuity of man could discover between this [Wesley's persuasion that he could ordain, in "obvious reference to the supposed inherent power of his order as a priest of the Catholic Church"], and *a body of laymen* who had never received any order at all, by a vote among themselves, which was carried by a simple majority, constituting themselves legitimate presbyters, we confess is beyond the powers of our minds to imagine. Even should the principle upon which Mr. Wesley's ordinations were performed, be conceded, the fact is clear that no number of laymen have any power to vote themselves into an order to which they had no previous pretensions." *Id.* p. 267.

CHAPTER XXIII.

METHODISM IN SEPARATION.

Wesley and High Churchmen.

A complete organization, and duly provided for as to its permanence, Wesley left Methodism *within the Church* of England, and the "People called Methodists" *strictly bound to the plan* which their Founder had with great wisdom designed, for that most noble object, "to reform the nation, more particularly the Church, and to spread scriptural holiness throughout the land." And so did the Methodists in their next Conference express their sense of the obligation which Mr. Wesley's repeated charge imposed—"*We engage to follow strictly* the plan which Mr. Wesley left us at his death." *Min.* i. 246.

The continuance of Methodism in communion with the Church depended mainly on two conditions:—1st, on the preachers' not assuming the Sacerdotal office; 2nd, on their services not being held in Church hours. And these, Wesley declared to be *essential to the integrity* of Methodism. For the preachers to administer the Sacraments, he said, would be a renunciation of its "first principle," and "a recantation of our Connexion:" to have service in Church hours, he said, would be "a formal separation from the Church;" and therefore "a sin;" and such, says he, "will see my face no more." *Mag.* 1790, pp. 235, 287; *Jl.* xxi. 26.

Nevertheless in 1793-4, three years after Mr. Wesley's death, these two prohibitions were withdrawn; and the severance, with all its momentous issues, was at once complete. (*Min.* i. 279, 299, 323.) The Methodists were not driven to take up this attitude by persecution (this, where it had not turned into favour, had all but ceased)—they were not thrust out—in spite of Mr. Wesley's warnings on this very head, prosperity did what persecution could never do. Dissenters had joined them in large numbers, and their influence in the Connexion everywhere made itself felt. (*Mag.* 1790, p. 215.) Preachers, ambitious to exceed their bounds (*Id.* 288), but controlled by the strong will of John Wesley during his lifetime, were in many cases unwilling to be held by the Conference in conformity to his principles after his death. In every place the Society was divided, some members being for the old plan, some for the new. The Conference felt the difficulty, unwilling, on the one hand, to lose any of its members, on the other, to appear in opposi-

Wesley and High Churchmen.

tion to the principles of their Founder, it cast lots; for a year the strife was allayed; then the decision was reversed, and Methodism, for sixty years nursed within the Church of England, by Church of England Ministers, took up its position without.*

In their new position the Methodists immediately cast about for arguments wherewith to defend their separation. It was said (it is repeated unto this day) that Mr. Wesley himself, by his admission of special exceptions prepared, and even indicated the way for their subsequent separation. Unfortunately, Mr. Wesley forestalls the plea, and pointedly protests against its use. " Observe !" said he, " This is done *not to prepare for*, but to *prevent* separation." (*Jl.* xxi. 143; *Mag.* 1790, 288.) The few exceptions were all of this nature: either permissive of service in regular hours, in order to keep the members of the Society from attending dissenting meeting-houses, and thereby contracting a disaffection to the Church; or, such as naturally resulted from his own peculiar notion as to the relation of πρεσβύτερος to ἐπίσκοπος. Even the Methodist historian and biographer, Mr. Smith, admits that until, and for some time after, Mr. Wesley's death, the Methodists " were not permitted to receive from the hands of their own preachers those sacred ordinances ;" nor was " preaching in church hours ... permitted except for special reasons." *History of Wesleyan Methodism*, ii. 2, 3, and 691, 692.

But it was seen that even this plea could not serve the cause of their separation so long as Wesley's latest and most emphatic declarations stood witnessing against them. *These therefore were suppressed.* His solemn protestation to the preachers, that in assuming the priestly office—in administering Sacraments—they would recant their connection with Methodism, and commit the sin of Korah, Dathan, and Abiram. 2, That to have service in church hours would be a formal separation from the Church—that consequently it would be a sin, and that such would see his face no more. 3, That to " leave the Church and set up for yourselves" ... would be to " frustrate the design of Providence, the very end for which God raised you up." All these, Wesley's most emphatic declara-

---

* Those early Methodists who were not content that the Methodist discipline—as it had been maintained for more than fifty years, and which Wesley had declared (*Mag.* 1787, p. 100) to be essential to their existence as a spiritually living body—should be thus overthrown, have uniformly set these facts out in somewhat stronger colours: the Irish Primitive Wesleyan Methodists, for example : these, in an official publication, say, " Many of the Preachers who were disaffected to the Church, as we have seen, had long wished for an entire separation from it, but were frustrated in their designs during Mr. Wesley's life, by his power and authority. But that which they were unable to effect during the time they were under his control, they succeeded in bringing about immediately after he was removed from their head. The Conference felt no hesitation, as soon as they were left to transact their own affairs, to vote themselves into the office of the priesthood, and to adopt the principle of Sacramental administration." *Centenary*, p. 265.

I.

Wesley and High Churchmen.

tions, made chiefly within a few months of his death, were never after it allowed to appear; in every subsequent edition of his Works they were suppressed; until, in 1828, the suppression was pointed out and complained of by one of Mr. Wesley's surviving friends.

This concealment of Mr. Wesley's will and design in order to the settlement of Modern Methodism, does of course manifestly prove that Modern Methodism is not in accordance therewith: and those who—living while he lived—had the best opportunity of knowing both, have thus left on indelible record their uneasy consciousness of it. But as deviation from Mr. Wesley's plan is now stoutly denied,* it may be well to add that "the highest authority in Methodism," the Conference, in that day both *admitted* and *pleaded excuses for* their deviation and departure from the "plan" which, say they, "was left us by our Venerable Father." In a Circular Letter, addressed by the Conference to the Members of the Methodist Societies, 1793; it is said — "Our Venerable Father, who is gone to his great reward, lived and died a member and friend of the Church of England. His attachment to it was so strong and so unshaken, that nothing but irresistible necessity induced him to deviate from it in any degree. In many instances God Himself obliged

---

* *Deviations* from Mr. Wesley's plan have been freely admitted on all hands by the Methodists when the supposed necessity of maintaining the contrary has not been immediately pressing upon them:—

"It has always appeared to us, that the fathers of 1795 and 1797 made a mistake, either in not retaining, *in its integrity*, the institute as Mr. Wesley left it, or in not dealing with the questions brought before them somewhat more largely than they did. In other words, we think that either the Society form should have been continued without alteration, or a more complete Church organization ought to have been adopted." *Methodism of the Future*, by a Wesleyan Minister, p. 35.

"The subject which created most alarm was, respecting that strict adherence to the National Church, which Mr. Wesley so *strenuously endeavoured and recommended*. Some of the members who had long been accustomed to receive the Lord's Supper in the Established Church, and to attend its public worship during Mr. Wesley's life, were vehemently opposed to any alteration in the Discipline of Methodism which would interfere with the former practice." *Chronicles of Wesleyan Methodism*, by S. Warren, LL.D., Vol. I., p. x.

"It is a question somewhat difficult to be settled whether it would not have been a prudent measure if Mr. Wesley—when he at length saw that a change in the relation of his Societies to the Church of England must take place after his death—*had prepared* for that event by some such moderate alterations as the Conference afterwards found it necessary to adopt." *Watson's Observations on Southey's Life of Wesley*, p. 145.

To give three such testimonies as these is like thrice slaying the slain: "but"—to continue the last extract—"certainly nothing can more strongly refute" the pretension that Wesley prepared the way for the subsequent event; or show with such unerring certainty that the Methodists since his death have deviated from their Founder's plan in allowing service in Church hours and the lay-preachers to administer the Sacraments: rather than which, "he preferred," says Mr. Watson, "to leave the Connexion to the hazard of the conflicts of different parties." Thus in this one point, all Methodists, both those opposed, and those favourable to the "innovating plan," were substantially agreed: in the words of the former, "the Conference of preachers voted themselves into the office of the priesthood;" in the words of the latter, "from that time a part of the societies assumed the form and substantive character of a regular religious body."

Wesley and High Churchmen.

him to do this"—*i.e.*, in field-preaching and in the employment of lay preachers. "A dilemma, or difficulty, of a similar kind, has been experienced by us since the death of Mr. Wesley. A few of our Societies have repeatedly importuned us to grant them the liberty of receiving the Lord's Supper from their own Preachers. But, *desirous of adhering most strictly to the plan which Mr. Wesley laid down, we again and again denied their request* ... You may see clearly from hence, dear brethren, that it is *the people** in the instances referred to who have forced us into this *further deviation* from our union to the Church of England." *Min.* i. 280, 1.

In a second Letter of the same date, similarly addressed, the Conference says:—

"We have not departed from the plan which was left us by our Venerable Father *except in the few exempt cases* where the people have been unanimous for the Lord's Supper, and would not be contented without it." The "few exempt cases"! in the Conference Minutes of 1794, are given in print—101 in number besides "the other places"!

A "further deviation," and "departure" from the plan "left them" by their Venerable Father, followed in 1795. Services were thenceforth allowed to be in Church hours "where the Society desired it." *Min.* i. 323.

The above association by the Conference of things so essentially different in their nature, as field-preaching and the employment of lay preachers on the one hand, and the intrusion into the priestly office and separation from the Church on the other, under the one common name of deviation—that under the edge of Wesley's shield they may find some shelter—is extremely disingenuous, and would

---

* The disingenuousness of this plea—not to use a stronger word which it well deserves—is apparent to everyone who knows anything of the history of Methodism. For points of discipline of much less consequence the Conference has maintained that attitude of firmness which has more than once rent the Connexion in twain. But Methodist writers, both English and Irish, have shown on other grounds that this plea is a *peculiarly* dishonest one. "We may observe," says the Wesleyan biographer Dr. Whitehead, "that this dissatisfaction originated with a few preachers, and from them spread like a contagious disease to the people. This was the case at first, and has always been the case since, whenever the people have desired any alteration in the original constitution of the Methodist Societies. Their method of proceeding to effect their purpose is rather curious, and shows to what means men will sometimes resort, to support a particular cause. For as soon as these preachers had, by various methods, influenced a few persons in any society to desire to receive the Lord's Supper from them, they pleaded this circumstance as a reason why the innovation should take place." In Ireland the case was the same. Mr. W. Stewart, a member of the Conference, in a letter addressed to the Methodist preachers in 1814 (two years before they had succeeded by these methods in carrying their point) not only pleads powerfully that as a matter "even of moral honesty," their public pledges, repeatedly given—in collecting funds, in raising chapels, in enlisting members, in conciliating opponents, in making friends—may be respected and adhered to, "but also charges some of his junior brethren amongst the preachers, with being the sole cause of that agitation which had been created throughout the Societies." *Centenary of Methodism,* 242, 280.

Wesley and High Churchmen.

merit severe reprobation, were it not that Wesley has so effectively disposed of it:—the latter, he says, it would be *a sin to do;* the former, a sin *not* to do. *Mag.*, 1790, p. 287.

The question now is no longer between πρεσβύτερος and ἐπίσκοπος: it is whether there be any order of ministers at all, deriving a spiritual power and authority by an outward channel from Christ; and consequently whether laymen can rightfully assume the sacerdotal office. The Preachers who acted with Wesley were never regarded in any other light than as "Evangelists,"[*] and "extraordinary messengers." He could never be brought to recognize them as clergymen: his last solemn warning addressed to them was on this very head;—against the sin of invading the priest's office, which God so signally punished in the instance of Korah, Dathan, and Abiram. And the few clergymen who, as ministers of the Sacraments, were associated with him, were, after his death, regarded with a feeling of considerable jealousy by the Preachers in general; and it consequently became the policy of the Conference to treat all equally as "Preachers of the Gospel," and let no difference of order appear: a policy which received its formal expression in that direction of the Conference — "The distinction between ordained and unordained preachers shall be dropped." *Min.* i. 278.

Hence, among other reasons, it was that not even Presbyterian Orders, nor indeed Orders of any kind could ever be claimed by the Methodists. So far indeed were the Methodists of that generation from pretending to anything of the sort, that they wholly disclaimed the slightest notion of it—"We have never sanctioned Ordination in England, either in this Conference or in any other, in any degree, or ever attempted to do it." (*Min.* i. 281.) Nor was even the outward form—the laying on of hands—ever assumed until a few years ago; viz., in 1836.

It is a matter of the deepest regret, that the dishonest policy of suppressing Mr. Wesley's final declarations, should have been followed by Methodists of respectability committing themselves to the untrue statement that the Wesleyan Ministers have *presbyterian orders:* (see, *e.g.*, Mr. Jackson's Second Letter, 1868). Now, Mr.

---

[*] There is a curious argument urged by Mr. Moore in his *Life of Wesley*, and reproduced by no less an authority than Dr. Rigg, which for its beautiful simplicity deserves to stand on permanent record. In a conversation, which the former preacher says he had with Mr. Wesley in reference to the famous sermon on Heb. v. 4, he addressed him thus, "Sir, you know the *Evangelists* Timothy and Titus were ordered by the Apostles to ordain Bishops in every place; and surely they could not impart to them an authority which they did not *themselves possess*," *i.e.*, a power to administer Sacraments. Wesley, it is said, was silent. "We must not forget" this! gravely urges Dr. Rigg. Wesley might well be silent. Even a well instructed Christian child would not need to be told that a Bishop may be—nay, should always be—an Evangelist, but this by no means invests a simple Evangelist or "Preacher of the Gospel" with the authority and power of a Bishop.

Wesley and High Churchmen.

Jackson knows perfectly well—1. That every opposition to Mr. Wesley's preachers and also every apology for them proceeded on the ground of their *lay* character; and that such as they were in Mr. Wesley's lifetime, such they continued after his death. 2. That as well after as before that event, the "official act" by which the Methodist preachers were admitted to the full exercise of their office was a formal delivering to them the Large Minutes.* 3. That the Conference in 1793 expressly renounced any idea of ordination, and never assumed it till 1836; when it was begun, and thenceforth continued, by men as destitute of "presbyterian ordination" as those upon whom they professed to confer it. If this function had been carefully committed to those clergymen or presbyters whose services for this purpose the Conference might have commanded, the present claim would have been defensible, but it was not—quite irrespective of any such consideration—it was committed to the President, the Ex-President, and the two senior preachers. If these senior brethren were presbyters *without* ordination, those junior preachers upon whom they laid their hands similarly did not need it; if these latter did need it, the former were not presbyters without it. This is a friendly representation, derived wholly from "the highest authority in the Wesleyan community," the Conference Minutes.

If, to escape this difficulty, Mr. Jackson should contend that the usual formal *recognition* was virtual ordination, then he places himself in entire opposition to the above Conference which denied it; if he takes the only other ground, and maintains that a layman does by laying hands on a brother preacher make him a Presbyter in Holy Orders, then he is bound to say that this is all that is meant in claiming for the present ministers *presbyterian ordination.*

To this same period 1835-1845, must be assigned the *outward manifestation* of Methodism as a separated community. The Conference of 1793, in order to quiet those Methodists who had taken alarm at the deviations from Mr. Wesley's plan which were being made, had tried to conceal from them the divisive character of their course:—" We do assure you, that we have no design or desire of making our Societies *separate churches.*" (*Min.* i. 281.) Notwithstanding this disclaimer, the early "deviations" of 1793, especially that one of allowing the Preachers to administer the Sacraments,

---

* " The giving and receiving this Instrument is considered as an official act, *by which* the person who receives it is admitted into full Connexion as a Travelling Preacher, and entitled to all the privileges of an accredited member." Dr. Warren, 1827. (*Chronicles of Wesleyan Methodism*, p. viii.)

" When he (the Probationer) has been on trial four years, if recommended by the Assistant, he may be received into full Connexion *by giving him the Minutes* inscribed thus:—As long as you freely consent to, and earnestly endeavour to walk by these rules, we shall rejoice to acknowledge you as a fellow-labourer." John Wesley, 1789. (*Large Minutes. Id.* p. 88.)

Wesley and High Churchmen.

fairly carried within them all subsequent "departures." And when this practice had become peaceably accepted by all the Societies, and the recognized rule instead of the rare exception, there was no further reason for concealing that the separation, whether for good or evil, was an accomplished fact. Wesley's standing injunction was "Warn the people not to call our preachers *Ministers*, and our Society a *Church*: but when the Preachers had assumed every ministerial function, and the Society had for every purpose superseded the Church, no desirable object could be served by any longer withholding what consistency required—an open acknowledgment of the altered relationship of Methodism to the Church. So in the year 1839, "Our Body," is classed by the Conference, "in common with all other protestant churches." The year after, the old term "preacher," is quietly dropped by the Conference, and "Minister" takes its place. Thenceforth the new style becomes the usual one, and fresh measures are taken to secure the due administration of *all* the Christian ordinances in *all* the Chapels. "As *Ministers* of our common Methodist *Church*, we resolve to do all that we can to provide for the devout and regular observance of *all Christian ordinances* in our numerous places of worship." Accordingly, "The Conference directs the use of the Liturgy," and "the Superintendents are required, without delay, to see that every Chapel in their respective Circuits be supplied with at least Mr. Wesley's Abridgment for this purpose." Conferences 1840, 1842. (N.B. Not for *this* purpose abridged by Mr. Wesley, but for the use of the Methodists in America, in districts where the Liturgy was unknown.—See page 56.) During these years, the Circuits one by one took up the new designation, and issued "The Wesleyan Methodist Preachers' Plan" with its improved heading, "Wesleyan *Ministers* and Local Preacher's Plan." Now also, with Ordination by imposition of hands and the assumption of titles, came in another novelty: for the first time in Methodism, the Travelling Preachers began to apply to the Local Preachers and all other members by way of contradistinction, the term, "laymen" or "the laity," (see Minutes of these years): not indeed without some grumbling and protesting on the part of the *local* brethren, who forcibly as well as truly pointed out, "Are they Ministers of Christ?" Why then "So are we." And judged by the same standard, as the other brethren had raised whereby to authorize themselves—*i.e.*, an inward call, ministerial fitness, and seals to their ministry—"with quite as much scriptural authority to discharge all the functions of Ministers of Christ, both to their Societies and to the world."

Of course, I do not expect that this Exposition will draw towards me the love of that section of my separated brethren who petulantly complain that "the Church of England in the persons of many of

Wesley and High Churchmen.

her sons insults us constantly, by insolent denials of our ecclesiastical claims, or by proposals for absorption." * (*Methodist Recorder*: Conference Sketches.) Nevertheless, I have so spoken—" the truth in love "—on the principle that the laying bare a wound, so that it be tenderly done, is the first step towards surely healing it.

It is doubtless open to any admirers of John Wesley to receive just so much only of his teaching as pleases them, and to adapt to their own supposed necessities the system which he founded, according to their own free will: but if there be one historical conclusion which may be called certain, it is that those who claim peculiarly to themselves his name, and profess to be guided by his principles, should in the main adhere to his doctrines, and above all remain stedfast to the Church of England. It is strange, to be told by the most venerable representative of those whose teaching is professedly the same as John Wesley's, that the Church " can expect no sympathy from Wesleyan Methodism," as " many of the Clergy preach the doctrines of Popery;" when there is not a single doctrine of the kind preached in even the *highest* of our churches, or attacked in any newspaper within the realm, which John Wesley in his day did not defend, as is exhibited within these pages, and also by references proved. It is stranger still, that the same venerable authority, the Ex-President of the Wesleyan Conference, should tell us that the Church of Wesley's days, when nearly by all his name was cast out as evil, and he was called " Papist," " Jesuit," " fanatic," " bigot," " firebrand," should be esteemed as alone worthy of their adherence, and be deemed a truer and better exponent of " New Testament Christianity " than the Church of this day, which reveres his name, teaches his doctrine, and in a spirit of love calls to all his children to return to their spiritual mother. This certainly shows either the strangest ignorance of, or the farthest departure from, the views and principles of their " Venerable Father." It seems somewhat more to the purpose, when the same authority, on behalf

---

* Willingly do I suffer contumely and reproach, in company with my Methodist brethren of former days, who have incurred it in making the same attempt. The Rev. Adam Averell, for example, " an aged and venerable minister of Christ," who had for many years at his own expense represented his brethren in the English Conference, and had also " with disinterested zeal, devoted his time, his talents, and a considerable part of his property, to the maintainence of Methodism ;" he, on being requested by the aggrieved minority, to open a correspondence with the innovating brethren on the subject of the restoration of Methodism to its original plan, " considered the proposed object a desirable one, and accordingly addressed a circular letter to the preachers respectively, calling upon them to join in 'replacing Methodism on its original basis in Ireland, as it stood at the period of the decease of the late reverend and venerable John Wesley.' To this letter, which was conceived in such a spirit of Christian love and conciliation as did honour to the writer, a circular reply was issued by the preachers who were then stationed in Dublin, in which the appellations of a *wolf*, an *Ahitophel*, and a *Judas* were liberally bestowed upon Mr. Averell, as an indication of their gratitude for his former services rendered to the Connexion." *Centenary*, 294.

of the Methodists, points to the existence of Rationalism within the Church of England, as a reason why they and he should not return to the fold. And yet, on their own showing, as if by affording this double answer they would overwhelm their pleas for continuing in separation with utter confusion, the case was precisely the same in Wesley's days, when they *did* adhere stedfast:—" Strenuous efforts," said the very same Ex-President in 1839, "were then made by several ecclesiastics to introduce deadly heresy into the Church. The learned Dr. S. Clarke, occupying the influential post of Rector of S. James's, and enjoying the friendship of Sir Isaac Newton, and the patronage of the Queen, openly appeared as the advocate of Arianism, and was assisted by the erudite and indefatigable Whiston, with other writers of less note. A noisy prelate, Bishop Hoadley, the friend of Clarke, appears to have given up all that is peculiar in Christianity in compliment to the Deists, who cannot endure mysteries, and to have espoused substantially the Socinian heresy, while at the same time he retained his office and preferment in the Established Church." (*Cent. of W. Methodism*, p. 3.) Could the parallel between that day and this have been more striking? But when we add the mention of this attendant difference, that in Wesley's days Convocation was forcibly silenced, lest it should condemn this prelate for his apostacy from the Faith; now the heretical prelate is deposed, and excommunicated, and another sent to take his office—the futility of the plea for separation is complete.

Also, on their own showing, does it appear that it is no new thing for Clergy of the Church of England, both Bishops and Priests, to refuse to regard as authoritative the opinions of the Reformers. " There was," then, continues the same Ex-President, " on the part of the great body of the Episcopal Clergy, an evident departure from some of the most important theological principles of the Reformation:" " such writers as Tillotson, Bull, and Waterland," for instance. So that, right or wrong, as a plea for a changed attitude towards the Church of England, it has fairly no place.

But it cannot be too distinctly understood that the Church of England stands by the settlement of 1662, which was a deliberate return towards the earlier settlement of 1549, passing over the later one of 1552 as due mainly to foreign and improper influences. Yet it is exactly to the period commencing 1552 that men point for "the principles of the Reformation."

As to the views of the Reformers, they have precisely the same claim to our agreement as the views of any other individuals of similar standing, before or since: the claim is valid in exact proportion to their *own* agreement with the early and undivided Church. But when we are told, and this by a Bishop (*Charge* of Bishop of Worcester, 1868), " It is patent to all inquirers that in the undivided

Church ... in the public acts of Councils, and in the recognized usages of Divine worship, are to be found some of the greatest errors (!) against which the Reformers of our Church protested;" we simply reply, "So much the worse for the Reformers:" just as when a Methodist author announces a discourse on "The Errors of the Apostolic Fathers," he bids us expect an exhibition of his own. To say that those who were taught by Apostles were not Methodistical in their belief, or that the early and undivided Church taught a doctrine different from Cranmer and Calvin, is simply another way of saying, that Methodists, or Reformers, *are wrong.* The overweening arrogance of the men, who rate their own soundness so highly, that they must needs condemn the whole Church of Christ, and the Apostolic Fathers into the bargain, is only comparable with the ludicrous absurdity of the country bumpkin who should insist upon keeping the time for Greenwich by his own watch.

Of the Reformers, Wesley certainly spoke very guardedly: he showed that none of them were to be commended, much less followed, in all their practices or opinions; that they were neither so immaculate, nor so infallible, as they have been painted; that their death, when violent, had more of retribution in it than of glory; while those on whose commands they waited, were so far lost to all good, that they "had not one spark of public virtue left." xv. 124, 183-4. xxvii. 268, 290. *Jl.* xix. 72.

Wesley uniformly looked beyond the 16th Century to the pure and yet undivided Church for testimony to The Faith, to whose witness, as "the most authentic commentators on Holy Scripture," both the Reformers and we must bow: and never varied in his prayer, "May we be followers of them, in all things, as they were of Christ."

But, included amongst other charges, is one which in itself is sufficient condemnation in the eyes of all—except indeed such as read their Bible, and the words of Him who prayed "that they all may be one"—"they desire union with Rome." So they do: and so did Wesley: and set a greater number of people praying for it than the whole body of the A. P. U. C.:*—"Especially bless Thy Holy Catholic Church, and fill it with truth and grace; where it is corrupt purge it; where it is in error rectify it; where it is right confirm it; *where it is divided and rent asunder heal the breaches thereof.*" (x. 47.) If Mr. Jackson, or any other accuser of the brethren, says that High Churchmen desire a "healing of the breaches," and not also "truth and grace," he says that which he has ample means of knowing is false.

That "portentous development of Sacramental principles," is also

---

* Association for Promoting the Unity of Christendom.

Wesley and High Churchmen.

a charge which lies quite as much against John Wesley and the early Methodists, as it does against us. In fact, what Laud was in the 17th century, and Pusey is in the 19th, that Wesley was in the 18th,—the *foremost teacher* of these "Sacramental principles." From a disciple of Laud, Dr. Brevint, he received them; and to us, in his writings and *Hymns*, he is teaching them still. In this, Dr. Brevint's Treatise on "The Christian Sacrifice," and yet more in the Sacramental *Hymns* "by John and Charles Wesley," these principles are fully developed; and we have in words which follow, the authority of even the Ex-President Mr. Jackson himself, for saying that no book of the Wesleys stamped with its own character the early Methodists so much as this:—"This very pious Manual," says Mr. Jackson, "was in great request, and in increasing demand, as long as the authors lived. Few of the books which they published passed through so many editions; for the writers had succeeded in impressing upon the minds of their Societies the great importance of frequent Communion. They administered the Lord's Supper in London every Sabbath day; and urged the people everywhere, at all opportunities, to eat of This Bread and drink of This Cup."

The seed which Wesley then sowed in our fields is now bearing fruit. Thoughtful Methodists who use his *Prayers* and read his *Christian Pattern*, form no inconsiderable share of our harvest. Those who would follow his advice, in attending Daily Prayer and Weekly Communion. have nowhere else to go. What becomes then of Mr. Jackson's bold assertions that " Mr. Wesley was a protestant to the backbone," and that the High Church Clergy are preachers of Popery? Whichever of these be true, this one fact is undeniable—the men who abide in the Church, who set up therein Daily Prayer and the Weekly Eucharist, do not shrink from Confession, do not fear lay-preaching, and are not afraid to win souls in a barn, are the only true representatives of John Wesley that now remain. And who these are, all men know; the choice is between "The *Ritualists*" and —none else. But because there are faithful followers of John Wesley within the Church, his reputed followers outside, prefer there to remain, in order to keep themselves wholly free from the influence of their "dear Father's" principles and teaching.

Such, and such only, were the reasons given on a late occasion,* by the authorized spokesman of Modern Methodism, why the Methodists do and must continue in separation from the Church.

When we consider their relevancy, and mark the spirit with which they were made, we cannot but grieve and point out to them the judgment of their "Venerable Father"—"*The pretences for separation may be innumerable, but want of love is always the real cause.*" Ss. ii. 196.

* The Wesleyan Methodist Conference, 1868.

CHAPTER XXIV.
METHODISM AGAIN IN UNITY.

Wesley and High Churchmen.

The day which sees the Methodists return to their former and better mind will be a bright one for the Church of our common Lord. And happily, no real difficulties lie in the way, except such as sticklers for "things as they are" amongst them, or ourselves, may raise.* If the movement called Methodism had arisen in these days, High Churchmen of this generation would have had a foremost place in it; or if High Churchmen had done their present work in Wesley's days, the Methodists would have had their part and share in it. All that is now wanted is, that with our correcter principles and greater appreciation of Evangelistic agencies, there should be simply a return to *original Methodism*. As Wesley left Methodism, so let Methodism remain. We can very well accept it *in its integrity*, if those called by his name can do the same. Religious men, who have an inner bond of union amongst themselves, as well as an outer one with the Church at large, are no longer our fear. We can welcome as labourers in the Church's field lay-preachers, exhorters, leaders, in buildings or in the open air. Class meetings, prayer meetings, love-feasts, and bands, we can receive, with every other means that can arouse, strengthen, or instruct. Wesley's (not Luther's—chap. xi.) teaching on Justification by faith, *i.e.*, *by grace alone*, we do receive. Conversion, Christian (not sinless—*Ss.* I., No. xiii.) perfection, the necessity of heart-religion, we constantly teach, and with the same distinctness as he. His teaching on the Sacraments is ours also, and will so remain. Two things alone are of necessity required:—1. That there be no intrusion by unordained persons into the Service of the Altar; 2. That unless for special or sufficient reason there be no Service in Church hours.

With judgment and discretion, and a spirit of love on both sides, the relations would be readily adjusted. In country parishes the general rule might be, the Church morning and afternoon, the

---

* "It is not beyond the bounds of reasonable hope, that, conforming itself to the original intention of its founders, it may again draw towards the Establishment, from which it has seceded, and deserve to be recognized as an auxiliary institution, its ministers being analogous to the regulars, and its members to the tertiaries and various confraternities of the Romish Church. The obstacles to this are surely not insuperable, perhaps not so difficult as they may appear. And were this effected, John Wesley would then be ranked, not only among the most remarkable and influential men of his age, but among the great benefactors of his country and his kind."
Robert Southey: Life of Wesley, ii. 289.

Wesley and High Churchmen.

affiliated Chapel at night, as *already it usually is*. Particular exceptions might be left for individual arrangement. In towns also, where church accommodation is not in excess, the *present* custom might continue—Churches and Chapels at all times in full use; the Sacraments being there administered by Methodist priests, under their own direction.

In any parish where either the Clergyman or the Methodist part of his parishioners objected to unite in holy worship, there need be no obligation. Temporary reasons time will outrun. Methodist priests might as now itinerate to meet such cases. (*Min.* ii. 26.) So would there be neither "aggrieved parishioners," nor *aggrieved priests*.

The Itinerant Ministers might be encouraged to accept Holy Orders; those who declined might do so, and continue their *present* work as Evangelists, forbearing only to administer Sacraments; if not for the sake of Truth, at least for Love and Peace. The Local Preachers* might continue their useful labours exactly *as at present*, with the encouragement and sympathy of the resident Clergy, instead of with feelings very naturally the exact opposite.

All that the Methodists teach we teach also; and that which they don't hold with us, we should not oblige them to accept. They might go on in strict accordance with Mr. Wesley's *Sermons* and *Notes*, preaching repentance, faith, conversion, death, and judgment-to-come. Sacramental verities they might leave alone, as they do now. They are, in general, right in what they affirm, wrong only in what they deny.† *Myles' Chronolog. History*, p. 479.

Foreign Missions also might as opportunity favoured be brought into the same amicable relation: their management being still left in the hands of those who have set them a-foot, as they are for the most part even amongst ourselves.

---

* I can confidently affirm, from the most certain knowledge—that derived from twenty years familiar intercourse with the Methodist Preachers—that it is no question of Doctrine or of Ritual which keeps this invaluable body of labourers out of the Church's field: it is simply because the Church of England has not at present opened her doors to such labourers in the Lord's Vineyard, that they continue—and feel they must continue—separate from us.

† Three "Articles of Agreement" drawn up by Mr. Wesley himself, in view of his death, would preserve the integrity of Methodism on its *original plan:*—

"I. To devote ourselves entirely to God; denying ourselves, taking up our cross daily, steadily aiming at one thing—to save our own souls, and them that hear us.

"II. To preach the *old Methodist doctrines*, and no other, contained in the Minutes of the Conferences.

"III. To observe and enforce the *whole Methodist discipline* laid down in the said Minutes."

The *Large Minutes* contain all which is here indicated and made of perpetual obligation. A copy of which was given by Mr. Wesley to all his preachers, "as the Rules by which they were to walk." "This Document," says the Methodist Chronicler, Dr. Warren, in 1827, "is held by all the Preachers as the collection of the most important and official Rules *by which they are to be governed.*"

Wesley and High Churchmen.

The whole machinery of Methodism, Trust Deeds, and Connexional Property, might continue to stand exactly *as at present*, and yet be all brought into entire conformity with Mr. Wesley's will and design, and be made of the highest utility to the Church of which he lived and died a member.

Our mutual gains would be many. The facility offered to any Pastor more fitted for an Evangelist of assuming that office; and *vice versâ* of any Itinerant Minister assuming for a like reason the pastorate of a flock. We have those amongst ourselves who impatiently long for an extended field wherein to broad-cast the seed; and Methodists have those who would gladly cultivate the soil, and in patience wait for the precious fruits thereof. The education of the Methodists' children throughout the country falls into the hands of the rural Clergy; and such young people of ours as are most desirous of some Christian work generally pass into the service of Methodism; and are thenceforth, unhappily for both them and us, our hinderers rather than our helpers. Our Church attenders who have most self-will, and are least patient of reproof, betake themselves to the neighbouring Chapel; and such as have attended Chapel while in health and strength, look to the Church for visitation, spiritual comfort, and alms, in times of sickness and old age. Such are a few of the vexatious anomalies which are without remedy as matters stand. We have sad need of an extended evangelistic agency, the Methodists have equal want of a resident pastorate. By joining our forces we should work into each others hands, and the deficiency of each would be met by the excellency of the other. " And," interjects Wesley, in advocating this very thing, "would it not be better for the whole work of God, which would then deepen and widen on every side?" xxxi. 294.

Besides, we should gain what is above all, Christian charity, and unity between brethren. And can we doubt that this would be attended with a more abundant blessing from "the Giver of all good things"?

But we are told that the proposed union between the Church and the Methodists "is *legally, morally,* and *religiously impossible.*" So was Wesley told in his day when he made the overture, and pleaded earnestly, that the Clergy and the Methodists being engaged in one common work, should work in unity together. Only it was *the Churchman then* who said. " It will never be: it is utterly impossible." Wesley with unabated hope replied: " Certainly it is with men. Who imagines we can do this? That it can be effected by any human power? All nature is against it, every infirmity, every wrong temper and passion; love of honour and praise, of power, of pre-eminence; anger, resentment, and pride; long contracted habit, and prejudice lurking in ten thousand forms. The devil and all his angels are against it; for if this takes place how shall his kingdom stand? But surely with God all things are possible. Therefore all things are possible to him that believeth. And this union is proposed only to them that believe, that show their faith by their works." Having said this (xxxi. 295), while "Mr. C. was objecting the impossibility of ever effecting such an union," Wesley did what must be his instruction to us under the same circumstances— he betook himself to Prayer:—

"*O God the Father of our Lord Jesus Christ, our only Saviour, the Prince of Peace; Give us grace seriously to lay to heart the great dangers we are in by our unhappy divisions. Take away all hatred and prejudice and whatsoever else may hinder us from godly union and concord: that, as there is but One Body, and One Spirit, and One Hope of our calling, One Lord, One Faith, One Baptism, One God and Father of us all, so we may henceforth be all of One Heart and of One Soul, united in One holy bond of Truth and Peace, of Faith and Charity, and may with One Mind and One Mouth glorify Thee; through Jesus Christ our Lord. Amen.*" Amen.

Laus Deo.

"THE WESLEYAN CONTROVERSY:"

Correspondence

BETWEEN

JAMES H. RIGG, D.D.,

Editor of the *London Quarterly Review*, and Principal of the Wesleyan Training College, Westminster.

AND

H. W. HOLDEN,

Assistant Priest of St. Andrew's, Middleton-on-the-Wolds, York.

Reprinted from the "Guardian" Newspaper;
Nov. 25, 1868—March 3, 1869.

With the Transcription from the original editions of Mr. Wesley's writings of some Passages, which after his death, were suppressed.

"Well worth reprinting. And it is not a little amusing to see the way in which Mr. Holden's antagonist turns and doubles to try and draw him off the line of his argument. Dr. Rigg is evidently a practised controversialist, and knows that when he has a bad case the best course is to raise some other issue, and then, under cover of the dust raised in its discussion, to escape from closing on the main point of the discussion; but in this instance he has met with an opponent who will not be tempted to let him go, and the result is that the correspondence is very diverting. But it is valuable as well."—*The Literary Churchman.*

www.ingramcontent.com/pod-product-compliance
Lightning Source LLC
Chambersburg PA
CBHW020308170426
43202CB00008B/544